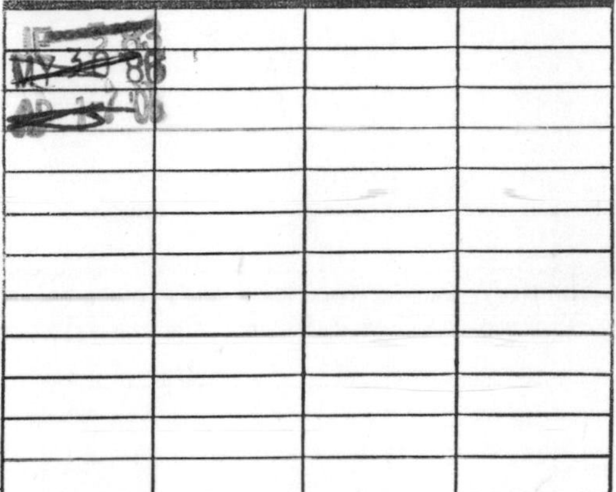

Developing Artistic and Perceptual Awareness

Developing Artistic and Perceptual Awareness

Art Practice in the Elementary Classroom

Fourth Edition

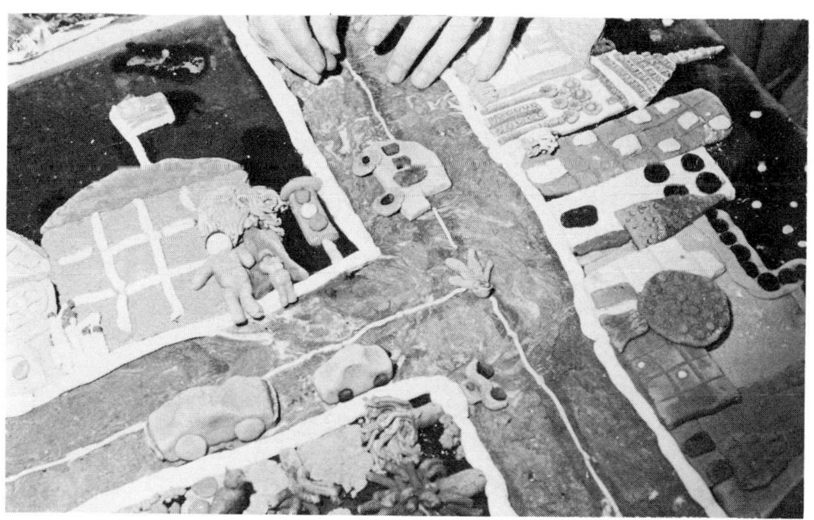

Earl W. Linderman
Arizona State University

Donald W. Herberholz
California State University, Sacramento

wcb

Wm. C. Brown Company Publishers
Dubuque, Iowa

Consulting Editor

Willard F. Wankelman
Bowling Green State University

Library of Congress Catalog Card Number: 77–77984

ISBN 0–697–03203–5

Third Printing, 1981

Printed in the United States of America

Contents

"I am certain of nothing but the holiness of the heart's affections and the truth of imagination—what the imagination seizes as beauty must be truth whether it existed before or not."

Letter to
Benjamin Bailey from John Keats,
November 22, 1817

Foreword

Modern life with all its complexities and all its abstractions seems to add a bar each day of our lives so that, like canaries, we are in danger of becoming prisoners of life. It is only the wise and the persistent who flee regularly from their cages to touch the real earth through a direct experience, coming face to face with nature, face to face with fellow men, or face to face with a simple lump of clay. It is in this direct experience that man is called on to use his own thoughts, feelings and actions. Regardless of the simplicity of the experience, the individual must construct responses in his own way. What most of us take for granted as a normal pattern of growth is in reality a series of most serious struggles which go on within every individual. Growth implies change and change can be frightening. Even mature artists sometimes admit to a real fear when faced with the emptiness, the challenge of a blank canvas; for standing alone, unassisted, the individual is now entirely dependent on his own resources—energy and motivation must create the answers which are his truths.

When one can stand apart from a group of children engaged in their creative activities and single out any one of the group for detailed observation, objectively analysing behavior, working habits, sequences of actions and responses, ability or inability to perceive, and interactions, one begins to sense, if only in a small way, the problems and frustrations of growth and change. For many years educators have had the benefit of the experience of inspiring intuitive teachers like Cizek and Cole and brilliant scholars like Lowenfeld, Read and Arnheim who have coupled research with intuition. More recently, younger scholars like Beittel, Barkan, McFee, Burkhart and others have supplied additional information and insight into the nature of child art and learning in the arts. Many of their insights are such that simple verbalization rarely explains them and there are, of course, dangers inherent in only synoptic adoption of insights. Sometimes those things which are most meaningful to one may be lost on a follower unless it is possible to reach the same depth of understanding and to work under similar conditions. How futile it would be to ape Cizek, whose culture-environment and children differed so greatly from ours. Mr. Linderman, Mr. Herberholz and I agree that each teacher must create his own rich environment to nurture the creative potential of his flock.

This book presents an open condition in which a multitude of findings are laid bare before the reader and gives original sources of much inspired thought. Digging deeper helps us elude the danger of oversimplification in one of the most important facets of the child's growth—his creative development. More important here, however, is the feeling of excitement which rubs off onto the reader the minute the pages are turned. Clearly, the classroom teacher is expected to teach, and to teach in an inspired way. The factor of chance is hardly considered a worthy approach in education. Art education has suffered occasionally through the casualness of chance success, in many cases by the mere misunderstanding of the relationship between the child's art product and the process of making it. The common misinterpretation of process versus product, particularly at the elementary school level, has led to all kinds of perversions of a most important and meaningful concept. Teachers have sometimes adopted the notion that anything a child does is both good and acceptable. I watched a class being taught one day in which the teacher walked through the group lifting every piece and gushing "oohs" and "aahs" in the most public sort of way. Any scratch or blob was loudly praised for its freshness, vitality or spontaneity. As I watched, I noticed one small boy who had caught on to the fact that the teacher praised indiscriminately. Playfully turning his back to his paper and with a loaded brush, he proceeded to slosh the paper heavily. As he anticipated, his paper warranted a fair share of high praise. This created a dilemma, for the teacher was right in wanting to encourage each child and yet as she was discovered to be praising everything indiscriminately, she was losing the confidence of her students. The accidental paper of the little boy may have been aesthetically the most pleasing piece in the class, but the mere fact that the child sensed insincerity in the teacher was most damaging.

The notion of process and product might better be thought of as inseparable. A weak product is merely a record of a poor process, which in turn may be the result of diffuse motivation. On the other hand, a good product is the record of a strong period of process and high motivation. This whole matter is further complicated by the fact that the teacher is expected to be a skilled and mature person whose job it is to assist each child to attain levels of achievement that he might not otherwise reach. Everyone who has taught recognizes the fact that children are sometimes so highly motivated that the teacher seems only to be in the way. But left only to his own resources, the child may reach a plateau from which he can no longer seem to ascend. It is here that the sensitive teacher guides, suggests and stimulates the child so that his spark of desire is reignited and he is challenged and aided in his desire to seek new solutions. Once renewed, he goes on to achieve new levels of accomplishment. All this is tied up with the matter of growth which is sometimes falsely considered to be an automatic part of the years in school. It is easy to deceive oneself into believing that, by merely having a few token art lessons, the child will pass smoothly through the various developmental levels which are recognized by most art educators. This, in part, is so, but what happens is that the child may pass through each level with the weakest kinds of concepts, failing to lay the necessary foundations for the stages which follow. Ultimately his concepts become so weak and insignificant the child loses confidence in them and thus rejects his own means of expression and communication. Growth and change are difficult for the child, and successful growth is very dependent on teachers who care, or perhaps I should say teachers "who care to give the very best."

Some years ago I began a collection of virtually all the drawings and paintings of a single child in order to try to determine the manner in which concepts change. This collection grew until it amounted to thousands of drawings and paintings. The various stages of development were clearly evident, but a study of all the drawings in chronological order revealed many clues to the struggles of growth. During the period around six years of age the child developed over thirty different kinds of noses for his people, trying to arrive at a concept that would satisfy him. This was not a steady progression, but rather an irregular moving forward with a periodical return to older symbols, an occasional modification and a sudden new surge forward. I began to see what hard work it was to be involved in all of these discoveries. Occasionally an enormous forward thrust appeared which resulted from increased perceptual awareness, no doubt brought about by a sensitive teacher who had provided a good experience or stimulation. How important it was that the teacher found the means to help the child remain open and receptive as well as flexible in his approach. These are characteristics which will serve him well throughout all life's activities. The teacher finds himself frequently walking a tightrope to maintain a balance between too easily satisfied children and those who are too quickly satisfied.

One of the conditions of achieving the full potential of every child is a sustained program of opportunities with the presence of materials and equipment and circumstances necessary for performance. The child must have the opportunity to fully explore his abilities, for no potential will ever be realized, or even be discovered, unless a child tries an activity and freely participates. As teachers, we receive the finest kind of raw material. When one considers the potential of a simple chunk of coal which can be turned into any of thousands of products, one is staggered by the potential of a classroom full of children. Most children come with an openness, ready to absorb the stuff of education. The tiny child is all perception: tasting, touching, seeing, smelling, hearing and asking. The most formidable task of education is to keep this perception open and to help it develop both sensitivity and selectivity.

Life cannot absorb everything indiscriminately, for ultimately life takes on direction and focus. Such a challenge requires teachers who care deeply and teachers who regard teaching as a great adventure of the human spirit. The authors of this book, Earl Linderman and Donald Herberholz, are creative artists who have sought their own personal truths in both artistic production and creative teaching. They recognize that what is "right" is an elusive something that each teacher must seek and find for himself. This search requires a grasp of fundamental concepts plus the teacher's own intuition. All this does not suggest any radical reorganization of the programs of the classroom, it simply suggests a means to a richer environment in which creative growth can take place through greater awareness and greater sensitivity.

Edward L. Mattil
Chairman, Department of Art Education
Pennsylvania State University

Acknowledgments

The authors wish to thank the following organizations and individuals for permission to quote:

The American Crayon Company for the quotation from *Everyday Art* by Yar G. Chomicky.

Art Education: Journal of the National Art Education Association for a quotation by Howard Conant from a symposium held at the Philadelphia Museum College of Art on Dec. 11, 1962.

Arts and Activities for quotations from "Let's Learn About Art" by Earl W. Linderman.

Crocker Art Gallery and *Everyday Art Magazine* for photographs. All photographs are by the authors unless otherwise noted.

Davis Publications, Inc., for quotations from *Art Activities for the Very Young* by F. Louis Hoover and *Painting in the Classroom* by Arne W. Randall and Ruth Elise Halvorsen.

Ed Mattil for the quotation by Allan Kaprow.

Frederick A. Praeger for the quotation from *Matisse: A Portrait of the Artist and Man,* by Henri Matisse.

Grade Teacher for "Child Art and the Teacher" by Earl W. Linderman.

Harper and Row, Publishers for quotations from *Creativity and Its Cultivation* edited by Harold Anderson.

Harper and Row, Publishers for the quotation from *Self-Renewal* by John Gardner.

Houghton Mifflin Company for the quotation from *The Natural Way to Draw* by Kimon Nicolaides.

International Textbook Co. for quotations from *Spontaneous and Deliberate Ways of Learning* by Robert C. Burkhart and *Art: Search and Self-Discovery* by James A. Schinneller.

J. B. Lippincott Co. for the quotation from *The Art Spirit* by Robert Henri.

McGraw-Hill for the quotation from *Understanding Media* by Marshall McLuhan.

The Macmillan Company for quotations from *Your Child and His Art* and *Creative and Mental Growth* by Viktor Lowenfeld.

New York State College of Home Economics for the quotation from *Children's Art* by W. Lambert Brittain in the Cornell Extension Bulletin, 1067.

Pantheon Books, Inc., for the quotation from *Education through Art* by Herbert Read.

Prentice-Hall, Inc., for the quotation from *Meaning in Crafts* by Edward L. Mattil and the quotation by Wassily Kandinsky from *Modern Artists on Art.*

The Ronald Press Company for the quotation from *A Foundation for Art Education* by Manuel Barkan.

Saturday Review for the quotation from "What Makes a Person Creative" by Donald W. MacKinnon and a quotation from "Art, Adrenalin and the Enjoyment of Living" by Norman Cousins.

Scientific American for the quotation from "Psychology of Imagination" by Frank Barron.

Syracuse University Press for the quotation from *Creativity and Psychological Health* by Michael F. Andrews.

Vision for the quotation from "Seeing Things" by Arthur Syverson.

Wadsworth Publishing Co., Inc., for quotations from *Preparation for Art* by June King McFee and *Creativity: Invitations and Instances* by Alice Miel et al.

The authors wish also to express their gratitude to their wives, Marlene Linderman and Barbara Herberholz, for their continual understanding and help during the creation of this book.

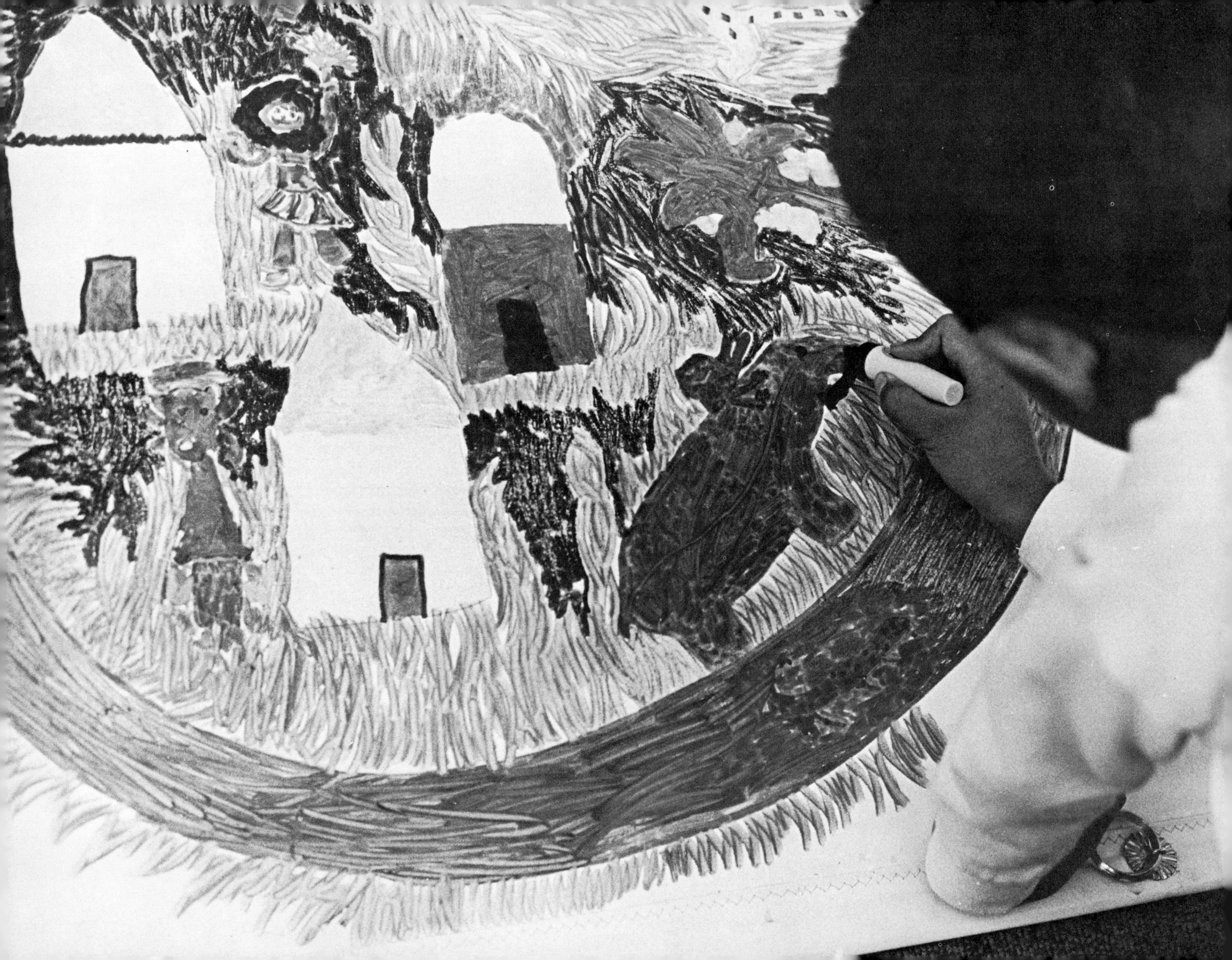

For the self-renewing man the development of his own potentialities and the process of self-discovery never end. Exploration of the full range of his potentialities is not something that the self-renewing man leaves to the chances of life. It is something he pursues systematically, or at least avidly, to the end of his days. He looks forward to an endless and unpredictable dialogue between his potentialities and the claims of life—not only the claims he encounters but the claims he invents. And by potentialities I mean not just skills, but the full range of his capacities for sensing, wondering, learning, understanding, loving and aspiring.

Self-Renewal by John W. Gardner,
New York: Harper and Row, Publishers, 1965,
Harper Colophon Books, pp. 10-12

Introduction

In a highly standardized, mechanistic society loss of human rights and dignities is threatened by a lack of the individual's opportunities to create. Individual innovation is being replaced by a national mass-mediocre-mindedness. Man is being stripped of many of his powers to perceive, imagine, explore and invent. The loss of this ability can be overcome through the exercising of the individual sensibilities and the seeking of basic principles through a creative search. The ideas contained in this book are intended to amplify the creative individualism of man and to "sense art's overwhelming power, the near-blinding beauty of its white-hot, aesthetic core"[1] through a depth of experiences in art practices.

This guide is written to help teachers and parents stimulate in children experiences which are basic to a rich unfolding of their creative expression. The ideas contained in this book are not merely theoretical but have resulted from carefully reasoned insights gained through successful teaching experiences with children. In addition, evidence based on extensive scientific research done in the fields of child psychology and art education form the nucleus of this presentation.

This book is especially designed to help the parent or teacher experience once again the beauty of life through fresh eyes. This fresh vision in experiencing the world will be an aid in teaching children an appreciation of its wonder and beauties. Children will learn to discover their own aesthetic and artistic imagery when they learn to open the magic door of their awareness and are encouraged to step into the wonderment of art experiences.

Before exploring these exciting experiences which are fundamental to art and to growing, we must first clarify our own thinking. What are we seeking? Basically, we are trying to lead children into experiences which will involve them in *touching, seeing, tasting, hearing* and *smelling* the things in their world; and we also want them to become involved in experiences which lead to *imagining, exploring, reasoning, inventing, experimenting, investigating* and *selecting*, so that these experiences will be not only rich in themselves but lead to personal creative growth.

Basic to this book is the underlying premise that early stimulation of the child's *sensory* mechanisms is essential to free his creative power. In the words of Viktor Lowenfeld, a great art educator:

> *We cannot start early enough in life. There are no limitations. Expose the baby to the lulling noise of a brook; make him conscious of it by saying, "listen." Let him listen to the singing of a bird, the hushing of the wind through the trees. Make him aware of the brittle sounds of the fall foliage under your feet. Let him hold and touch whatever the opportunity offers. Open his eyes to whatever you are able to take in. One of my most precious memories is the moment in my childhood when I walked with my mother through the fields and saw the miracles of nature she made me see. Whatever you can do to encourage your child in his sensitive use of his eyes, ears, fingers and entire body will increase his reservoir of experience and thus help him in his art.*[2]

It therefore is the responsibility of both parent and teacher to provide the child with opportunities which will increase his understanding of the natural and man-made world. In our hands rest the means to make the child's vision flow with wonder, to quicken his imagination and to awaken him to the joys of living. We have the opportunity to let him discover the softness of furry kittens, the scent of freshly cut lumber, the echo of a train in the night, glistening raindrops on a petal, cool mist against his cheek. In a sense, we want him to capture the full flavor of life. Awakening children to experiences of this sort is normal and precious to all human beings. Such aesthetic feelings must be cultivated deeply for they govern the inner harmony which is so vital to the fundamental structuring of a keen mind. We must always remember that the child's mind needs to be stretched and his eyes opened to all he can perceive.

This book is for all who desire to enrich their own awareness and sensitivity to art. We must be courageous enough to take this plunge into what may at first seem foreign to our present thinking and behavior. Unless we have confidence in our own desire to explore and investigate the world, we will be hesitant in stretching the frontiers of our children's imaginations. As we engage in these experiences with children, we will take pleasure in seeing the awakening of new vistas in ourselves.

The photographs contained in the body of the text relate to the general theme of the book, although one may not necessarily find a direct reference to the text. The pictures are intended to enhance the main theme in a visually communicable form.

The use of the senses stressed in chapter 2 takes on great significance in our electronic age when the child has a greater need to visualize and express his personal feelings in the private dialogue of art. He will also participate in public dialogue because of his heightened perceptual awareness to his visual environment.

Chapter 4 provides the framework for motivational dialogue between student and teacher. In utilizing both the cognitive and affective domains in a motivation, the child can grasp a more active way of entering his culture. The problem-solving aspect emphasized in chapter 1 and again in chapters 4 and 5 will always remain central to any theory of art education, whether it be for seeking unique answers to personal problems or to problems of our society.

Emphasis throughout the book stresses the development of one's artistic and perceptual awareness through a personal and group search toward self-discovery. The authors hope that several options for discovery will open for the classroom teacher, student, and parent in finding possibilities for steering art awareness toward the front edge of our discovery. The book tries to indicate that sensitive awareness to art, to self, and to others depends on developing articulate use of the senses at an early age. These artistic and perceptual experiences can greatly enrich the child's approach to the wonderful world of art.

Just as our own responses and attitudes about art vary, so will those of the children in our classroom because of individual and cultural differences. We need to plan a sequence of learning experiences to guide children in their creative, perceptual, and aesthetic responses. This learning process can be facilitated by both parents and teachers by:

knowing and valuing the make-up of an artist or creative person;

knowing and developing a child's perceptual intake of seeing and feeling experiences in his life;

knowing and encouraging a child to value and express his ideas, images, and feelings through in-depth motivations;

knowing and helping a child learn an in-depth approach to understanding and exploring materials and tools of the artist to produce an aesthetically organized visual whole;

knowing and guiding a child's aesthetic judgment in relation to his environment, as well as enriching his sense of culture through art history.

In this fourth edition, the authors have clarified and expanded the opportunities for students, parents, and teachers to discover the joy and continuing adventure that art experiences offer to both mind and spirit. The consistency and flow of the previous editions have been maintained and reinforced through careful addition of relevant new material, and to a contemporary adaptation of current issues and philosophies pertinent to classroom art teaching. As before, we encourage each person who utilizes this book to grow in the many facets of the art experience, and ultimately to make art an important part of their lives, as well as those they teach.

Throughout the text the pronouns he and she have been used to refer to artists, teachers, and students. This is used for succinctness and does not imply that any one of these groups is limited to a specific sex.

References

[1]Quote by Howard Conant, as reported in *Art Education, Journal of the National Art Education Association*, from a symposium held at the Philadelphia Museum College of Art on December 11, 1962.

[2]VIKTOR LOWENFELD, *Your Child and His Art* (New York: The Macmillan Company, 1960), p. 26.

The landscape is filled with infinite glimpses, each transitory, each displaced by another, and another. A seed floats on the air. A fringe of mist creeps and rises from a pine-spiked ridge. A rock looks about, shoulder-deep in the snow. An apple tree scratches at a December sky. A weed, dead-brown, tangles with twig and blown leaf in a wind-trodden patch. A quarry wall resists the widening pit . . . a tumbling kaleidoscope of awesome, fleeting visual fragments.

Yar G. Chomicky,
from *Everyday Art* vol. 36,
spring, 1958, p. 11

Chapter 1

The Nature of Art and Creative Thinking

How often have we heard a person exclaim, "Creative—why I can't even draw a straight line!" Yet, this very same individual may abound with untold creative power! Our first hurdle, therefore, consists in understanding what we mean by such a term as *creativity*. Before we discuss this new world of creative thinking one essential point must be stated: It is possible to be a creative person without becoming a professional artist. It is true that artists are very creative people. However, there are also creative bricklayers, chemists, doctors, chefs, electricians, salesmen, parents and teachers! The key in understanding this point is to remember that all creative people do not deal in *special-talent* products. Your type of creativeness refers to your ideas, feelings and human experiences. For our purpose, let's begin right now by thinking of creativeness as a special way of learning, thinking and perceiving—your own life style.

Most individuals have the natural endowments necessary to become more creative persons. However, not everyone's creativeness has been stirred. In many it lies slumbering beneath the surface, waiting for the moment when it can awaken and enrich fresh, unique ways of seeing. When creative potential remains in such a passive state it collects mental dust. The term *creative functioning* is applied to those teachers, students and parents who seek to brush away the cobwebs of dull routines and conventional living (the villains of creative thinking).

What Do the Experts Say About Creativeness?

Before we embark on our new adventure into the ever-changing, always-challenging arena of creative exploration, it is important that we first understand what the experts mean when they speak of the creative person. As a point of reference, we have carefully chosen selected personnel from the sciences and the visual arts as our group of experts. Here is what they say about creativity:

Creativity is the ability to invent new symbols and ideas, to improvise on established symbols, to rearrange established organizations into new organizations, and to integrate new or borrowed ideas into previously organized systems or situations.

June King McFee[1]

Creativity is a process of individual experience which enhances the self. It is an expression of one's uniqueness. To be creative then is to be oneself.

Michael F. Andrews[2]

Creativity is an instinct which all people possess, an instinct with which we were born. It is the instinct which we primarily use to solve and express life's problems . . . Creativity, the ability to explore and investigate, belongs to one of the Basic Drives, a drive without which man cannot exist.

Viktor Lowenfeld[3]

Creativity is action by an individual through a medium. There are many avenues in human experience for creative action, but they vary according to the potentialities and the character of the particular media they offer.

Manuel Barkan[4]

Creativity as interactive learning brings in life. The process becomes a matter of responsiveness to all in life that is coming in and going out, and thus refers to a continual process of rejecting and accepting, making and destroying, revising and adding, and failing and succeeding.

Robert C. Burkhart[5]

We are concerned here with the development of people who think imaginatively, who have original ideas and welcome opportunities to put them into action.

F. Louis Hoover[6]

Creativity is found in people, but not by the use of a microscope or dissecting instruments. Rather, according to the literature, it can be found in how people behave: inventing, planning, compromising, constructing—behaving in such a way that others would call them creative.

W. Lambert Brittain[7]

The creative person is both more primitive and more cultured, more destructive and more constructive, crazier and saner, than the average person.

Frank Barron[8]

The creative individual . . . has revealed himself . . . it is his high level of effective intelligence, his openness to experience, his esthetic sensitivity, his independence in thought and action, his high level of creativity energy . . . and his unceasing striving for solutions to the ever more difficult problems that he constantly sets for himself.

Donald W. MacKinnon[9]

Creativity requires freedom—freedom to rebel against stifling conditions, freedom to make decisions differing from those made yesterday and differing from those made by others—but it is not unlimited freedom.

Alice Miel[10]

. . . Creative thinkers are flexible thinkers. They readily desert old ways of thinking and strike out in new directions. . . . In the area of creativity one should certainly expect to find a trait of originality.

J. P. Guilford[11]

My definition, then, of the creative process is that it is the emergence in action of a novel relational product, growing out of the uniqueness of the individual on the one hand, and the materials, events, people, or circumstances of his life on the other.

Carl R. Rogers[12]

My subjects were different from the average person in another characteristic that makes creativity more likely. Self-actualizing people are relatively unfrightened by the unknown, the mysterious, the puzzling, and often are positively attracted by it.

Abraham H. Maslow[13]

Creative learners learn by questioning, inquiring, searching, manipulating, experimenting, even playing around, but always trying to find out the truth.

E. Paul Torrance[14]

Where there is faith that there will be an emergent intuition of wholeness concerning a real and internalized problem, accompanied by a readiness for commitment to its pursuit, we may speak cautiously of "creativeness." It is said to involve an open perception of self and the world and of their interaction for the sake of that which is to come. As such, it suffers the joy, despair, and dictates of a continuous, unpredictable, and irreversible dialogue with the future, for which nothing is either necessary or irrelevant. 'Up' may be 'down,' 'in' may be 'out,' 'old' may be 'new,' but the form left behind will emanate vitality, rightness, and conviction, even though it all might have been otherwise. The courage and faith to act this way I call 'creativeness,' no matter where or when or in whom it may be found.

KENNETH R. BEITTEL[15]

Creativity is a quality of uniqueness, originality, newness, or freshness which an individual voluntarily, perhaps intuitively, contributes to the conception and development of an idea.

Creativity, in my sense of its meaning, must be affected by, though it is not identical with, aesthetics. Probably because the two main ingredients of the arts are uniqueness (or creativity) and superbly high quality (or aesthetics), I see creativity as one of two fundamentally inseparable elements of the arts, and I frankly cannot see it used as a synonym for new ways of advertising products, managing personnel, building scientific devices, mailing letters, or sailing a boat.

HOWARD CONANT[16]

After a careful consideration of the many divergent avenues the experts have taken in trying to assess the creative individual we begin to see the complexity of the endeavor and gain a greater insight into how a creative person operates in his behavior, personality, the values he holds, and how he thinks creatively.

What Are Artistic or Creative People Like?

Herbert Read has stated that we need to teach children not only to know, but also to create, for art is a way to become a sensitive, aesthetically oriented person. Further clarification on the creative process in art is offered by Norman Cousins:

The electrical engineer who checks for short circuits in a Boeing 707 may be impressively adroit and he is essential but he is not an artist; he must not depart from a fixed purpose or technique. The artist doesn't need such tight wiring, he would strangle himself with it if he did. His natural habitat is full of magnificent short circuits. For his job is to supply the sparks for jumping the gaps, which is what distinguishes the creative process from the functional one.[17]

NORMAN COUSINS[17]

Our experts have provided us with a composite picture. Let us slow this action down and see what traits are unique to creative people. Creative people seem to have many characteristics in common. Here are some of them:

1. Creative people are extremely alert perceptually. That is,
   - They are observant of the world about them.
   - They are aware of the way things feel to the touch.
   - They listen to the sounds of life around them.
   - They have a sensitivity for the way things smell.
   - They are aware of the taste of things.

2. Creative people are builders of their ideas. That is,
   - They like to construct things in materials.
   - They prefer to rearrange old ideas into new relationships.
   - They like to experiment with various approaches and media.
   - They like to try out new methods and techniques.
   - They prefer to manipulate their ideas in various ways.
   - They like to solve problems which they set for themselves.
   - They seek to push the boundaries of their thinking.

3. Creative people like to explore new ideas. That is,
   - They are very original in their thoughts about things.
   - They like to invent new ways of saying and telling.
   - They like to dream about new possibilities.
   - They like to imagine and pretend.

4. Creative people have confidence in their inner resources. That is,
   - They are flexible in their approaches to situations.
   - They like to be independent and on their own.
   - They are outwardly expressive about what they have to say.
   - They are not afraid to have emotional feelings and to show them.

5. Creative people like to investigate the nature of things. That is,
   They like to search for the meaning of things.
   They question available data and information.
   They like to inquire into unknown quantities.
   They discover new relationships.
   They desire to uncover new meanings.
6. Creative people are sensitive to aesthetic stimuli. That is,
   They are sensitive to the beauty in man and nature.
   They appreciate beauty that man has made.
   They have a feeling for harmony and rhythm.
   They like to sing, dance and write.

The picture of the artist or creative person developed thus far is that of one who creates out of a vast wealth of knowledge. Some of this knowledge is conceptual, while a great deal is perceptual. Perceptual knowledge is arrived at from his sensory experiences which he then puts together to form a visual statement. The creative person has specific attributes, abilities, or skills that he uses during the creative process or art experience. These attributes are sensitivity to problems (awareness), ideational and associational fluency (many ideas), flexibility (ability to change), originality (unusual responses), and redefinition (ability to improvise and adapt). Everyone has these creative abilities to some degree (Lowenfeld[18] and Guilford).[19]

How is the elementary teacher to use this information in her classroom in order to encourage creativity? She must provide art learning tasks that challenge the child to discover his abilities or uncover them. A teacher also needs to encourage the child to value his art tasks and to *push boundaries* in working out new ideas (Eisner).[20] The child should be discouraged from using the same idea over and over in his art production. Encouragement of the student to listen to his intuition during the art process is an important part of learning creative behavior.

Some Personal Statements Regarding Art and Creativeness

What are the factors which cause an artist to decide to take, or not to take, the steps he does in his work? We can only speculate here, but some of them may be the following: (A) his particular itch, bugginess, obsession, neurosis or whatever name one wants to give it; (B) his knowledge of existing alternatives of action, historical and contemporary; (C) his continuing sense of discovery in what he does, or equally, his continuing sense of confirmation of suppositions and intimations he has had all along; (D) his sensitivity to day-by-day opinion, voiced by colleagues, critics, public and family; (E) his notion (sub specie aeternitatus) of his place, or non-place, in history; and (F) his feeling of being someone special: a seer, prophet, elected victim of society, philosopher, moralist, priest, etc.

ALLAN KAPROW, artist[21]

For in the electric age there is no longer any sense in talking about the artist's being ahead of his time. Our technology is, also, ahead of its time, if we reckon by the ability to recognize it for what it is. To prevent undue wreckage in society, the artist tends now to move from the ivory tower to the control tower of society. Just as higher education is no longer a frill or luxury but a stark need of production and operational design in the electric age, so the artist is indispensable in the shaping and analysis and understanding of the life forms, and structures created by electric technology.

MARSHALL MCLUHAN, author[22]

Painting is a thundering collision of different worlds, intended to create a new world in, and from, the struggle with one another, a new world which is the work of art. Each work originates just as does the cosmos—through catastrophes which out of the chaotic din of instruments ultimately create a symphony, the music of the spheres. The creation of works of art is the creation of the world.

WASSILY KANDINSKY, artist[23]

I put down my tones without preconceived ideas. If at first, and without perhaps my knowing it, a tone has delighted or struck me, I usually find when I have finished my picture that I have respected that tone, whereas I have gradually modified and transformed all the others. The expressive qualities of colours impress me purely instinctively. To paint an autumn landscape, I should not try to remember what colours were proper to that season, I should only be inspired by the sensation they gave me: the icy purity of the sky, which is an acid blue, would express the season just as well as the colours of the leaves. My sensation itself can vary: autumn can be sweet and warm like a prolonging of summer, or conversely cool with a cold sky and lemon-yellow trees, which give an impression of cold and already foretell the winter.

HENRI MATISSE, artist[24]

Life's experiences can be interpreted in all kinds of ways and as an artist you define them in your own way. All through our lives we seek a direction and in the process, as men and artists, we evolve

Art is a way to enrich individual awareness and understanding of the world.

Awareness develops when individuals have opportunities to investigate and explore the detailed nature of objects.

principles and beliefs. These beliefs are not separate from our art; in fact, they are the underlying pulse.

YASUO KUNIYOSHI, artist[25]

How Do We Define a Classroom Teacher of Art?

From the statements by our experts, we begin to perceive creative models of the teacher of art. The creative person is one who can change his mind and ideas about things, can have many ideas on one subject, can solve problems and relate to people, can come up with strange new ideas, and can combine old and new ideas. This is the *model* of the artist or creative person the art teacher will want to project to his students. It will not be the *old model* of the artist hidden in his studio unrelated to the real world, but as a person who has deep feelings about his humanness. The art teacher must remember that an *art experience* occurs not only in producing an art work, but that one can also have an art experience in looking at art works. The *model* of the *artist* in the studio neglects the *art critic* and *art historian* models that are also to be projected by the art teacher. The art teacher must project the creative side of the *art critic* model who makes aesthetic judgments as he critically evaluates art works relative to their cultural heritage.[26] The teacher should also project the *art historian* model, as one who relates art historically and gives us new insights into different cultures. Therefore the teacher of art is more likely to be multi-dimensional in the *model* that he projects. Our creative model of the teacher of art has three sides: *artist, art critic, art historian.* An art teacher (a classroom teacher who teaches art to his pupils) is someone who can translate the essence of art into linguistics that children can discover at their particular developmental level. He (she) is, above all, a teacher who has a supreme interest in children and the courage to learn about art himself so that he can teach it to his students. He is a person who continues to create in a media of his own choosing in order to blaze toward the frontiers of his own discovery. The creative teacher places first emphasis on encouraging in his students options for self-discovery, through media exploration, subject search, learning to evaluate and knowing what to look for in art.

What Are the Major Objectives of a Good Art Program?

As one becomes involved with the ideas and approaches in this book, the term creative thinking can be exchanged for what is meant by art experiences. This book has four major objectives. First, it intends to enrich the sensory perceptions and visual thinking of the teacher, and ultimately to enrich the creative thinking of those whom he will teach. Second, it intends to expand one's knowledge and skills in practicing art. Third, it intends to enlarge the way in which a person evaluates his aesthetic judgment—it gives him a structure or map with which to appraise art works. Fourth, in the area of art history, it intends to develop the understanding of our cultural heritage, both past and present. Leading art educators and organizations, such as the National Assessments of Educational Progress: Art Objectives,[27] the California Art Education Framework,[28] the Essentials of a Quality School Art Program, National Art Education Association,[29] Art Education: Elementary, NAEA,[30] support these four major objectives in teaching art in the elementary school.

What Is the Content of a Good Art Program?

Our individual and natural concern for aesthetic quality and harmony with our ecology is a growing concern which is highly related to the role that art education plays in our educational systems. The National Art Education Association has emphasized a quality elementary school art program in the following statement:

> Art in the school is both a body of knowledge and a series of activities which the teacher organizes to provide experiences related to specific goals. The sequence and depth of these experiences are determined by the nature of the art discipline, the objectives desired, and by the interests, abilities, and needs of children at different levels of growth.

There are four major objectives supported by the NAEA in carrying out an effective quality art program in the elementary school:

1. Seeing and feeling visual relationships
2. The making of art
3. The study of works of art
4. Critical evaluation of art

The Art Education Framework of California Public Schools also states four similar major goals:

1. Development of visual and tactile perception
2. Encouragement of creative expression
3. Study of art heritage
4. Development of aesthetic judgment

The California Framework states that these components should blend into a curriculum that is appropriate to the maturity and abilities of the students involved.

The National Assessment of Educational Progress states its objectives as follows:

1. Perceive and respond to aspects of art
2. Value art as an important realm of human experience
3. Produce works of art
4. Know about art
5. Make and justify judgments about the aesthetic merit and quality of works of art

The National Assessment of Educational Progress has established an operational definition for art objects and experiences with objects such as the following:

> painting, drawing, sculpture, the graphic arts (woodcuts, engravings, etchings, and lithographs) photography, films, assemblages, collages, mobiles, and happenings, crafts (pottery, weaving, jewelry, metal work), the environmental arts (architecture, city planning, landscape architecture, interior design, product design), and the popular arts (advertisements, television commercials, clothing, record covers, and comic strips).

An effective classroom teacher will consider and creatively utilize the four major objectives as delineated here and throughout the following chapters.

Art Practice and Creative Thinking

Art is a way to *develop skills* in the use of art materials through experimentation, manipulation, and practice.

Art is a way to *enrich critical appreciation* of artists, art works, and aesthetic forms.

Art is a way to *become a creative person.*

Art is a way to *become a flexible, confident* person through telling and saying your ideas in a visual language.

Art is a way to *clarify and fix ideas* in the mind through visual reiteration, by strengthening what has been learned about something.

Every effort should be made by the classroom teacher of art to project a clear picture of how the artist or creative person works. Adults, teachers, and children should have a clear image of the artist as a creative worker who works at doing his thing just like the milkman, mailman, or policeman does his thing. Workers can only be productive when they have developed their individual skills in relation to their particular kind of work. The artist should not be viewed as a different worker but only as one who responds with a visual form that reflects how he as a human being relates to himself, others, and his environment. When he does this he then becomes a fully functioning being and should be viewed for his humanness and how it is stated by him in the art product. Looking at the creative person and the artist from this point of view makes one see and realize the human side of the individual which often times does not come through in his work. Sometimes we have projected a picture of the artist as withdrawn and unrelated to society. This is far from the truth. The art product is then viewed as the artist's concern for the human condition as he sees it. Eisner[31] and Feldman[32] point out that art is one of the means through which we can exercise our humanness by relating to man's visions as expressed through his art forms. The perception of these visual forms, their primary sources and their meaning, becomes a vital component or objective in the teaching of art (see Chapters 2 and 6).

Summary

The artist has the attributes of sensitivity to problems, flexibility, fluency, and originality because he is a creative person. The teacher should understand and be able to use this model of the creative person or artist in her classroom.

The teacher of art should have a total picture of the model of a creative art teacher as one who has three distinct sides: the studio-artist, the art critic, and the art historian. The teacher must have a depth of knowledge of each, so that she can project the models to her students.

Since we understand best the artist-studio model, we probably project it more clearly than the other two, those of art critic and art historian. The artist-studio model gives us a person who is excited about his work and about life, can change his feelings and ideas about things, can have many ideas, can combine the old with the new, and has deep feelings about his humanness.

The art teacher should also project the art critic model as one who makes aesthetic judgments as he critically evaluates works of art relative to his cultural heritage. The art critic model as defined here can be a high motivator in the classroom. The art critic model for the teacher to project is one who emphasizes the use of perceptual awareness and aesthetic judgment, is highly verbal, and is a question prober. He (she) deals with the excitement of taking in information and visual knowledge, and enjoys making an aesthetic quality judgment. This is as exciting as the making of art. The creative process is as much involved in the perception of this model as in the artist-studio model.

The art teacher should also project the art historian model as one who relates art historically and helps us gain new insights into our own and other cultures. When we neglect the art historian model our students will have missed the joy and delight that they could have gained through a knowledge of their artistic heritage. A great deal of knowledge the studio artist needs comes from the study of historical models. It should be one of the greatest sources of inspiration for the young artist.

None of the three artist models should become stereotyped into any way or pattern of doing art. They have certain overriding attributes in common, but each have their unique individual way of carrying it out. There is no one artist-studio model that should be projected, but rather many. The same applies to the art critic and art historian models. Art has many diverse approaches and all of them are highly creative. For example one artist-studio model might start with an idea, another with materials, another with the external images, another with internal images, another based on dreams; these and many more types should be projected by the art teacher.

The meaning of the term art has a broad base in our culture, as expressed by the NAEP, which ranges from painting to the comic strips.

The School Art Program has four major objectives:

1. Training of sensory perception
2. Skill in making art
3. Skill in making critical evaluations in art
4. Knowledge of art history

The practice of art and creative thinking implements these four major art objectives which gives meaning to art in our culture.

Ways to Involvement

The following involvement activities will help the student increase his understanding of some of the ideas presented. Some suggestions for the student to engage in for a deeper personal discovery of how some aspects of his emotional, intellectual and perceptual powers work in a creative way are listed here.

1. The use of J. P. Guilford's "Brick" test, which has been widely publicized, is a good example to demonstrate *uniqueness of point of view* and how *rigid* one's thinking can be without his awareness of it. One can make up any number of tests similar to this type and try them out.

2. E. Paul Torrance and R. E. Myers, in a book designed for grade school children called *Invitations to Thinking and Doing*,[33] offers ways to help even the adult understand how he does or does not understand relationships which are essential to creative ways of thinking in the arts or any subject. An example of this is one exercise called "What Do They Have in Common?" The student is asked to give as many ways as he can to show how *newspaper, blood* and *air* are related. These exercises also indicate to us how limited our thinking might be. We cannot overcome deficiencies in our ways of thinking unless we ourselves know better what the barriers are.

3. Several other operational techniques to encourage creative thinking are offered by Myers and Torrance in *Can You Imagine?*[34] *For Those Who Wonder,*[35] *Plots; Puzzles and Plots,*[36] *Invitations to Speaking and Writing Creatively.*[37]

4. A record titled *Sounds and Images*[38] by B. F. Cunnington and E. P. Torrance is designed to help one discover and overcome blocks to creative thinking. It is a deliberate attempt to expand the imagination by pushing one idea rather than moving to another idea. Torrance believes that we drop many good ideas and do not expand them as far as we might. The more thoroughly we become acquainted with an idea, the more ideas we are able to relate imaginatively to it.

5. *The Violinist,*[39] *Adventures of the Asterisk*[40] and *Flatland*[41] are films of a type which depict some aspects of our society in relation to the creative person. They emphasize the role of environment and its effect on the individual. Other aspects stressed are the need of the individual for peer and parental sanction and the role society plays in making the individual conform. The beginning portion of the film *The Information Machine,*[42] demonstrates how a person creates from things he has perceived and then later relates them into a visual product. The film *Clay*[43] explores the fluency and flexibility of one medium in depth and is a delightful aesthetic experience.

6. Torrance offers some exercises in Appendix A and B of *Rewarding Creative Behavior,*[44] that will give some idea as to how creative thinking patterns operate. Samson does similar exercises in *The Mind Builder*[45] and *The Language Ladder.*[46] They are fun to work out and at the same time they indicate how one does or does not think creatively. Many of these are not art tests, but they are tests that will help one to a deeper understanding of oneself and how one thinks creatively. Parnes, in his *Workbook for Creative Problem-Solving Institutes and Courses,*[47] gives some very specific art problems to be worked out in a creative way. Many of these help develop flexibility, fluency, divergent thinking and other attributes of the creative person. Chapter 2 of *The Mind,* Life Science Library,[48] indicates how some of our perceptual habits make us see things that are really not there and also how different individuals interpret the same sensory stimuli differently.

7. Gordon and Wyman[49] in their *Primer of Perception* suggest many ideas for perceptual training by using visual images. They offer a number of exercises to extend the ideas they illustrate. Try some of the exercises at the end of the book.

8. Lee Scherz,[50] in a book about an amazing new pencil pastime, *Imagi-Noodles,* offers a fun way to help you stretch your imagination by looking at ordinary shapes and then trying to see how many different objects you can make from each shape.

All the above authors attempt to offer ways which stimulate an individual to gain more insight into his own creative thinking. Difficulties will be encountered because new relationships are being formed and established and old ones are being rejected. You will begin to realize that the creative person in art as well as in any field uses analytical and creative thinking in resolving the problems he has set for himself. Doing some of the exercises suggested or constructing similar ones of your own will increase your understanding of some of the limits in your particular way of thinking and also help you realize the complexity and divergency of the creative mind at work.

References

[1]June King McFee, *Preparation for Art,* Belmont, Calif.: Wadsworth Publishing Co., Inc., 1961.

[2]Michael F. Andrews, "The Dialectics of Creativity and Mental Health," *Creativity and Psychological Health,* Syracuse: Syracuse University Press, 1961.

[3]Viktor Lowenfeld, *Creative and Mental Growth,* New York: The Macmillan Company, 1960.

[4]Manuel Barkan, *A Foundation for Art Education,* New York: The Ronald Press Company, 1955.

[5]Robert C. Burkhart, *Spontaneous and Deliberate Ways of Learning,* Scranton: International Textbook Co., 1962.

[6]F. Louis Hoover, *Art Activities for the Very Young,* Worcester, Mass.: Davis Publications, Inc., 1961.

[7]W. Lambert Brittain, *Children's Art,* Cornell Extension Bulletin 1067, New York State College of Home Economics, August, 1961.

[8]Frank Barron, "Psychology of Imagination," *Scientific American,* 199:50, 150-156, September, 1958.

[9]Donald W. MacKinnon, "What Makes a Person Creative?" *Saturday Review,* February 10, 1962, pp. 15-17.

[10]Alice Miel, *et al., Creativity in Teaching: Invitations and Instances,* Belmont, Calif.: Wadsworth Publishing Co., Inc., 1961.

[11]J. P. Guilford, *Creativity and Its Cultivation,* ed. by Harold H. Anderson, New York: Harper & Row, Publishers, 1959.

[12]Carl R. Rogers, *Creativity and Its Cultivation,* ed. by Harold H. Anderson, New York: Harper & Row, Publishers, 1959.

[13]Abraham H. Maslow, *Creativity and Its Cultivation,* ed. by Harold H. Anderson, New York: Harper & Row, Publishers, 1959.

[14]E. Paul Torrance, statement from an address presented at Sacramento State College, California, Spring, 1962.

[15]Kenneth R. Beittel, Statement frcm the context of a letter sent to the authors. Professor Beittel is Director of Research for the Department of Art Education at Pennsylvania State University, 1963.

[16]Howard Conant, Statement from an address delivered at the George Peabody College for Teachers, Nashville, Tennessee, July 9, 1963. Title of the talk was "An Artist-Educator Views Creativity and Aesthetics."

[17]Norman Cousins, *Saturday Review,* April 20, 1968, p. 22.

[18]J. P. Guilford, "Creative Abilities in the Arts," *Readings in Art Education,* edited by Elliot Eisner, Waltham, Mass.: Blaisdell Publishing Co., 1966, pp. 283-291 .

[19]Viktor Lowenfeld, "Creativity: Education's Stepchild," *A Source Book for Creative Thinking,* edited by Sidney J. Parnes, New York: Charles Scribner's Sons, 1962, pp. 9-18.

[20]Elliot W. Eisner, *Educating Artistic Vision,* New York: The Macmillan Company, 1972, pp. 217-220.

[21]Allan Kaprow, *The Creation of Art and the Creation of Art Education,* Cooperative Research Project V-002, A Seminar in Art Education for Research and Curriculum Development, Edward L. Mattil, Project Director, Pennsylvania State University, 1966, pp. 74-75.

[22]Marshall McLuhan, *Understanding Media: the Extensions of Man,* New York: McGraw-Hill Book Company, 1965, p. 65.

[23]Robert L. Herbert, ed., *Modern Artists on Art,* Kandinsky, Wassily, from "Reminiscences," Englewood Cliffs, N.J.: Prentice-Hall, Inc., 1964, p. 35.

[24]Henri Matisse, *Matisse: A Portrait of the Artist and the Man,* New York: Frederick A. Praeger, Inc., 1960, p. 82.

[25]Statement by Kuniyoshi, from an exhibit catalogue letter *40 American Painters* 1940-1950, University Gallery, Department of Art, University of Minnesota.

[26]Guilford, "Creative Abilities in the Arts."

[27]"The Essentials of a Quality School Art Program, A Position Statement by the National Art Education Association," *Art Education,* April 1973, Vol. 26, No. 4, pp. 21-26.

[28]*Art Education Framework,* California State Department of Education, Sacramento, Calif., 1971.

[29]*Art Objectives,* National Assessment of Educational Progress, Ann Arbor Offices: Room 201A Huron Towers, 2222 Fuller Road, Ann Arbor, Michigan, 48105.

[30]*Art Education: Elementary,* National Art Education Association, 1201 16th St., N.W., Washington, D.C., 228 pp.

[31]Eisner, *Educating Artistic Vision.*

[32]Edmund Feldman, *Becoming Human Through Art, Aesthetic Experience in the School,* Englewood Cliffs, New Jersey: Prentice-Hall, Inc., 1970.

[33]R. E. Myers and E. P. Torrance, *Invitations to Thinking and Doing,* Boston: Ginn and Company,

[34]———, *Can You Imagine,* Boston: Ginn and Company,

[35]———, *For Those Who Wonder,* Boston: Ginn and Company,

[36]———, *Plots; Puzzles and Plots,* Boston: Ginn and Company, 1966.

[37]———, *Invitations to Speaking and Writing Creatively,* Boston: Ginn and Company, 1965.

[38]Bert F. Cunningham and E. P. Torrance, *Sounds and Images* (record), Imagi Craft Series, Boston: Ginn and Company, 1965.

[39]Western Cenima, *The Violonist* (*films*), 244 Kearny, San Francisco.
[40]Ed. Harrison, *Adventures of the Asterisk*, 1201 Broadway, New York.
[41]*Flatland*, Contemporary Films. 1211 Polk St., San Francisco.
[42]*The Information Machine* (free film), contact local IBM office.
[43]*Clay: The Origin of Species* (film), Contemporary Films, 1211 Polk St., San Francisco.
[44]E. P. Torrance, *Rewarding Creative Behavior*, Englewood Cliffs, N.J.: Prentice-Hall, Inc., 1965.
[45]R. W. Samson, *The Mind Builder, A Self-Teaching Guide to Creative Thinking & Analysis*, New York: E. P. Dutton & Co., Inc., 1965.
[46]———, *The Language Ladder*, New York: E. P. Dutton & Co., Inc., 1967.
[47]S. Parnes, *Workbook for Creative Problem-Solving Institutes and Courses*, Buffalo: Bookstore, State University of New York, 1966.
[48]John Wilson, *The Mind*, Life Science Library, Time Inc., New York, 1964.
[49]Gordon Stephen and Jenifer Wyman, *Primer of Perception*, New York: Reinhold Publishing Corp., 1967.
[50]Lee Scherz, *Imagi-Noodles*, New York: Grosset and Dunlap, 1973, p. 96.

Additional References

Anderson, Harold, ed., *Creativity and Its Cultivation*, New York: Harper & Row, Publishers, 1959.

Barkan, Manuel, *Through Art to Creativity*, Boston: Allyn & Bacon, Inc., 1962.

Brittain, W. Lambert, "An Experiment Toward Measuring Creativity," *Research in Art Education 7th Yearbook*, National Art Education Association, 1956.

———, ed., *Creativity and Art Education*, National Art Education, 1964, 147 pp.

D'Amico, Victor, *Experiments in Creative Teaching*, New York: The Museum of Modern Art, 1960.

Eisner, Elliot W., *Think With Me About Creativity*, Danville, N.Y.: F. A. Owen Publishing Co., 1964.

Grigsby, J. Eugene, Jr., *Art and Ethnics: Background for Teaching Youth in a Pluralistic Society*, Dubuque, Ia.: Wm. C. Brown Company Publishers, 1977.

Gruber, Howard E., *Contemporary Approaches to Creative Thinking*, New York: Atherton Press, 1963.

Hyman, Ray, *Creativity and the Prepared Mind*, Research Monograph No. 1., National Art Education Association, 1965, 32 pp.

Koestler, Arthur, *The Act of Creation*, London: Hatchinson & Co., 1964.

Krathwohl, David R., Benjamin S. Bloom, Bertram B. Masia, *Taxonomy of Educational Objectives*, The Classification of Educational Goals, Handbook II: Affective Domain, New York: David McKay Co., Inc., 1964.

Linderman, Earl W., "How Do We Stimulate Children To Be Creative?", *California Parent-Teacher*, January, 1962.

Linderman, Earl W. and Linderman, Marlene M., *Crafts for the Classroom*, New York: Macmillan Co., 1977.

Linderman, Marlene M., *Art in the Elementary School*, Dubuque, Ia.: Wm. C. Brown Company Publishers, 1974.

Lowenfeld, Viktor, "Basic Aspects of Creative Teaching," *Creativity and Psychological Health*, Syracuse: Syracuse University Press, 1961.

———, "Creativity and Art Education," *School Arts*, October, 1959.

Massialas, Byron G. and Jack Zevin, *Creative Encounters in the Classroom, Teaching and Learning through Discovery*, New York: John Wiley & Sons, Inc., 1967.

Osborn, Alex F., *Applied Imagination: Principles and Procedures of Creative Thinking*, New York: Charles Scribner's Sons, 1957.

"Perceiving, Behaving, Becoming," *Association for Supervision and Curriculum Development, 1962 Yearbook*, National Education Association, 1962.

Saunders, Robert J., *Relating Art and Humanities to the Classroom*, Dubuque, Ia.: Wm. C. Brown Company Publishers, 1977.

Stein, Morris I. and Shirley J. Heinze, *Creativity and the Individual*, Glencoe, Ill.: The Free Press, 1960.

Film References

Eye of Man, Counterpoint Films, 5823 Santa Monica Blvd., Hollywood, Calif.

Perception-Structure or Flow, National Film Board of Canada, 44 Montgomery St., San Francisco, Calif.

Why Man Creates. Pyramid Film Productions, P. O. Box 1084, Santa Monica, Calif.

Photo Credit: Marlene Linderman.

"We are all prone to accept our preconception instead of investigating a thing fully and anew. Once we have had an experience, the repetition of the experience becomes muffled and not clear. We anticipate and in anticipating we lose the significance, the meaningful details.

Kimon Nicolaides,
from *The Natural Way to Draw,*
Boston: Houghton Mifflin Co.,
1941, pp. 67-68

Chapter 2

Developing Readiness for Art Expression Through Awareness

One of the most important things that a teacher or parent can help children retain as they mature is their awareness of experiences through the use of their senses and emotions. The creative person keeps his openness to experience and in this respect he is childlike. The child does not feel that a new experience will be a risk to him. He perceives the world without thinking that he has to make judgments about it. During early childhood he collects much raw material without deciding "what" or "how" he will use it. How much information is collected and what is done with it will determine his creative potential not only as a child but as an adult.

In order to have a sharper picture of how important awareness is, it would be well to understand how awareness fits into the creative process. The central characteristics of the creative process might well be defined as 1. awareness, 2. focus, 3. working process, 4. art product. In this order, the first stage becomes all important to creativity of any kind.[1] *Awareness* entails letting the data in so that the information can be processed and stored for use. Processing and storing involves the total act of perceptual awareness. It means taking in all sensory impressions without immediately judging them. The second stage in the creative process is that of refining the data absorbed, in other words, *focusing*. Here we begin to structure, to make form out of the formless. We relate the new data to our existing information until we have a clearer idea. Then we attempt to create or work out our focus to produce the art product.

How an Artist or Creative Person Processes Information Through the Senses

The following descriptions of two *creative process models* clearly explain how the artist or creative person processes information through the senses:

Creative Process Model Number 1

AWARENESS

1. Learning to take in information without prejudging it.
2. Being uninhibited and more free inwardly to receive information.
3. Delaying structure.
4. Trying to deliberately take in more information than usual.
5. Continuing to question a situation, observation or judgment.
6. Getting oneself into the mood, warming up, getting into the spirit of the situation.
7. Learning to look at things from more than one point of view.

FOCUS

1. Occurs when we begin to narrow the field of data.
2. Imposes a form on things.
3. Searches over the information perceived.
4. Relates ideas, facts, sense impressions, feeling and moods.
5. Uses the imagination to break barriers and seek new relationships.
6. Orders our experiences.
7. Keeps ideas fluid.
8. Begins to structure bits of information.
9. Begins to put the data into an order. If it does not fit, go to awareness again. Awareness and focus are interrelated.

WORKING PROCESS

1. Refers to production, the activity or creative process.
2. Refers to intense and total involvement.
3. Refers to the skill of the person.
4. Refers to ordering, working hard, forming, being responsible.

ART PRODUCT

1. Refers to the finished product.
2. Refers to the feeling of being finished for the moment.
3. Refers to the culmination of the previous stages.
4. Refers to making the final judgment to stop.
5. Refers to the expression of the person as seen in the product.

Creative Process Model Number 2

The act of learning or *creative process* as described by Bruner[2] is very useful in helping us understand the importance of perceptual awareness. He has divided the act of learning into three phases:

1. Acquisition of knowledge
2. Transformation
3. Evaluation

Perceptual awareness is the taking in of knowledge and is of first consideration in the *creative process*. For example, the "visual knowledge" of an object is its color, texture, shape, line, light and art patterns. If we attend to the object being perceived from this

Knowledge stems from a point of view. A trec is made of many visually and tactually perceived details. What details can we remember about trees? How many ways can wc think of to increase our awareness? How have these pictures modified our concept of a tree?

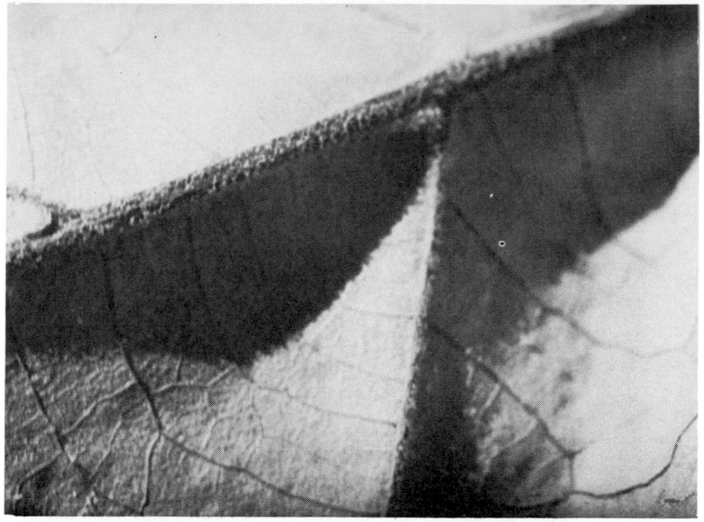

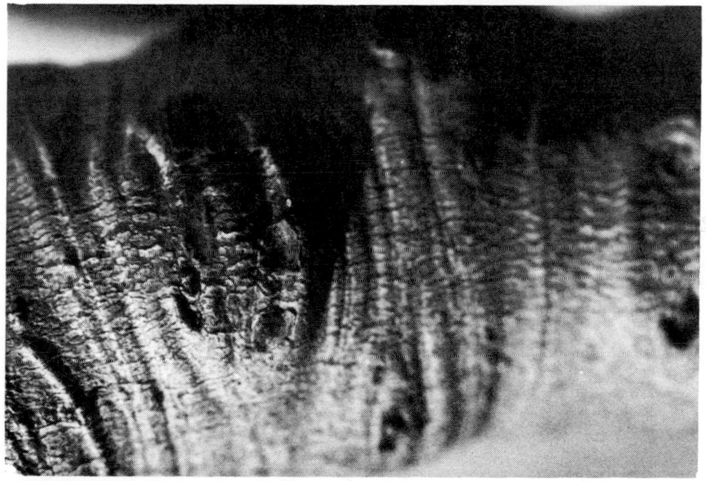

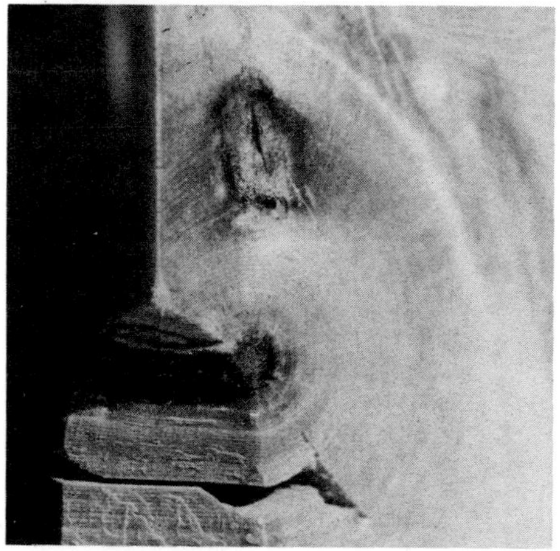

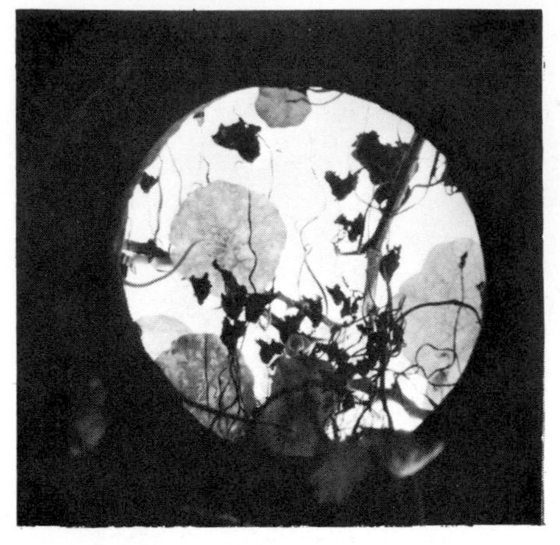

The point of observation changes the meaning of an object and may bring out details previously missed. Looking UP and looking DOWN, as well as looking straight ahead can increase awareness.

point of view, the "visual knowledge" will be increased and the recall later will be greater because specific details were taken in at the time of viewing.

The transformation stage is similar to the focus and working process stages given above. It is during this part of the act of learning or the creative process that the individual has free play in how he transforms knowledge (thinking, feeling, perceiving) which he has taken in during the unstructured awareness stage.

Evaluation becomes very critical because without it the inner demands of the individual remain diffuse and his self-motivation to deeper levels of knowledge and involvement is likely to diminish.

Krathwohl, Bloom and Masia[3] in *Taxonomy of Educational Objectives*, Handbook II: Affective Domain, gives some attention to awareness under the behavioral objectives of "receiving." "Awareness" lists educational objectives which reflect many of the primary experiences of the young child. Many of the items from the three check charts in this chapter could be listed under the "cognitive domain" as "visual knowledge." Visual knowledge as used here implies an assessment of the qualities of the stimulus (object) perceived. The student can then relate his perception of the visual quality of an object in his art product or express verbally his aesthetic judgment of the art work. An example of a visualized model of the creative process is presented in *Discovering Ideas For Art*,[4] a film that makes individual awareness more than passive receiving. This film directs one's attention to the taking in of visual art elements in viewing a variety of objects. During the awareness stage one takes in information through the different senses in different ways, but the information is not always abstracted and then stored in memory traces. Rather, impressions are retained and intermingled with other impressions to be triggered later by perhaps verbal or nonverbal stimuli which will bring forth a personalized visual product. It is the inventive use of things we see that produces creative art products.

The important aspect of attending to and perceiving one's environment in great detail from many points of view is a vital part of any elementary art program.

Breaking Barriers To Awareness

In order to be able to assist the child in developing awareness we must be more open to our *own* experiences. We must develop our *own* sensitivity, our *own* awareness. One effective method is to start with those children's books which are written with a high degree of sensitivity. Many of these offer unique avenues of exploration. Such an example of enriching the concept for one specific detail is dealt with in a book called *A Tail Is a Tail*, by Katherine Mace.[5] This little book tells all about animal tails and what some of them are used for.

Many approaches that we use to develop awareness are indirect and are not a conscious dissecting. They involve aesthetic experiences by exposure. Openness is referred to as the exposure stage by some psychologists. They explain that during this period the individual takes in or absorbs raw material for later use in creative expression. It is important to lead the child into experiences but to let him discover things for himself. He must perceive his environment in his own way. He should not be told how a thing smells. Rather, encourage him to explain what the smell is like or what it means to him. Experiences such as these should involve ordinary things that occur daily. Awareness requires daily practice. Do not hurry the child to answer because this forces him to a premature focus. Encourage him to perceive but not to judge; to enjoy the entire aesthetic experiences of a flower rather than just naming its parts.

For the person who has become "dulled" to the world, an unusual, or oddball approach is needed to reawaken his sensibilities. In order to penetrate into the details he must again become an observer investigating the detailed visual relationships which form the total impression. As Lowenfeld states, "Unless we penetrate into an experience, whatever its nature may be, it will remain superficial and as such cannot serve as the basis for creativity."[6]

Awareness Means to Eliminate the Risk to the Inner Self

Probably one of the most important points to remember when considering whether we have what it takes to be more creative persons is to remember that we are competing only with ourselves. We tend to set up our own set of stumbling blocks. To avoid taking a risk, we may use devices such as, "I can't do that," "I don't know how to draw a straight line," "I have never done that before," "I can't think of anything to paint," or "I don't know what to do." These all are ways we have of protecting ourselves from a threat, the threat of doing something we have not tried before.

So that we can better compare a person who has more perceptual openness to one who maintains a more conventional attitude toward openness let us look at the following characteristics that are somewhat typical of the two types:

The Teacher Who Is Highly Aware Is More:	The Teacher Who Is Not as Highly Aware Is More:
expressive in his personality and encourages this in his students.	dependent on previous routines that have been established as "practical."
open to vast quantities of raw materials in his environment.	likely to rely on set routines and patterns.
flexible and fluent in ideas and adaptable to new situations.	highly dependent on "how-to-do-it" routines that give a predetermined result.
interested in searching, exploring and experimenting with materials.	inclined to reject all new ideas as threatening to the status quo; keeps his mind closed to new or unusual approaches.
free and unthreatened by mysterious and unknown situations that arise, and is rather excited and attracted by such possibilities.	likely to travel the well-trodden paths and close his eyes once general recognition is made.
humorous in his approaches.	likely to have no time for humor or play, stick to tried and true methods.
inclined to try new methods of enriching learning.	inflexible, conforming, has only solutions or ideas he used in previous situations.
likely to encourage and stress independence in thought and action that leads to individual initiative and decision.	

Awareness is what Herbert Read[7] refers to as the refined use of the senses. A second meaning refers to the ability to have a high degree of awareness with the experience undergone. Third, emphasis is placed on having more empathy with a given object.

A person who has awareness perceives more of the "raw" data from his environment through his senses, experiences and his capacity for empathy. He reaches total awareness when he is receptive to his feelings and experiences so that he can take in new information and see things in new relationships.

Awareness to objects through refined use of our senses thus means that we discipline ourselves in such a manner that much more *detail* than usual can be perceived. To be aware, one should cultivate the discipline or habit of unstructured perceptual awareness to objects in the environment.

An eighteen-month-old child is very open to his environment through his senses in that he does not have barriers, does not feel threatened, does not immediately judge the material he takes in, does not relate it, does not structure, nor does he focus or make closure on what he perceives. We might compare our own way of using our senses to the open manner in which a young child perceives a new object. In one study, when given two empty tin cans to play with, a child grasped them by the open ends in each hand. As he did so, he brought them near his face and noticed the shiny insides of the cans. He then tried to place one can inside the other by holding one under his arm and putting the other can inside the one he was holding. This did not work so he then placed one on the floor and placed the other on top of it. This worked, and one can stood on top of the other. He then tried to pick them up but did not succeed and knocked them over. He tried several times to restack them and then picked them up two at a time, but did not succeed. He then picked up one of the cans and shouted into it and seemed to enjoy the echo of the sound. Later he put the can into his mouth and tried to bite it. At the same time he tasted it and repeated his action several times. He then dropped the can and watched it roll. Then he got up and kicked it to make it roll some more. After picking up one of the cans, he dropped an object into it and listened to the noise it made.

In this experience, the child used many of his senses to experience the tin can. He found it made a noise when he dropped it, his voice sounded different when he shouted into it. He tasted it, touched it with his tongue, found that it was hard when he bit it and that it was cold. He kicked it. He noticed the surface reflected his image. He discovered many things about an object because he was free to explore it and did not approach it already focused or with a set pattern in mind.

Another example of how "closed" adults sometimes are to the use of the sense impressions is indicated in a quote from *Vision* magazine.

> *Helen Keller tells of a friend of hers who walked through the woods. When she was asked what she saw on her walk she replied, "Nothing in particular." Miss Keller could not imagine how anyone could possibly walk through the woods and see "nothing in particular." Helen Keller must "see" through her fingers, because she lost her eyesight through severe illness when she was a very small child. Yet Miss Keller can appreciate the symmetry, texture, and variety of the leaves. She thrills at the touch of the smooth bark of the birch tree and the tough bark of the elm tree. She delights at the feel of the first buds on the branches and the special fragrance that announces that it is springtime.*[8]

Developing Awareness Through Experiencing Details

Another way that will help you obtain a better understanding of your own awareness is to remember in detail your perceptual personal experiences or for the first time direct your attention to the details listed while observing a flower. Check the "yes" column if you have ever thought about:

DETAIL CHECK CHART

	Yes	No
the weight of the flower		
how soft or hard the petals are		
how long the petals are		
how easily the petals break or fall off		
how easily the petals bend		
the amount of moisture in the flower		
how fragile and hollow the stem is		
where the stamen is		
where the nectar is		
the hair follicles growing on the petals		
whether or not the petals have veins		
whether the stem breaks easily		
the shape of the petals		
what it feels like to rub the petals on your cheek		
how the flower might taste		
how it smells		
how the color in the petals changes or blends		

The key to richer awareness lies in the development of our *sensory equipment*. We must learn to investigate, explore, search and experiment. Nothing in our environment is too small or unimportant to overlook.

Awareness to one's experience means first of all the ability to perceive, and second, the ability to recall in vivid detail the thoughts, perceptions and feelings derived from an experience.

This ability to form a harmonious relationship is undoubtedly more difficult for the average adult to accomplish than simply being open to his own sensory impressions.

The recall and relating of details as expressed by Laird[9] will be greater if the individual has structured the perception in a "meaningful way" at the time he perceived it. The "meaningful way" could assume a number of different patterns:

1. Have the student become involved in a physical act of moving, if possible, while taking in the information. This same physical act will help later in the recall of the information taken in.

2. Have the student relate the new knowledge or perception to something he already knows.

3. Do not tell him exactly what or how to perceive. Let him discover as much as he can by himself and then ask questions that will help him structure and continue his inquiry.

4. Use the actual object, if possible, while increasing knowledge and awareness. Do not try to do everything at the abstract verbal level.

5. Practice remembering things about people you meet by doing the following:

Associate the person's name with an unusual relationship

Concentrate on the specific features of the face: color of eyes; teeth; shape of nose; eyebrows; skin texture;

Look for cues that describe the person's uniqueness

Concentration can help you achieve a new in-depth awareness. Try to arrange yourself so that you limit your awareness to a single unchanging source of stimulation for a period of time. All of one's energies are focused on the movement, the visual object, the smell, the sound, or the color.

One way we can concentrate or return to the process of awareness is to slightly vary our habitual or automatic way that we do something. We do this in our art class by looking at a picture upside down or drawing with the left hand if right-handed, or drawing the back of the head instead of the face. These and similar methods of altering our usual way of looking or experiencing will help us return to a more "open" awareness. This slight change eliminates all outside distractions, removes habitual actions, and frees individuals to give full attention to whatever they are taking in. In his statement about creative people MacKinnon states that creative people tend to prefer perceiving to judging. Or when one is concentrating on his awareness he is not judging, acting, or initiating action, he is simply observing. We need to develop this power of concentration since our past experiences tune out a lot of perceptual information.

In relating his experiences the adult faces a greater threat to his inner self and therefore is very likely to react by saying he cannot do something he is requested to do, thus eliminating the threat. Part of this attitude undoubtedly stems from the fact that since early childhood we are told not to have feelings and later as an adult we are told to hide our feelings. We are told not to cry when we are injured (It didn't hurt, did it!) until we become so protective of ourselves that we can no longer identify with our emotions.

In speaking of a child's emotional reactions we mean how he felt when he was lost in a big store; how excited he was when he took a train ride; how sad he felt when his canary died; how happy he was at his birthday party; how he enjoyed sharing popcorn with a friend; how he loves to have Daddy read to him at bedtime; how sorry he felt when he hurt a playmate; and how angry he was when an older child took his tricycle away from him. His "feeling" might sometimes be more physical in nature and deal with such common experiences as a stomachache, or falling and hurting his knee. These are all experiences he has gone through, been a part of, participated in. He will also have sensory perceptions to relate to the emotional experiences when asked to express his reaction through art materials.

Developing Awareness Through Experiences

To help you identify with your own awareness to your experiences, respond to the questions on the following chart. We will use experiences with flowers again in order to clarify the three areas of openness being considered. Check under "yes" if you have ever:

Experience Check Chart

	Yes	No
planted flower seeds and watch them grow		
bought a bouquet of flowers		
picked or cut flowers		
given someone a present of flowers on some special occasion		
smelled flowers in relation to funerals, weddings, state fairs, etc.		
held or carried flowers on May Day, for a wedding, or for your mother as she cut them		
worn a flower for a special occasion		
arranged flowers for the table		
visited a florist shop, flower garden		
destroyed a flower to see how it is put together		

You have experienced "flowers" in many ways. Let us take the first point on the list and ask ourselves some questions to deepen and broaden our understanding of an experience. When you planted the flower seeds, did you notice the size, shape, weight and color? Was the ground warm and moist? Did you crumble the dirt in your hands and smell it? Were your knees tired from kneeling on the ground? Did you uncover worms as you dug? Did you make straight rows for the seeds? Did you mark the spot where you planted them? Did you cover them with soft earth, etc., etc.?

Developing Awareness Through Empathy or Identification

The third and final way to perceptual awareness is through empathy or identification with the object in the sense that you become the object. You can use the example of the flower again. In checking the following, you should begin not only to gain an

understanding of empathy, but also to increase your understanding of it by stretching your own barriers a little. Have you ever thought how it feels:

Empathy Check Chart

	Yes	No
to have the sun warm you		
to open in the morning and close at night		
to fall off the bush		
to feel the dew collect on you at night		
to have a bee take nectar from you		
to wave in the wind and bump into other flowers		
to get cold at night		
to turn and face the sun		
to be pulled, picked, or cut off		
to have someone put his nose in your face and sniff		
to have bugs crawl over you, maybe even eat you		
to feel the rain beat on you during a thunderstorm		
to be a flower of many colors		
to open from a tiny bud to a full blossom		
to change from the flower to the seed		

If you checked "yes" many times on each chart you are well on your way to creative thinking. If you answered many of them "no" you need more practice to develop your skill in observation of details, awareness of experiences, and empathy.

Sensory Awareness Discovery Lists and Games

Test your awareness for being sharp and alert by utilizing your senses! Study each discovery list described below, and check each experience that is similar to your own background. Add to each list in the space provided! If you scored more than half, you are at the beginning of a new discovery awareness of your world. If you experienced all things listed, you are at the front edge of your awareness!

Sights We Discover

How many sights have you observed?

	Yes	No
rays of sunshine through the clouds		
frosty windows in winter		
a wet spider web		
a full moon		
a baby sleeping		
polliwog eggs with little black specks inside of them		
an anthill		
the cream-colored pattern on top of a crab shell		
watch armed robbers pass 3 feet in front of you		
changing of the sea during an entire day		
dark brown eyes		
the endlessness of looking across the ocean		
dog rubbing his nose with his paw		
a snake in the grass		
freshly picked peaches		
gum stuck to the bottom of one's shoe		
catching the eye of someone in a shared experience		
the surface of your tongue		
the inside of a dog's ear		
pools of sunlight under the trees		
a thick fog starting to roll in		
snow blowing past a lamp		
add some unusual experiences here		

Sounds That We Discover

How Many Sounds Have You Heard?

	Yes	No
rain on a roof		
trains in the night		
roosters crowing		
car horns tooting		
dripping faucet		
dental drill (emotional reaction)		
jackhammer		
water rushing over rocks		
birds singing in the morning		
wood crackling in the fireplace		
wind in the trees		
squeaking hinge		
thunder in the distant sky		
hiss of a snake		
crunch of snow beneath our feet		
walking in wet tennis shoes		
lonely sound of a gull in the wind		
sound of the ocean		
throaty buzz of a chain saw		
chatter of an old dog's teeth		
smack of a kiss		
whine of wire when stretched tightly		
sound of a sickle in the grass		
cows chewing hay		
lambs nursing on bottles		
thump on a watermelon		
water breaking against bow of ship		
click of a light switch		
scratching our skin		
hanging up the telephone		
tea kettle boiling		
a telephone in the night		
squealing brakes		
fingernail on the blackboard		
crying of an adult		
radio static		
a cat yowling		
supersonic boom of a jet		
cracking of knuckles		
growling of the stomach		
gum cracking		
add more sounds to the list here		

Increased awareness of height and size can be experienced in many ways. We can experience perceptive qualities through other parts of our body, such as hands and knees, as well as our eyes. In this way, basic information vital to art expression develops.

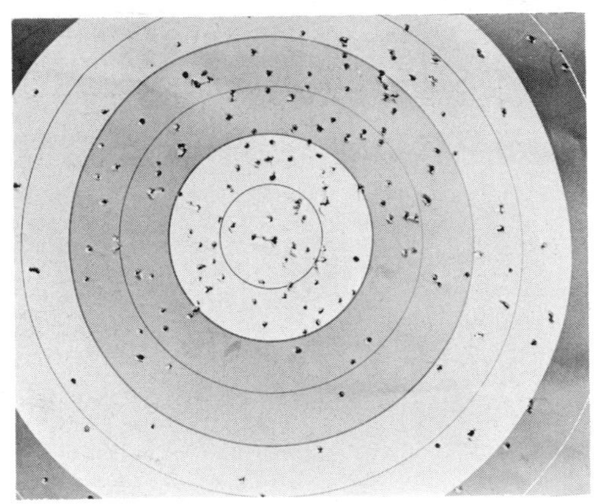

Enlarging or magnifying parts reveals new meanings about common objects we have viewed many times before, and missed.

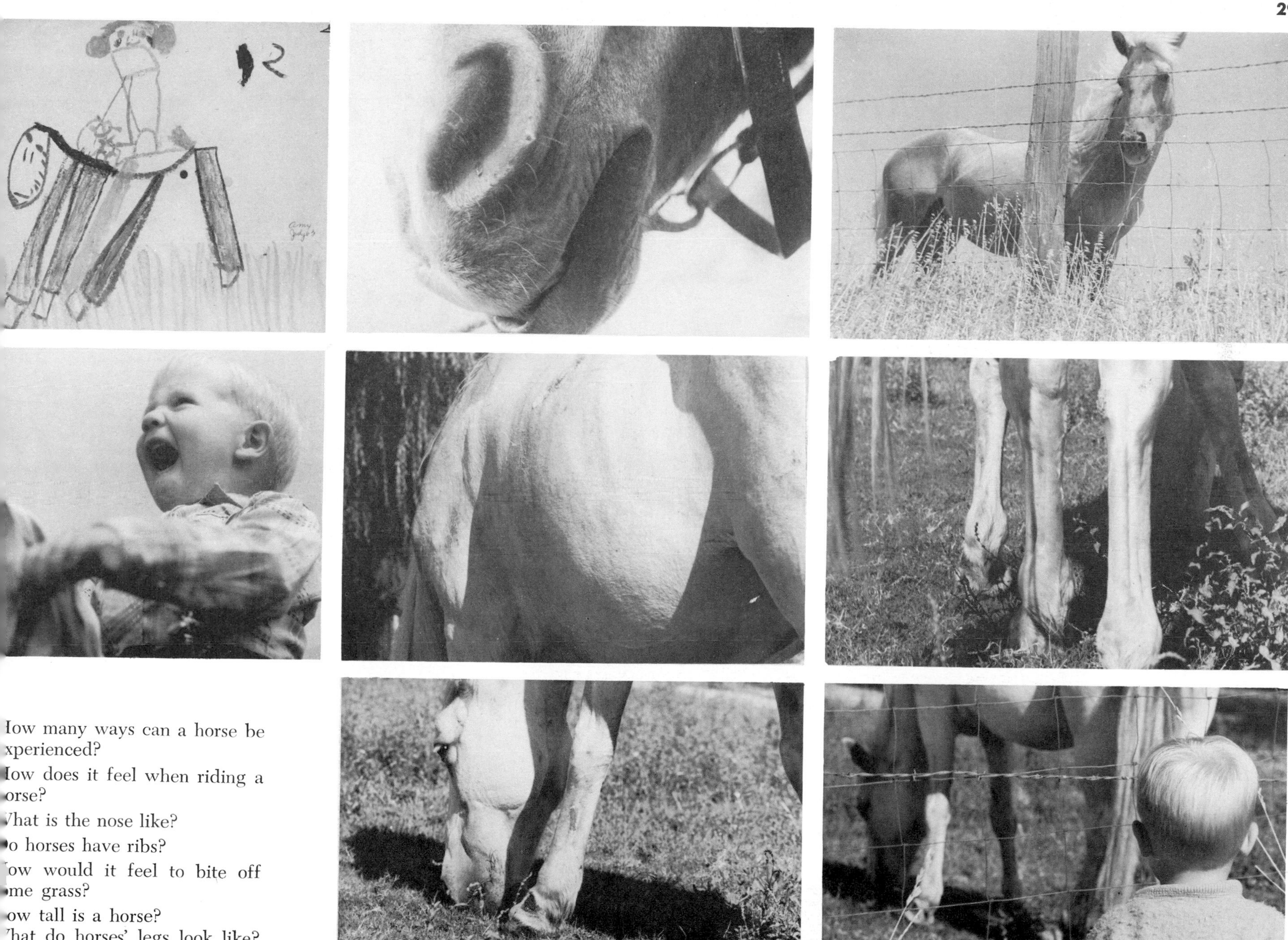

Iow many ways can a horse be xperienced?

Iow does it feel when riding a orse?

Vhat is the nose like?

o horses have ribs?

'ow would it feel to bite off me grass?

ow tall is a horse?

'hat do horses' legs look like?

The birds on these two pages were drawn by first grade children, while using actual photographs as models. Notice the high degree of interpretation evident in each picture, as well as the personal approach of each child.

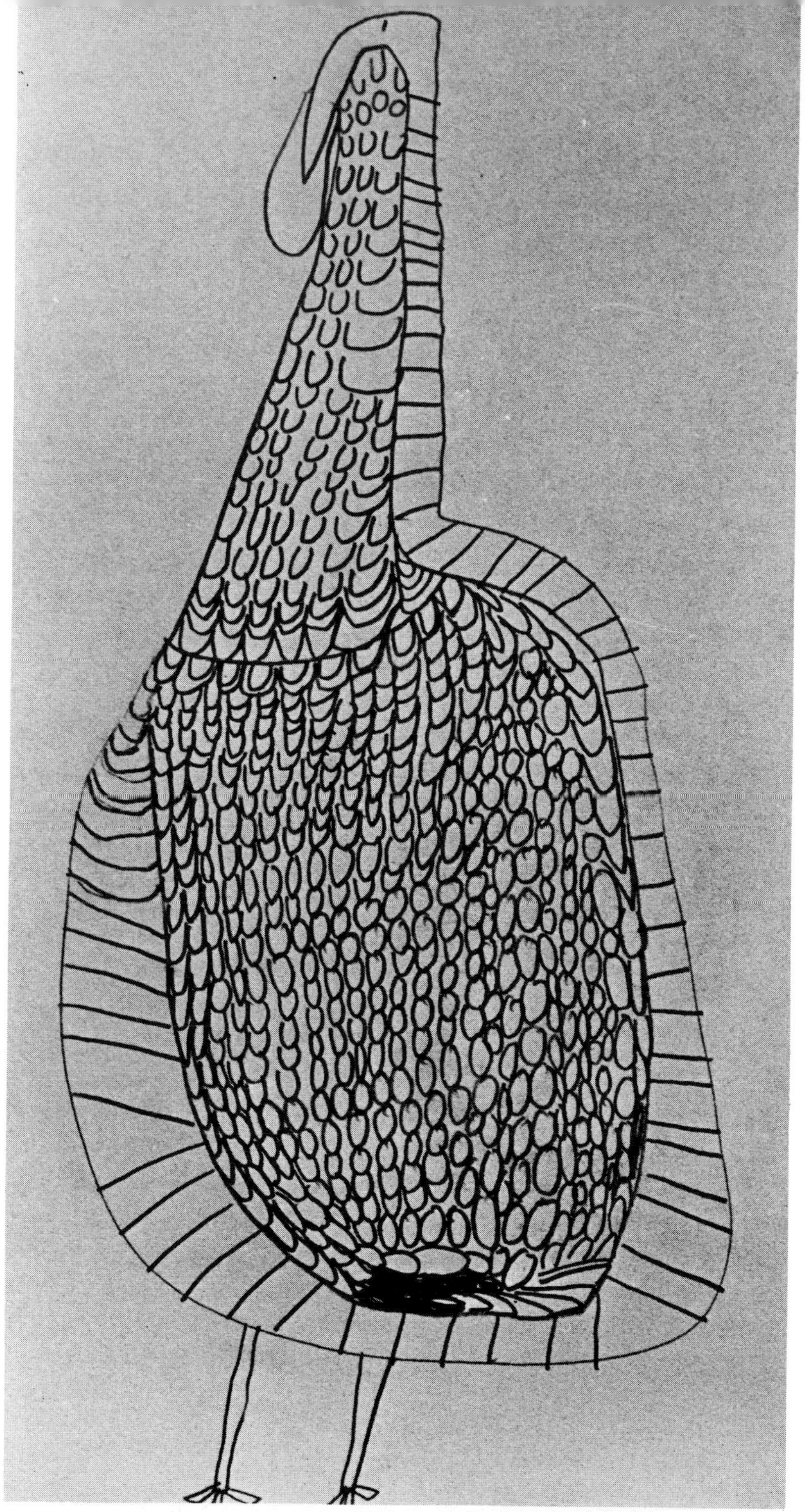

When we imagine, we extend our vision and increase our openness. Where do the insects live? Are there craters on the moon? Do the gears move? Is there a parking lot? What else can you see?

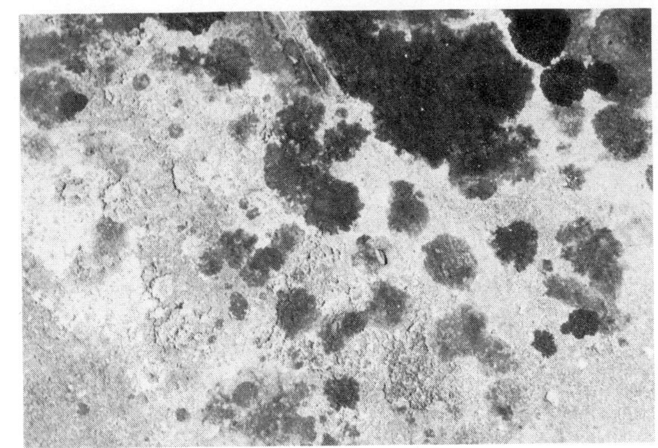

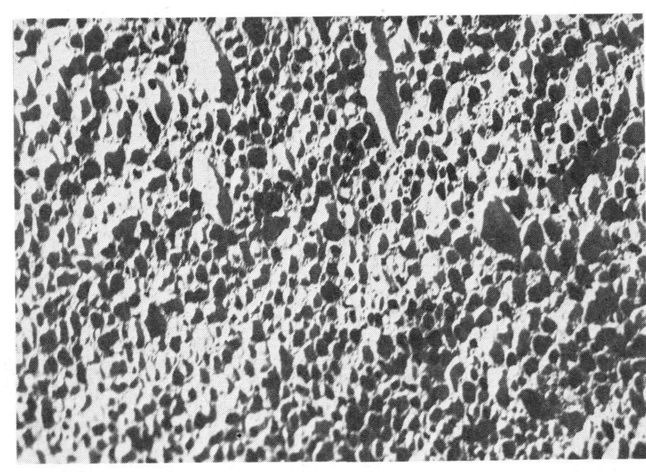

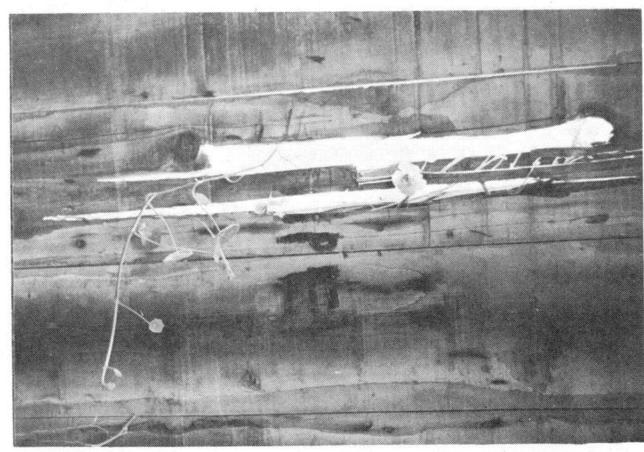

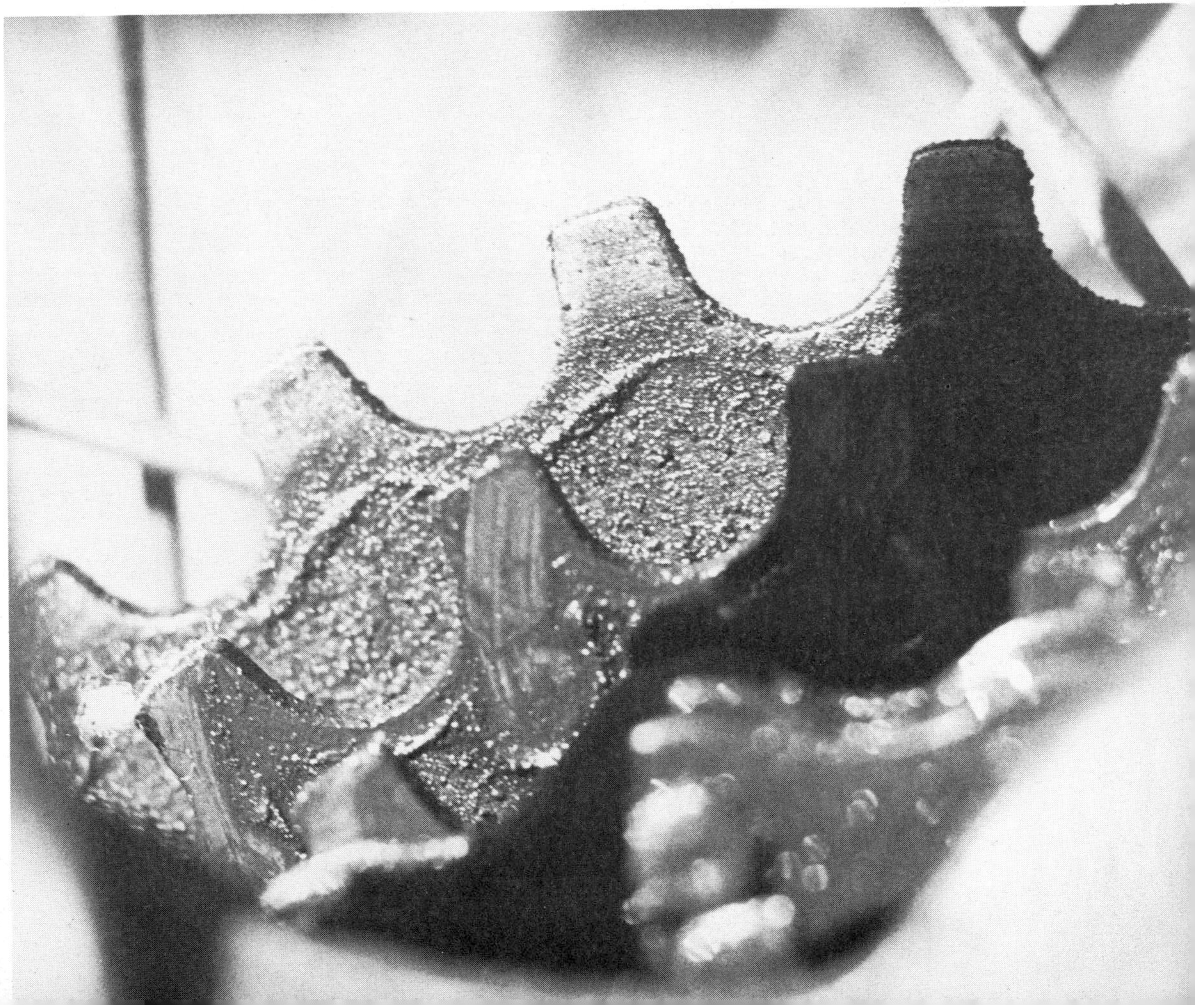

Artistic awareness is a continual experiencing of the world through all of the senses, again and again.

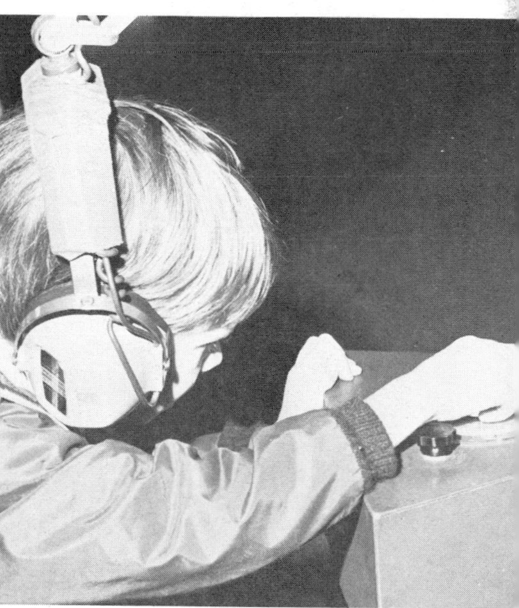

Artists use many of their senses other than vision in order to express feelings and emotions and to develop imagery in their art work. Smells in our immediate environment can provoke strong visual images, such as the ones listed below. Add your own personally remembered smells to this list. Share and exchange your list with a friend. See Ways to Involvement, item 5, Chapter 2, for another smelling game that you can construct.

Smells We Discover

How Many Smells Have You Noticed?

	Yes	No
after-shave lotion		
coffee perking		
new shoes		
freshly cut grass		
hot tar		
cigar smoke		
wet dog		
sour milk (repugnant)		
hayfield		
baby right after bath		
onion factory		
wet bathing suits		
the air after a summer rain		
musty old books		
smell of the ocean		
bread from the oven		
dead whale on a beach		
closed-up rooms		
add more smells to your list here		

Some Teachers Relate Their Rediscovered Awareness To Smells

When I start really thinking about the smells around me, I find so many to like that it becomes difficult to express them. I like to stand outside on a warm day and smell freshly cut grass. I like the smell of evergreens and the smell of the ocean. The smell of an early morning is an exciting pleasant smell that makes me feel great to be alive. The smell, after a spring or summer shower, is fresh and pure and very pleasant. I like the smell of dust on a country road and of wind on a clear day. There are many smells outside of nature that are also very exciting to me. I like the smell of home and of a library or bookstore. I like the smell of my own pillow and of my husband's, and I like the smell of sheets that have hung on the line outside to dry. I like the smell of clean hair. I enjoy the smell of baby powder and of Chanel #5. I like the smell of a baby after a bath and the smell of Ivory Soap. I like the smell of fresh coffee in the morning and of bread baking in the oven. I like the smell of a bakery and a drugstore. I never realized just how much I enjoy smelling, until I started thinking about it.

Joyce Ramig

Many everyday smells that were once a part of my daily life have been replaced by secondary smells that express my total existence this summer.

The missing smells are those of my husband: after-shave lotions, spray deodorants, pipe tobacco, leather polish, car grease and oil, grass, and many others. These have been replaced by cigarette smokes, ashes, hair spray, perfumes of assorted smells, body lotion, cream deodorant, suntan oil and so forth, from my female roommate.

There are a few familiar smells from my past that I still sense. Our dog, Charlie, has many smells. He smells dirty after rolling in the soil. He smells like pine sol after his bath, and carries what we laughingly call "the essence of weeds" when he comes in from playing in the nearby field.

My car has many smells like warm air, suntan oil, sand, dog, and many others I would imagine. Our apartment has the smell of coolness from the absence of heat and closed curtains all day. The rug has a definite smell of dog and dirt, even after cleaning it!

I have tried many new recipes this summer so we always have a new smell in the kitchen.

I am aware of many smells in my life but wish this summer would go by real fast so I may encounter the smells of husband and

home once more. Familiar smells bring back many wonderful memories and help make the heart grow fonder.
PS. I think I will send my husband a perfumed letter today!
KAY EMMETT

Good listening is an art in itself. It takes practice, and it will aid you in your perceptive and artistic search. In order to increase your listening power, consider doing the following:

Concentrate on one thing: listening
Keep your mind alert but relaxed
Don't jump to premature conclusions
Let ideas and thoughts jell
Participate in the conversation
Listen for basic themes rather than every little fact
Try to comprehend what is being said
Don't become impatient
Try not to be distracted
Try to be objective
Tune in to other people's wavelengths

Listening to sounds with your eyes closed increases the intensity of the sounds that you hear. Listening to and not reading information permits the right side of the brain to relate and relay visual images more rapidly. Reading poetry to children or telling descriptive stories encourages them to use the right side of the brain to visualize their own personal art images.

Artistic Detective Game to Increase Visual Observation

Write down everything that you noticed about the person you just talked to. Then see how many of the following questions you can answer. You can also probably add some of your own.

1. Color of eyes ____________________
2. Shape of nose ____________________
3. Color of shoes ____________________
4. Color of hair ____________________
5. Do the ears stick out the same on each side? ____________________
6. How tall is the person? ____________________
7. What is the person wearing that is unusual? ____________________
8. What is the texture of the clothes? ________ color? ________ shape? ________
9. What is the shape of eyebrows? ____________________
10. Any scars, warts, moles? ____________________
11. Any tattoos? ____________________
12. Types of jewelry worn ____________________
13. Does the person have fillings in his/her teeth? ____________________

List 5 other items you noticed that are not listed above.

14. ____________________
15. ____________________
16. ____________________
17. ____________________
18. ____________________

Investigating Facial Details Game

This game increases awareness of facial features. Study photographs, paintings, drawings, comic strips, sculptures, TV commercials, graphic arts, toys to discover how many different ways artists have invented symbols for eye, nose, hair, mouth, ears, eyebrows, teeth.

Draw five different features you have discovered for each of the following:

Eye:

Nose:

Hair:

Mouth:

Ears:

Eyebrows:

Teeth:

Books: A Way to Discover Sensory Awareness

Children's books can help children discover the many ways creative authors relate their perceptual awareness of details, emotions, and experiences. Children's books can help adults experience the real joy of rediscovering aesthetic qualities inherent in each of us.

A Tail Is a Tail[10] by Katherine Mace is a book that demonstrates not only fluency about tails but helps one identify with an animal that has a tail. By the time we finish reading this book to a child, we are likely to look behind us to see if we have a tail; that is, if we have identified to a high degree with the material presented.

Of Course You Are A Horse[11] by Abner Graboff, is another child's book that could start one on the road to increased identification. The emphasis in this book is on pretending or imagining that we are something and then acting it out. There are many other books, records, pictures and films that can help us develop perceptual openness and empathy.

To help a child develop perceptual openness we should always refer to other aspects rather than merely learning the name of the object. Machines can be programmed to reiterate a whole category of names, but machines have never looked at an object, smelled it, listened to it, touched it or had any feelings about it. Your questions should be directed at the differences and similarities.

Hailstones and Halibut Bones[12] By Mary O'Neill is an excellent book for a teacher to read to a young child on the perception of color. *Do You Hear What I Hear?*[13] by Helen Borten is a book that deals with sounds from those beyond human range, such as the falling of a daisy petal, to the chords of a full symphony orchestra. When a child hears something ask him if it is loud, soft, muffled, rhythmic or hesitant. Can he relate this to some other perception of sound? In answering such questions he will learn to discriminate differences, subtle similarities and relate them to other sense impressions.

This is training for a more creative attitude since highly creative people (see McFee, Eisner, Guilford, Kelley, Torrance, Barron and Rogers) not only respond in unique ways to their experiences but also observe in greater detail and take in much more of the unique aspects of their environment. They also see more differences and similarities than the average person and bring more facts to bear on one aspect of a problem because they have perceived more through their senses.

Do You See What I See?[14] by Helen Borten is another example of the type of book adults could use for themselves or read to children to rediscover the sense of sight. It talks about the variety of shapes, lines and colors that surround us. *The Wing of a Flea*[15] is a book about shapes by Ed Emberley that points out shapes in our environment that we keep missing when we look at the world with dulled eyes. These books (see additional reference sources at end of chapter for a more extensive list) deal not only with the pure perception of sounds, shapes, colors and lines but also with the feelings they evoke in us.

It should be emphasized that all three aspects of perceptual awareness will be brought into play whenever the adult or child engages in the creative process. It is only when he brings all three into an aesthetic relationship that he achieves a momentary wholeness. As Herbert Read has stated of art, "no other subject is capable of giving the child a consciousness in which image and concept, sensation and thought, are correlated and unified . . ."[16]

Our awareness goals should be:

1. To try to be more open when faced with a situation involving sensory perceptions. Do not try to structure it before perceiving it!
2. To try to find new ways to "take in" something; an unusual view, whether through sound, sight or other senses.

3. To try to remember some of the delightful as well as the painful perceptual experiences of childhood and proceed in like manner to reexperience the world.
4. To try to identify with the experiences of others.

Education for sensory intelligence should become a part of every elementary art school curriculum. Art can enrich every preschool and elementary school youngster's environment.

How Does Perception Develop and Can It Be Learned Through Art Tasks?

Developing perceptual awareness is a way to increase one's ability to handle visual information through the senses. As a result of this information one has more aesthetic options to select from and more ways to relate himself to his world. Prepared with this visual information, he can be confident that his sense perceptions will help him to solve his art tasks with a higher degree of flexibility. A more thorough immersion in sensory experiences (all of the senses) should produce deeper personal feelings that will help the child's art expression at any level.

Art educators agree that developing visual readiness is one of the major goals of a good art program. As teachers, we should investigate recent research; for in understanding how individuals perceive, we can increase our teaching effectiveness in presenting art tasks.

Gestalt theory of perceptual development states that as children grow older they increase in their perceptual differentiation. That is, the child perceives simple wholes in the beginning, and as he grows older, he perceives the details within the whole. This suggests that differentiation of art elements and other art relationships can be taught through experiences in *doing* (art process) and *seeing* (aesthetic judgment). The child's frame of reference in seeing things is conditioned by the aesthetic and cultural environment that surrounds him.

We see through our subculture, whic . is the sum total of child rearing practices, religious belief, social interaction, economic condition, peer influence, and other family traits—all of which cause varying degrees of distortion in our perception. These same cultural influences affect each individual differently, and each reacts in terms of his own temperament and being.

Most other perceptual theories put forth very similiar proposals about perceptual development in children. Simply stated the young child first perceives wholes, later fills in details, then moves to a realistic attempt at representation in his art work.

A number of researchers[17, 18, 19, 20, 21, 22, 23, 24] in art education state that perception is learned or at least improved through training in *visual discrimination*. In observation or in drawing tasks, the teacher should point out such visually discriminating aspects as: shape of contours, the contrast of brightness, the structure of what is to be seen, figure and ground relationship, etc. For the teacher this means more visual showing and less verbal instructions.

Even with training in visual discrimination, the child seems to proceed through rather definite perceptual developmental patterns at an early age with more variation around twelve years.

The child basically starts with a whole (human schema) and begins to add basic parts to the whole as concepts become more differentiated. Soon the child has included the major features in his figures, and he continues to add elaborations (details) to his basic concept.

As the child's conceptual thought increases, the schema transforms itself into a more and more realistic rendering of the object perceived. This also applies to other objects the child uses in his art learning tasks, such as space, color, and form, that is, from schematic to realistic.

At about the age of eleven or twelve we may begin to notice differences in the way children perceive or react to their environment. These differences in perception have been accounted for in a number of different ways and have been given different emphasis by their interpretors.

The development of the child's sensory awareness is the most important beginning art task for every young child in his future role as artist, art critic, or art historian.

Summary

As teachers of art we should be able to give our students an understanding of how the creative process works in the artist or highly creative person. It should be made clear that this process involves not only the perception of information from our environment, but also the meaning we give to that information and how we communicate it to others.

Our understanding of modes of perception, in a general way, allows us to help children to perceive their environment. Since perception is learned, we can provide learning tasks to increase their perception abilities.

We know that individual perception modes and habits of perception vary a great deal and we, as teachers of art, should provide for these differences. The three *awareness charts,* of details, experience, and empathy, give us many ways to develop percepts and concepts which the child can use in his art work. The *sensory awareness discovery lists and games* give many suggestions on how to use our senses for an in-depth divergent sensory experience.

Imagination or visualization is the creative faculty of the mind which involves recall of sensory images and emotional impressions. Teachers should help children develop their powers to summon images and to form and reform them as they create.[26] By selecting and arranging their personal images children can create unique pictures, invent new ways to use crayons, or perceive other solutions to artistic problems that arise.

The use of children's books (lists at end of Chapter 2) to help

both the child and the teacher to increase or overcome sensory perception is an important aid for the teacher to use in her classroom. It may be a painting, a poem, a song you sing, a dance step to be tried, a beautiful discovery in nature—the education of the senses comes through all of the *arts.*

Ways To Involvement

The following are some suggested exercises which will create a greater understanding in depth of the material presented in this chapter through group or individual involvement.

1. Construct an "awareness is" book. What does "awareness" mean to you? What art elements can you become more aware of? How do you feel about an object, person, persons or current topic? Express your *new* awareness to ideas about something that has moved you deeply. Start by writing down as many ideas as you can about what you want to say. Leave them unstructured, unrelated, unorganized. Select pictures from magazines which relate to your idea or topic, or make your own drawings. Now try to relate the written statements and pictures to make a personal statement. Put them together in the form of a book. When you have finished share the booklet with a friend or child. Record their reactions.

2. Look through some of the children's books listed at the end of the chapter, or similar books, and become aware of the illustrations used. Try to discover some of the different kinds of materials and tools used by the artist in creating the illustration. Does the artist present a unique point of view? Does the artist combine several art media in one illustration?

3. Develop your own "awareness charts." Use either the *detail, experience* or *empathy* approach (pp. 23-25) in a personal way and relate it to the geographical location in which you live or plan to teach and for which you have deep feelings.

4. Compile your own personal list of children's books in relation to awareness to details, experience and empathy.

5. Collect twelve bottles with small covers or stoppers. Select several items from your kitchen and deposit them into the bottles. Add water. You might add food coloring to the liquid to disguise the natural color of the item you have placed in the bottle. Number the bottles. Have your friends see if they can identify the odor in each bottle. This should give you some idea of how little we use our sense of smell and how we rely almost entirely on the visual sense for the identification of many things in our environment.

6. Draw objects such as an eye, leaf, bridge and a tree, and then observe the same actual object or collect many different photographs of each and consider them from the point of view of color, line, texture and shape. Then redraw each of the objects previously drawn and compare. This is a good way to demonstrate the fact that it is often a lack of visual knowledge, that prevents us from producing an art product.

7. Robert H. McKim in his book *Experiences in Visual Thinking*,[25] not only explains how necessary visual thinking is to the creative person but also gives many exercises for the adult to use to recenter perception. Chapter 3 will help you understand how you see. Do some of the exercises at the end of this chapter. This book is written for the nonart student.

8. Keep a sensory diary of some object in your environment that you can experience daily. Record something new about it that you perceive each day for a week or month. Try to look at it from a new point of view, side, top, underneath, etc. Try to imagine seeing things in it. Touch it and record your feelings. How could I change it or modify it to make it pretty, ugly, or more fun to play with? How would the color change make me feel? How would it look in different surroundings? Can I relate the color, texture, shapes in a new way to give a different aesthetic effect? How has the artist used the object in his works? If it has never been used in an art product, how could it be used?

9. To increase your ability to perceive space try several of the following:

1. Make a drawing while looking through a reflex viewer of a 35 mm camera with a wide angle lens.
2. Trace around the reflection of your face in a mirror with a crayon.
3. View a landscape or other scene through a small window and make a drawing of it (sit about four feet away from the window).
4. Look through a large window or glass door and paint what you see directly on the glass.

10. *Seeing with the Mind's Eye, The History, Techniques and Uses of Visualization* by Mike and Nancy Samuels is an excellent source book to help you understand not only how visualization works but also how to make it work for you. Chapters 9 and 15 present some ways in which you can learn to visualize mental images that you can use in your art work.

11. Check the library for one of these books and try some of the exercises to make you more aware of your self and your senses. Have your friends and some children try some. Record their reactions.

HENDRICKS, GAY, and WILLS, RUSSEL, *The Centering Book, Awareness Activities for Children, Parents, and Teachers*, Englewood Cliffs, N.J.: Prentice-Hall, Inc., 1975, 178 pages.

COOK, HAROLD, and DAVITZ, JOEL, *60 Seconds to Mind Expansion*, New York: Random House, 1975, 105 pages.

KIRST, WERNER, *Creativity Training: Become Creative in 30 Minutes a Day*, New York: Peter H. Wyden, Inc., Publisher, 1971, 122 pages.

References

[1]ARTHUR FOSHAY, "The Creative Process Described," in *Creativity in Teaching*, ed. by Alice Miel, Belmont, Calif.: Wadsworth Publishing Co., Inc., 1961.

[2]J. BRUNER, *The Process of Education*, New York: John Wiley & Sons, Inc., 1962.

[3]D. Krathwohl, B. Bloom and B. Masia, *Taxonomy of Educational Objectives, Handbook II: Affective Domain,* New York: David McKay Co., Inc., 1964.

[4]*Discovering Ideas for Art,* Color, 14 minutes, Film Associates of California, Santa Monica, 1967.

[5]Katherine Mace, *A Tail Is a Tail,* New York: Abelard-Schuman, Limited, 1960.

[6]Viktor Lowenfeld, "Basic Aspects of Creative Teaching," *Creativity and Psychological Health,* ed., by Michael F. Andrews, Syracuse: Syracuse University Press, 1961.

[7]Herbert Read, *Education Through Art,* London: Faber and Faber, Ltd., 1944.

[8]Arthur, Syverson, "Seeing Things," *Vision,* March 12, 1961.

[9]Donald and Eleanor Laird, *Techniques for Efficient Remembering,* New York: McGraw-Hill Book Company, 1960.

[10]Mace, *Ibid.*

[11]Abner Graboff, *Of Course You Are A Horse,* New York: Abelard-Schuman, Limited, 1961.

[12]Mary O'Neill, *Hailstones and Halibut Bones,* Garden City, N. Y.: Doubleday & Company, Inc., 1961.

[13]Helen Borten, *Do You Hear What I Hear?* New York: Abelard-Schuman, Limited, 1960.

[14]*Ibid.*

[15]Ed Emberley, *The Wing of a Flea,* Boston: Little Brown and Company, 1960.

[16]Read, *Ibid.*

[17]Rudolph Arnheim, *Art and Visual Perception,* Berkeley: Univ. of Calif. Press, 1965.

[18]Dale Harris, *Children's Drawings as Measures of Intellectual Maturity,* New York: Harcourt, Brace, and World, 1963, p. 194.

[19]Pearl Greenberg, Task Force Chairman, "Art Approached as Perception," *Art Educations Elementary,* National Art Education Association, 1972, pp. 23-24.

[20]Gordon L. Kensler, "The Effects of Perceptual Training and Modes of Perceiving Art Upon Individual Differences in Ability to Learn Perspective Drawing," *Studies in Art Education,* vol. 7, no. 1, 1965, pp. 34-42.

[21]Richard Salome, "Two Pilot Investigations of Perceptual Training in Four- and Five-Year-Old Kindergartners," *Studies in Art Education* v. 13, no. 2, 1972, pp. 3-9.

[22]Jessie J. Lovano, "Readiness, Research, and the Art Classroom," *Art Education* vol. 24, no. 5, May 1971, Journal of the National Art Education Association, pp. 12-17.

[23]Mary Rouse, "What Research Tells Us About Sequencing and Structuring Art Instruction," *Art Education,* vol. 24, no. 5, May 1971, Journal of the National Art Education Association, pp. 18-25.

[24]Helen James, "Conceptual Modes of Children in Responding to Art Objects," *Studies in Art Education* 11, no. 3, 1970, pp. 52-60.

[25]Robert H. McKim, *Experiences in Visual Thinking,* Belmont, Calif.: Wadsworth Publishing Company, Inc., 1972, p. 71.

[26]Mike and Nancy Samuels, *Seeing with the Mind's Eye, The History, Techniques and Uses of Visualization,* New York: Random House, Bookworks Book, 1975.

Additional References

Eisner, Elliot, "Children's Creativity in Art," *Studies in Art Education,* Spring, 1963.

Marrants, Kenneth, *A Bibliography of Children's Art Literature,* National Art Education Association, 1965.

"How to Encourage Creativity in Children," *Good Housekeeping,* August, 1962, pp. 136-137.

"Curriculum for Awareness," *Art Education,* June, 1964.

Linderman, Earl W., "A Magic Touch," *Arts and Activities,* May, 1962.

———, "A Thing of Beauty," *Grade Teacher,* April, 1963.

———, "What Is a Good Teacher?" *Arts and Activities,* October, 1963.

———, "Developing Perceptual Awareness," *Arts and Activities,* December, 1962.

———, "Let's Learn About Art," *Arts and Activities,* December, 1963.

Platt, John R., "The Fifth Need Of Man," *Horizon,* July, 1959.

Rannells, Edward, "Experience and Expression," *Art Education Bulletin,* November, 1961, pp. 14-18.

Taylor, Irving, "The Nature of The Creative Process," in *Creativity—An Examination of the Creative Process,* Paul Smith, ed., New York: Hastings House Publishers, Inc., 1959.

Von Bargen, Dora, "Motivating Young Children," *Arts and Activities,* February, 1962.

Books to Help Children Become Sensitized to One Subject, Exploring It From Many Viewpoints

Bartlett, Margaret, *Where the Brook Begins,* New York: Thomas Y. Crowell Company, 1959.

Conklin, Gladys, *I Like Caterpillars,* New York: Holiday House, 1958.

———, *I Like Butterflies,* New York: Holiday House, 1960.

de Regniers, Beatrice Schenk, *The Shadow Book,* New York: Harcourt Brace & World, 1960.

Gordon, Isabel, *The ABC Hunt,* New York: The Viking Press, Inc., 1961.

Hay, John and Arlene Strong, *A Sense of Nature,* New York: Doubleday & Company, Inc., 1962.

HUNTINGTON, HARRIET, *Let's Go Outdoors,* New York: Doubleday & Company, Inc., 1939.
MACE, KATHERINE, *A Tail Is a Tail,* New York: Abelard-Schuman Limited, 1960.
McGRATH, THOMAS, *The Beautiful Things,* New York: Vanguard Press, Inc., 1960.
MATHEWSON, ROBERT, *The How and Why Wonder Book of Birds,* New York: Wonder Books, 1960.
MONTRESOR, BENI, *House of Flowers, House of Stars,* New York: Alfred A. Knopf, Inc., 1962.
PASCHEL, HERBERT, *The First Book of Color,* New York: F. Franklin Watts, Inc., 1959.
ROOD, RONALD N., *The How and Why Wonder Book of Insects,* New York: Wonder Books, 1960.
SHUTTLESWORTH, DOROTHY, *The Story of Spiders,* Garden City, N. Y.: Doubleday & Company, Inc., 1959.
UDRY, JANICE MAY, *A Tree Is Nice,* New York: Harper & Row, Publishers, 1956.
WILLIAMSON, MARGARET, *The First Book of Bugs,* New York: Franklin Watts, Inc., 1949.
ZIM, HERBERT, *Goldfish,* New York: William Morrow & Co., Inc., 1947.

Books to Help Children Sharpen Their Senses of Seeing, Smelling, Hearing, Touching, Tasting

BORTEN, HELEN, *Do You Hear What I Hear?* New York: Abelard-Schuman Limited, 1960.
———, *Do You See What I See?* New York: Abelard-Schuman Limited, 1961.
ELKIN, BENJAMIN, *The Loudest Noise in the World,* New York: Viking Press, 1954.
EMBERLEY, ED, *The Wing of a Flea,* Boston: Little, Brown and Company, 1960.
FISHER, AILEEN, *Going Barefoot,* New York: Thomas Y. Crowell Company, 1960.
McGRATH, THOMAS, *The Beautiful Things,* New York: Vanguard Press, Inc., 1960.
MARKS, MARCIA, *Swing Me, Swing Tree,* Boston: Little, Brown and Company, 1959.
O'NEILL, MARY, *Hailstones and Halibut Bones,* Garden City, N. Y.: Doubleday & Company, Inc., 1961.
SCHWARTZ, J., *Through the Magnifying Glass,* New York: Whittlesey House, 1954.
SHOWERS, PAUL, *The Listening Walk,* New York: Thomas Y. Crowell Company, 1961.
———, *Find Out by Touching,* New York: Thomas Y. Crowell Company, 1961.
SPOONER, JANE, *Tony Plays with Sounds,* New York: The John Day Company, Inc., 1961.
WEBBER, IRMA E., *It Looks Like This,* New York: William R. Scott, Inc., 1958.

Books to Help Children Respond and Identify Emotionally With Other People, Objects, or Situations

BROWN, MARGARET WISE, *The House of a Hundred Windows,* New York: Harper & Row, Publishers, 1945.
———, *The Dead Bird,* New York: Young, Scott, Brooks, 1958.
BUCKLEY, PETER, *Jan of Holland,* New York: Franklin Watts, Inc., 1956.
CIARDI, JOHN, *I Met a Man,* Boston: Houghton Mifflin Company, 1961.
CONGER, MARION, *Who Has Seen the Wind?* New York: Abingdon Press, 1959.
CROWELL, PERS, *What Can a Horse Do That You Can't Do?* New York: Whittlesey House, 1954.
DE REGNIERS, BEATRICE and IRE HAAS, *Something Special,* New York: Harcourt Brace & World, Inc., 1958.
FENTON, EDWARD, *Fierce John,* Garden City, N. Y.: Doubleday & Company, Inc., 1959.
FISHER, AILEEN, *Going Barefoot,* New York: Thomas Y. Crowell Company, 1960. Could be used to stimulate awareness of ground and perhaps help produce a base line.
FREEMAN, DON, *A Rainbow of My Own,* illustrated by author, New York: The Viking Press, 1966. $2.96. To an imaginative boy—what a rainbow becomes—how to find a real rainbow. Can be useful for color experience: a prism, reflection of color, what are colors. Watercolor drawings are fress, free, show how watercolor should be, not flat like poster colors.
FROST, ROBERT, *You Come Too,* New York: Holt, Rinehart & Winston, Inc., 1959.
GARELICK, MAY, *Sounds of a Summer Night,* illustrated by Beni Montessor, Young, Scott Books, 1963. $3.25. Variety of words matched with simple mood pictures to bring on sleep of a midsummer night. Word sounds; ink drawings show pen and ink in a fascinating way.
GRABOFF, ABNER, *Of Course, You're a Horse,* New York: Abelard-Schuman Limited, 1959.
HATCHER, C., *How We Know Our Sources—Windows to Our World,* London: Golden Pleasure Books, 1962.
HUNTINGTON, HARRIET, *Let's Go Outdoors,* New York: Doubleday & Company, Inc., 1939.
ICENHOWER, J. B., *Antarctic,* New York: Franklin Watts, Inc., 1956.

KEATS, EZRA, J., *The Snowy Day*, New York: Viking Press, 1962.

LENSKI, LOIS, *Now It's Fall*, New York: Oxford University Press, 1948.

LIONNI, LEO, *Little Blue and Little Yellow*, New York: McDowell, Obolensky, 1959.

LIVINGSTON, MYRA COHN, *Whispers and Other Poems*, New York: Harcourt Brace & World, Inc., 1960.

RADLAUER, RUTH SHAW, *Good Times With Words*, Chicago: Melmont Publishers, 1963.

ROUNDS, GLEN, *Wildlife at Your Doorstep*, Englewood Cliffs, N. J.: Prentice-Hall, Inc., 1958.

RUSSELL, SOLVEIG, P., *What Good Is A Trail?* New York: The Bobbs-Merrill Co., Inc., 1962.

SCHULZ, CHARLIE, *Happiness Is a Warm Puppy*, San Francisco: Determined Productions, Inc., 1962.

———, *Security Is a Thumb and a Blanket*, San Francisco: Determined Productions, Inc., 1963.

TRESSEL, ALVIN, *White Snow, Bright Snow*, New York: Lothrop, Lee & Shepard Co., Inc., 1947.

Film References

Changing Art In A Changing World, A Paul Burnford Production in association with Jack Stoops, Ed. D., 21 min.

Discovering Creative Pattern, A Paul Burnford Production in association with Jack Stoops, Ed. D., 17 min.

Discovering Dark and Light, A Paul Burnford Production in association with Jack Stoops, Ed. D., 18 min.

Discovering Harmony In Art, A Paul Burnford Production, 16 min.

Discovering Composition In Art, A Paul Burnford Production, 16 min.

Discovering Form In Art, A Paul Burnford Production in association with Jack Stoops, Ed. D., 21 min.

Discovering Ideas For Art, A Paul Burnford Production, 15 1/2 min.

Discovering Color, Discovering art series, 16 min.

Discovering Line, Discovering art series, 17 min.

Discovering Perspective, Discovering art series, 14 min.

Discovering Texture, Discovering art series, 17 1/2 min.

This Is Red, A Paul Burnford Production, super 8mm, color series.

This Is Orange, A Paul Burnford Production, super 8mm.

This Is Yellow, A Paul Burnford Production, super 8mm.

This Is Green, A Paul Burnford Production, super 8mm.

This Is Blue, A Paul Burnford Production, super 8 mm.

This Is Purple, A Paul Burnford Production, super 8mm.

(All of the above films are from Film Associates of California.)

References

More books to help children sharpen their senses of seeing, smelling, hearing, touching, tasting, and feeling.

ANGLUND, JOAN WALSH, *Love Is a Special Way of Feeling*, Harcourt, Brace & World, Inc., 1960, K-4.

BURNINGHAM, JOHN, *Borka, The Adventures of a Goose with No Feathers*, illustrated by author, New York: Random House, Inc., 1963. Free splashing paint technique that children can appreciate with a story of a goose who is different from others, how he solves his problem.

COLE, WILLIAM and JULIA COLMORE, *The Poetry Drawing Book*, Books I and II K-4, New York: Simon & Schuster, 1962. Here is a delightful collection of poems for children to illustrate right on the spot. Let us hope they do not get the idea they can illustrate all books.

DE REGNIERS, BEATRICE SCHENK, *Cats, Cats, Cats, Cats, Cats*, drawing and design by Bill Sokol, New York: Pantheon Books, Inc., 1958. Awareness of an animal in words, sounds, feel. Drawings and form of book are imaginative, fun, could suggest a "creative writing" and art project on animals.

ELKIN, BENJAMIN, *Why the Sun Was Late*, illustrated by Jerome Snyder, Parent's Magazine Press, 1966. From an old African tale of "Why the fly says no more than buzz." Night drawings could suggest ways of creating crayon scrafitto.

EMBERLEY, BARBARA, adapter, *One Wide River to Cross*, illustrated by Ed Emberley, New York: Prentice-Hall, Inc., 1966. $3.39. From an old folk song, the spirit and humor of the animals as they file into the ark. Woodcuts of black on colored backgrounds suggest wonderful possibilities for woodcut and cardboard cut-out printing activities.

EMBERLEY, ED, *Rosebud*, illustrated by author, Boston: Little, Brown and Company, 1966. $3.14. Adventure of an ordinary turtle who sets out to become an extraordinary turtle. Brilliant, bold cut-out suggests ideas for colored paper cut-outs without crayon activities.

TENNYSON, ALFRED, *Charge of the Light Brigade*, illustrated by Alice and Martin Provensen, New York: Golden Press, 1966. $3.79.

SPILKA, ARNOLD, *Once Upon a Horse*, New York: Henry Z. Walck, Inc., 1966. $3.75. Sense and nonsense verses illustrated in blue, black and white.

O'NEILL, MARY L., *What Is that Sound!* drawings by Lois Ehlert, New York: Atheneum Publishers, 1966 $3.51. Poetry describing sounds: a giggle, a roar, a baa, a buzz, the sound of day, night, of cities, of life. Ink drawings.

CIARDI, JOHN, *The King Who Saved Himself from Being Saved*, drawings by Edward Gorey, Philadelphia: J. B. Lippincott Co., 1965. $2.95. Written in verse; satiric poem about a long-ago king who wanted to keep a quiet kingdom; ink drawings.

MERRIAM, EVE, *It Doesn't Always Have to Rhyme*, drawings by Malcolm Spooner, New York: Atheneum Publishers, 1966. $3.07. Collection of poetry that does not rhyme; sound and listening experience for mood of idea.

UPDIKE JOHN, *A Child's Calendar*, illustrated by Nancy Ekholm Burkert, New York: Alfred A. Knopf, Inc., 1965. $2.99. Seasoned poems by an adult author. Poems are sensitively matched by drawings of Nancy Ekholm Burkert.

LEAR, EDWARD, *Limericks by Lear*, pictures by Lois Ehlert, Cleveland: The World Publishing Company, 1965. $4.09. Oustanding color presentation of illustrations that enhance limericks by Edward Lear. Colorful cut-out shapes with printed ink forms over them. Combined media approach to poetry.

ROCKWELL, ANNE, *Sally's Caterpillar*, pictures by Harlow Rockwell, Parent's Day Magazine Press, 1966. $3.03. Simple story of Sally finding a caterpillar at the beach, then she takes it home where it becomes something else. Illustrations are simple, large, remind one of long ago. Children's books in outline form filled in with color.

ROUNDS, GLEN, *Rain in the Woods and Other Small Matters,* Cleveland: The World Publishing Company, 1964. $3.00. Good for read-aloud periods, good observation in word form to interest others to look about.

NEWMAN, CAROL, *Strella's Children*, illustrated by Fernando Krahn, New York: Antheneum Publishers, 1966. $3.41. Made-up animals—peak-ayuks, Frivvens, Lumpetees, Octopoppies, etc. with open ink drawings which fit the verse and animals.

DENNY, NORMAN and JOSEPHINE, FILMER-SANKEY, *The Bayeaux Tapestry*, New York: Antheneum Publishers, 1966. Actual running account of 1066 and the Norman Conquest as seen through the Bayeaux Tapestry. History recorded in an embroidery, historical cartoon of event. Could other events be recorded in tapestry form?

JARRELL, RANDALL, *The Bat-Poet*, pictures by Maurice Sendak, New York: The Macmillan Company, 1965. Sensitively drawn pen and ink pictures show a bat who wakes up in the day and makes up poems about what he sees. Others do not wish to listen to him—provacative idea.

———, *The Animal Family*, decorations by Maurice Sendak, New York: Pantheon Books, Inc., 1965. $3.39. Unusual theme, unusual format of old-fashioned printed books, unusually well-drawn pen and ink drawings of nature in detail.

MERRIAM, EVE, *A Gaggle of Geese*, illustrated by Paul Galdone, New York: Alfred A. Knopf, Inc., 1960. $3.29. Words that count groups of animals, fish and birds. Fun with words, could be good for picture making as well as for word awareness and numbers.

HODGES, MARGARET, *The Wave,* adapted from Lafcadio Hearn's Gleanings in Budda-Fields, illustrated by Blair Lent, Boston: Houghton Mifflin Company, 1964. $3.07. Picture book revision of Japanese folktale. Wonderful block prints that relate to the wave, the town, the old man.

CARSON, RACHEL, *The Sense of Wonder*, photos by Charles Pratt and others, New York: Harper & Row, Publishers, 1965. $5.34. Photos and text explore the sight, sound, smell and feel of the earth, sea and sky. Photography at its best. Involves reader, unites text. A real contribution to sense awareness.

LERNER, SHARON, *I Found a Leaf*, illustrated by author, Minneapolis: Lerner Publications Co., 1964. $2.75. Written in simple free verse style and illustrated with rubbings of actual leaves. This book lends itself to a leaf study that could be fun.

JORDAN, HELEN J., *How a Seed Grows*, illustrated by Joseph Low, New York: Thomas Y. Crowell Company, 1960. Easy to read but fun to see an awareness type of science book with wash drawings that enhance and explain as well.

PORTAL, COLETTE, *The Life of a Queen*, illustrated by author, New York: George Braziller, Inc., 1964. The story of the queen of the blue ants, who "alone possesses the future, the hope, the promise of her people," and "alone will found a city." The study of ants is enhanced by the magnificent tempera paintings which make these insects come alive.

Bring a Torch, Jeanette, Isabella, A Provencal carol, pictures by Adrienne Adams, New York: Charles Scribner's Sons, 1963. Pictures and music bring a new meaning to an old Christmas carol.

IENNER, PHYLLIS, *Giants and Witches and a Dragon or Two*, New York: Alfred A. Knopf, Inc., 1943, gr. 4-6. Excellent out of print stories.

IPCAR, DAHLOV, *The Calico Jungle*, illustrated by author, New York: Alfred A. Knopf, Inc., 1965. $3.29. Animals from calico quilt transformed into story form. Suggests what you can do with old material scraps; juxtaposition of print to print can be fun.

KEATS, EZRA JACK, *The Snowy Day*, New York: The Viking Press, Inc., 1962, 32 pp. A story of a small boy's personal discovery of snow and the very special magic of a winter day. Gives alomst a kinesthetic feeling for snow. Caldacott award 1962 for art work.

KIRN, ANN, *Nine in a Line*, from an old, old folktale, illustrated by author, Arabic by Leila Leonard, New York: W. W. Norton & Company, Inc., 1966. $3.28. Old Amin is horrified to count only eight camels when there should be nine. He looks everywhere for ninth until children remind him to count the camel he is riding on. Spattered background, brown, white, black with orange full figures. Arabic is lovely to see (counting).

KRUSS, JAMES, 3 x 3, *Three by Three,* pictures by Era Johanna Rubin, New York: The Macmillan Company, 1965. $3.24. Counting story of 3's. Stylized objects in European manner all in 3's.

LIONNI, LEO, *Tico and the Golden Wings,* New York: Pantheon Books, Inc., 1964. $2.19. A bird expresses "we are all different, each for his own memories and his own invisible golden dreams." Stylized bird-plant-nature forms in most poetic fashion.

LONERGEN, JOY, *There You Are,* illustrated by Lawrence Beall Smith, New York: Franklin Watts, Inc., 1962, 32 pp. A little girl sees a reflection of herself in various shiny objects, a bowl, in a silver spoon, in the eyes of someone who loves her. Yummy!

LUND, DORIS HEROLD, *Attic of the Wind,* illustrated by Ati Forberg, Parent's Magazine Press, 1966. $3.03. Written in verse. *In the Attic of the Wind* is to be found all the escaped balloons, hats, butterflies. Combined media paints, ink and cut-outs. (How the wind feels.)

MCCLOSKEY, ROBERT, *Time of Wonder,* New York: The Viking Press, Inc., 1956. The change of seasons on an island in Penobscot Bay in Maine is the subject of McCloskey's stunning picture book. The pictures are in wonderful, muted, imaginative colors with the human figures in minor focus and the landscape most important. Not a story, but a lyrical description of a loved region.

MCGOVERN, ANN, *Zoo Where Are You,* illustrated by Jack Keats, New York: Harper & Row, Publishers, 1964.

MEYERS, R. E. and E. PAUL TORRENCE, *Invitation to Thinking and Doing,* Minneapolis: Perceptive Publishing Co., 1961, gr. 4-6. Work in books designed to enhance creative ability. For grades 4-6 but ideas can be related to all levels.

MILES, BETTY, *A Day of Winter,* illustrated by Remy Charlip, New York: Alfred A. Knopf, Inc., 1961. $2.89. Black-white-blue suggests what winter feels like. Childlike simplicity of words and drawings.

PINTOFF, ERNEST, *Always Help a Bird* (especially with a broken leg), New York: Harper & Row, Publishers, 1964.

REID, JON, *Celestino Platti's Animal ABC,* New York: Atheneum Publishers, 1955. $4.50. Poster-like, Roualt black-lined animals go through the ABC's. Clear large animals and letters.

RASKIN, ELLEN, *Nothing Ever Happens on My Block,* New York: Atheneum Publishers, 1966. $2.95. Nothing can be seen by a boy on his city block. Against black and white drawings of the block, colors suggest what is really happening that he cannot see. Perhaps a suggestion that we do not see what is around us.

SCHNEIDER, LEO, *You and Your Senses,* New York: Harcourt, Brace & World, Inc., 1956. An explanation with accompanying experiments of intricate, mechanisms of the human body which enable us to see, taste, touch and hear.

SELDON, GEORGE, *I See What I See,* illustrated *by Roger Galster,* New York: Farrar, Straus & Giroux, Inc., 1962, 48 pp. The story of seven playmates in New York City. Six of them see all kinds of things through their imagination but the seventh spoils everything with his "I see what I see." The illustrations are marvelous especially the dragon.

SANDAK, MAURICE, *Where the Wild Things Are,* New York: Harper & Row, Publishers, 1964, K-4. Stimulates imagination yet child can identify with a real boy situation.

SCHWARTZ, J., *Through the Magnifying Glass,* New York: Whittlesey House, 1954.

UNGERER, TOMI, *Snail, Where Are You?* illustrated by author, New York: Harper & Row, Publishers, 1962. $2.57. A wordless picture book except for first and last pages. On each page a spiral snail is concealed in the picture. Good for preschool, prereader.

———, *One, Two, Where's My Shoe?* illustrated by author, New York: Harper & Row, Publishers, 1964. $2.57. No words—tells the story of a hunt for a lost shoe. Another look for the shape books.

MYRUS, DONALD and ALBERT SQUILLACE, *Story in the Sand,* New York: Crowell, Collier and Macmillan, Inc., 1963. $3.92. Unusually excellent use of photographs to capture the joy of a day at the beach, drawing in the sand. Creative experience and fun at the beach; varieties of what sand can be made to express.

MIZUMUTA, KAZUE, *I See the Winds,* New York: Thomas Y. Crowell Company, 1966. $2.65. As season turns, so does the wind. The spirit of Japanese haiku with Japanese brush drawings. Wonderful for poetry experience.

WITHERS, CARL, adaptor, *The Tale of a Black Cat,* illustrated by Allen Cober, New York: Holt, Rinehart & Winston, Inc., 1966, $2.78. A drawing tale. A folktale which narrator illustrates line by line as he develops story. Could stimulate other "drawing tale" by children.

ZEMACH, HARVE, adaptor, *The Speckled Hen,* a Russian nursery rhyme, illustrations by Margot Zemach, New York: Holt, Rinehart & Winston, Inc., 1966. $3.27. A speckled egg laid by speckled hen causes window panes to shatter, geese to scatter as whole household falls into chaos. Expressive ink drawings, very childlike, reflect spattering and movement. Extremely well done.

SINGER, ISAAC, *Zlateh the Goat and Other Stories,* pictures by Maurice Sendak, New York: Harper & Row, Publishers, 1966. $4.11. Yiddish tales that span the years, good for story telling. Mood set by good ink drawings.

Books to Help in Relating the Arts

These are science books but well written to satisfy curiosity about a lot of things.

BRANLEY, FRANKLIN M., *The Big Dipper,* illustrated by Ed Emberley, New York: Thomas Y. Crowell Company, 1962. This explanation of the stars in the big dipper and their relation to other heavenly bodies will further a child's understanding of questions often asked. This is more an information book than the rest recommended.

BULLA, CLYDE ROBERT, *What Makes a Shadow*, New York: Thomas Y. Crowell Company, 1962. 40 pp. Simple scientific discussion of shadows and what causes them. Experiments with shadows included.

CARSON, RACHEL, *The Sense of Wonder*, New York: Harper & Row, Publishers, 1965, gr. K-8.

CONKLIN, GLADYS, *I Like Caterpillars*, New York: Holiday House, Inc., 1958.

———, *I Like Butterflies*, New York: Holiday House, Inc., 1960.

HUNTINGTON, HARRIET, *Let's Go Outdoors*, Garden City, New York: Doubleday & Company, Inc., 1939, gr. 1-4.

———, *Let's Go to the Seashore*, Garden City, New York: Doubleday & Company, Inc., 1941, gr. 1-4.

———, *Let's Go to the Brook*, Garden City, New York: Doubleday & Company, Inc., 1952, gr. 1-4.

———, *Let's Go to the Desert*, Garden City, New York: Doubleday & Company, Inc., 1949, gr. 1-4. (Huntington's books give scientific answers to outdoor questions; excellent photographs.)

JORDAN, HELEN J., *Seeds by Wind and Water*, illustrated by Wils Wogner, New York: Thomas Y. Crowell Company, 1962, 42 pp. An introduction to the ways many seeds travel by wind and air and water before taking root.

KIRN, ANN, *Full of Wonder World*, 1959, K-6. Beauty of everyday objects is revealed by striking crayon rubbings. Prose; poems about objects employed.

ROOD, RONALD N., *The How and Why Wonder Book of Insects*, New York: Wonder Books, 1960.

SHOWERS, PAUL, *Look at Your Eyes*, illustrated by Paul Geldome, New York: Thomas Y. Crowell Company, 1962. Accurate answers to the many questions children ask about their eyes, including discussions of lashes, lids, pupils, and tears. A good book to use in conjunction with *There You Are* by Lonergen.

Life Series, the Atom, Math, Insects, and Reptiles, etc. K-8 Time-Life. Excellent series with information and beautiful photographs.

III. Poetry

Imagery fills the child's natural urge for sensuous impressions and fills him with the joy of rhythmic sound.

CUMMINGS, E. E., *Collected Poems and Other Collections*, New York: Harcourt, Brace & World, Inc. This man is a genius for sensory images. His *Balloon Man* is full of childlike delight and he even makes up words as children so often do like "mud-lucious" and "puddle-wonder."

ARBUTHNOT, MAY H., *Time for Poetry*, rev. ed., 1961, gr. K-4. A varied anthology of poems meant to be read aloud.

FISHER, AILEEN, *I Wonder How, I Wonder Why*, illustrated by Carol Baker, New York: Abelard-Schuman Limited, 1962. Poems reflecting a child's wonder at the world around him. The author effectively encourages curiosity about the moon, the spinning earth and eggs.

FROST, ROBERT, *You Come Too*, New York: Harper & Row, Publishers, 1959, gr. 5-up. A collection of Frost poems for young people; original wood engravings.

HOSS, PHOEBE W., *Noses Are for Roses*, illustrated by McGraffery, New York: McGraw-Hill Book Company, 1960. Here is a book that tells what you are. Attractively illustrated and with humorous verses, this book gives the child an idea of what he is and what he is for, from his head to his toe.

KUMIN, MAXINE, *No One Writes a Letter to the Snail*, illustrated by Allen, New York: G. P. Putnam's Sons, 1962. Here are 25 poems whose subjects are particularly familiar to children. The author has a most imaginative vocabulary and uses names to tickle tongues.

MONTRESER, BENI, *House of Flowers, House of Stars*, New York: Alfred A. Knopf, Inc., 1962, 48 pp. Here is a flight of fancy to a galaxy of houses both real and imaginary. The author-illustrator uses beautiful sun-drenched pictures to reinforce haunting poetic prose.

O'NEIL, MARY, *Words, Words, Words*, New York: Doubleday & Company, Inc., 1966.

READ, HERBERT, *This Was Delight*, New York: Pantheon Books, Inc., 1956, gr. 3-7. Introduces young readers to poetry whose inspiration is within the reach of their experience.

THOMPSON, BLANCHE JENNINGS, *Silver Pennies*, New York: The Macmillan Company, 1953, 129 pp., gr. 3-8. "You must have a silver penny to get into fairyland." This collection can be used with students of many ages. This philosophy is not to kill the interest that children may have in the magic of poetic words, but to foster it. This book plus music, pictures and discussion can set the mood for good reading aloud sessions.

ZOLOTOW, CHARLOTTE, *When the Wind Stops*, illustrated by Joe Losker, New York: Abelard-Schuman Limited, 1962, 48 pp. After a perfect day, a small boy wonders why it must come to a close. His mother explains in poetic prose why nothing ends, but becomes the beginning of something else. Lyrical dialogue of nature's wonders and changing forms.

IV. Creative Dramatics

BROAD, RUTH and STAN, *How Would You Act*, Skokie, Illinois: Rand McNally & Co., 1962, 32 pp. Develops a sense of rhyme through use of an appealing and whimsical game in verse such as "How would you act if you were a snail? I'd glide through the garden leaving a trail!"

This and other imaginative rhymes create many possibilities for creative dramatics.

CARLSON, BERNICE WELLS, *Act It Out,* illustrated by L. Matulay, Nashville: Abingdon Press, 1956. Simple dramatics for children divided into two parts: acting and puppet performances. Examples of each and directions for making puppets.

CHARLIP, REMY, *Mother, Mother I Feel Sick Send for the Doctor Quick, Quick, Quick,* Parent's Magazine Press, 1966. Picture book and shadow play.

COLEMAN, S. N., *Dancing Time,* New York: The John Day Company Inc., 1952, gr. K-3 Music for rhythmic activities. Simple piano arrangements. Within concepts of small children, hammering, hoeing.

DURLAND, FRANCES, *Creative Dramatics,* Yellow Springs, Ohio: Antioch Press, 1952. This book has a good bibliography to use with creative dramatics and suggests many new techniques.

SANDBURG, CARL, *The Wedding Procession of the Rag Doll and the Broom Handle and Who Was in It,* pictures by Harriet Pincus, New York: Harcourt, Brace & World, Inc., 1967.

A Boy Went Out to Gather Pears, an old verse with new pictures by Felix Hoffmann, New York: Harcourt, Brace & World, Inc., 1966.

SIKS, GERALDINE, *Creative Dramatics: an Art for Children,* New York: Harper & Row, Publishers, 1961. This is an excellent source book with a list of the stories that are best for dramatization with children.

WARD, WINIFRED, *Playmaking with Children,* New York: Appleton-Century-Crofts, 1957. I mention this on a children's list because it, and Siks' book, are helpful in stimulating creative thinking and dramatics. Ward is a pioneer in the field. Her thesis is based on the fact that every child is endowed with the sensitivities of the artist.

MERRIAM, EVE, *What Can You Do with a Pocket?* illustrated by Harriet Sherman, New York: Alfred A. Knopf, Inc., 1964.

Music for Art

ALEXANDER, CECIL, *All Things Bright and Beautiful,* illustrated by Lee Petit, New York: Charles Scribner's Sons, 1962.

BERNSTEIN, LEONARD, *The Joy of Music,* New York: Simon & Schuster, Inc., 1959, gr. 9-up.

FISHER, EDWARD, *The Animal Song Book,* New York: St. Martin's Press, Inc., 1963. Songs about lions, porcupines, a myriad of delicious creatures with music. Excellent for creative musical activities.

SEEGER, EDWARD, *American Folk Songs,* New York: Doubleday & Company, Inc., 1948. Good songs for singing, memorizing and dramatizing.

SPOONER, JANE, *Tony Plays with Sound,* New York: The John Day Company, Inc., 1961.

NO CONTROL

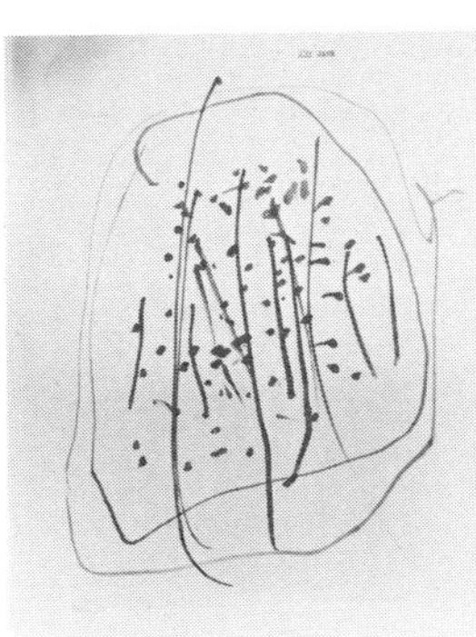

LINE CONTROL

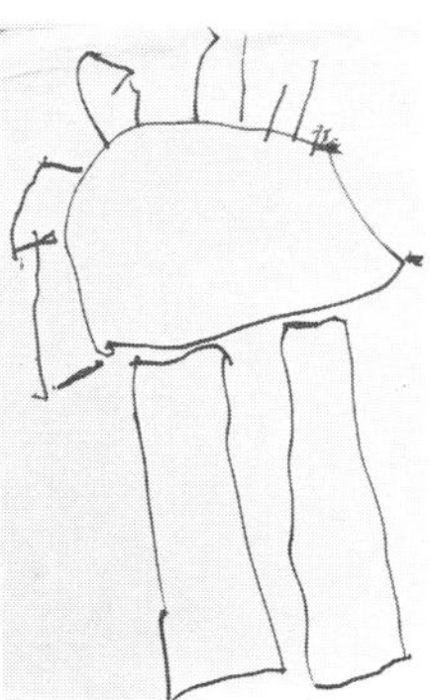

SHAPE CONTROL

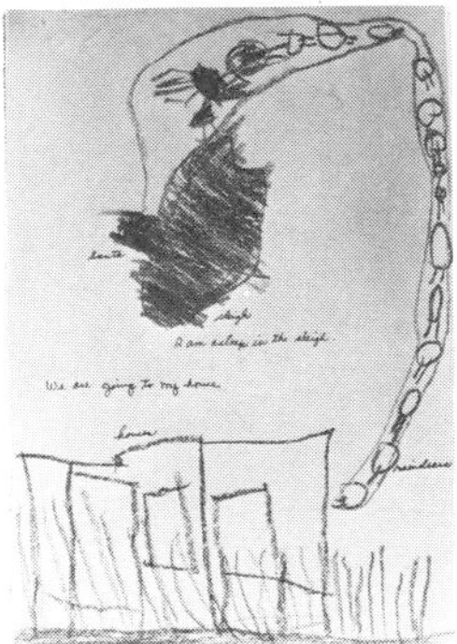

NAMING

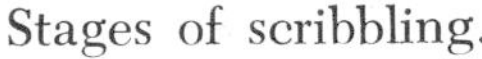

Stages of scribbling.

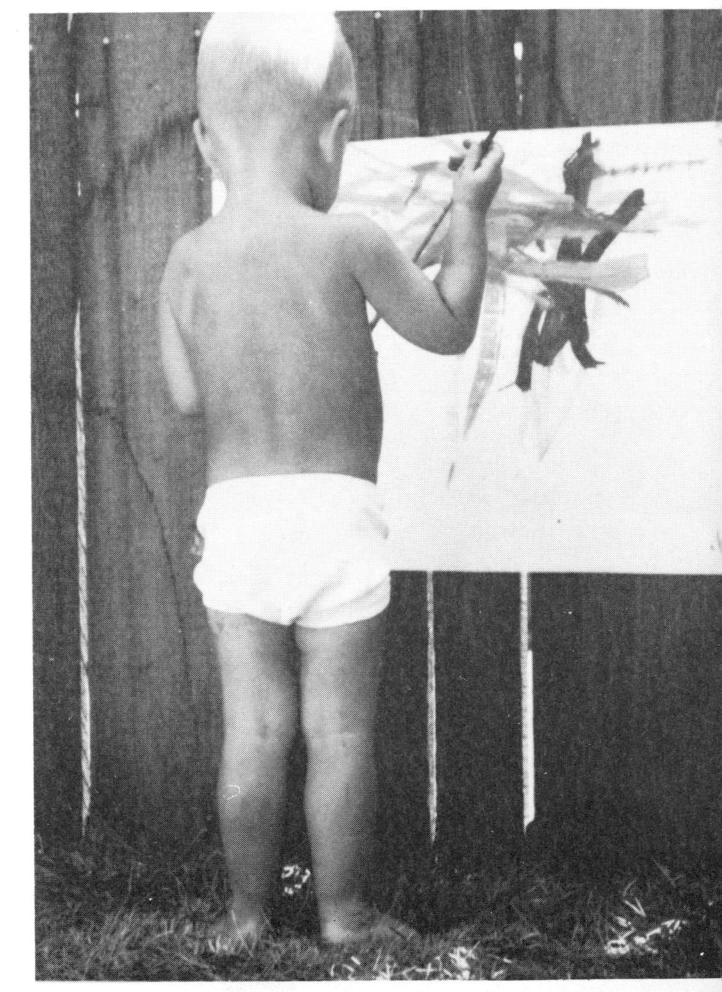

Children may be likened to a handful of seeds from many flowers. At first they may seem more similar than different in many respects. Place these seeds in the earth and nourish them. As they grow and mature their differences become marked. Some remain small and delicate while others are large and brilliant, some bloom early and some late. One thing they may have in common: Under good conditions they all bloom and have their own beauty.

Edward L. Mattil,
from *Meaning in Crafts*,
Englewood Cliffs, New Jersey: Prentice-Hall, Inc.,
1959, p. 3

Chapter 3

Child Art Development and Evaluation

A child's creative and mental growth sequences can be seen in three readily identifiable stages: scribbling or manipulative, symbolic or schematic, and representational or realistic.

The manipulative or scribbling stage is an action stage in which he enjoys the movement of himself, the movement of materials, the cutting of materials, and the pushing around of materials. He is not dealing with art images or art skills. He is learning about himself and about what happens when he hits things, bends things, and cuts things. It is a period of all action and movement.

Symbols or schemas to express ideas, and feelings – to communicate – gives the child a whole new world with which to interact, to consume through the senses, to digest, and to make into personal symbols through which he can tell others about himself.[1] When his world of images unfolds he does not have the verbal skills to make his personal statements, so he uses the only means at his disposal–visual images. His primary and basic information is obtained through the use of the senses. The unfolding of this artistic activity develops at a rapid pace and engages his mental and creative growth. He can now use symbols to communicate the excitement of his personal experiences and he takes great joy in doing so.

The realism stage is a whole new world for the child to investigate and explore. He takes on new challenges, the main one being how to make things look real—true visual images related to external objects. He also sees the possibilities of his art materials doing all kinds of new things that they could not do before. Colors can be changed to match things out there, shading can make flat things look round on a flat piece of paper, lines can be put together and then a person's hair looks like real hair, etc.

When the sequence of stages unfolds so that the child develops his maximum creative and mental growth, he will have developed a number of highly skilled tools or ways to deal with life.[2] His visual, emotional, and aesthetic life cannot be complete without art.

The Scribbling Stage of Art Development: Ages 2 to 4

Do not tell a soul, but Leonardo da Vinci was once a scribbler! Hard to believe? But alas! Each of us once scribbled! Fascinating as it may seem, the beginning of all artistic expression has its origin in the earliest scribblings of childhood. Let us tip the hourglass topsy-turvy for a moment and return to that magical, sugar-coated land of our early years.

How does art begin? At the very start the child begins by making indistinguishable marks on a table, wall or paper. He uses any available instrument: crayon, pencil, chalk, or even a spoonful of applesauce. The two- or three-year-old has little muscular control over his scribbling actions. He also cannot coordinate his drawing because of "the lack of a mental image that he can retain prevents him from drawing and from thinking intelligently."[3]

He is simply delighted to discover the lines he is able to make on a particular surface. In these early beginnings he is only aware of the discovery of a newly found ability. If the child has an opportunity to practice his scribbling while his cognitive powers are developing, he will more readily develop control and learn to guide the direction of his lines.

Generally speaking, children scribble between the ages of two and four. Children are in the beginning stages of art if they scribble in an uncontrolled fashion. When the child has had an opportunity to practice his art, his scribbles become more controlled. After the child has practiced his scribbling for a sufficient time, he will one day begin to tell stories in connection with his drawings.

As he draws he may converse to himself, for example,

> This is a train. Choo Choo Choo.
> This is a house.
> This is a bird.

When the child has reached this last level of "naming" his scribbles, he becomes more capable of retaining a mental image and thinking about concrete objects and events which Piaget refers to as the "intuitive thought" stage within the "concrete operations period."[4]

As pointed out in Chapter 2, if the child's attention is directed to detailed aspects of his environment, he will be able to become more involved and thus more aware of objects. This not only includes looking, but touching, smelling, tasting and listening to objects. Kamii and Radin[5] state that "only after thorough sensory-motor acquaintance with real things does the child become able to reproduce actions in the absence of objects." He must internalize sensory-motor actions before he can relate them into his own structured symbols.

For teachers who work with children who are at the scribbling stage, here is what can be done to help them in their art development:

1. Provide a work space where the child can draw his own scribbles.

2. Do *not* show him how to improve his scribbles by suggesting that he imitate adult masterpieces.
3. Do not interfere with his activity by asking questions about "what is it?" or otherwise distracting him.
4. Provide the proper art materials. Following is a list of the most suitable art materials for children who are in the scribbling stages of their art development.

Art Materials for Children 2 to 4 Years Old

1. Crayons of assorted colors and sizes (small and big)
2. Paper, white, manila, newsprint, colored construction
3. Brushes, nylon or stiff bristle 1/4" to 1/2"
4. Poster paint (water base opaque—liquid or powdered)
5. Smock or apron
6. Paint and water containers (can); sponge or rag to wipe brush
7. Chalk for chalkboard, sidewalk, paper
8. Modeling materials: salt and flour mix, playdough, baker's dough, modeling clay, water base clay
9. Collected materials (natural, discarded, and inexpensive non-art materials)

Summary

The scribbling period of the child art development includes four recognizable stages: (1) no control, when line is used and materials are just moved around, (2) line control where the line is repeated, (3) shape control where materials are controlled into a shape, and (4) naming of scribble or naming of other manipulated materials.

The parent or teacher should remember that children will be at different stages in their scribble development even though they are at the same chronological age. Some children are slower in both their physical and mental development, some children will have had opportunities to practice the manipulation of art materials, and some are offered much encouragement in art. In conclusion the child needs many experiences with materials and much encouragement to develop the skills that are necessary for him to have before he can successfully enter the symbol stage of expression.

The Symbol Stage of Art Development: Ages 4 to 8

To teachers and parents it sometimes seems as though the little child will never stop scribbling. Then one day when least expected, he begins to draw pictures which can no longer be considered scribbles. Hurray, we say! He is going to be an artist!

Would not it be wonderful if life were that simple! Of course, through the uninhibited vision of children, things do take on a pure, refreshing glow. When we look at children's art works it is very important that we also open our minds to the beauty of their artistic vision.

Through instruction and practice, the child will "obtain both competence and satisfaction in the visual arts."[6] The "naming" of scribbling evolves to more concrete images as the child's mental ability develops, and the former scribbles evolve into rudimentary figures of all sorts.

The first signs of such a change can be visually detected at the kindergarten level. Circular motions become heads and tree tops, while longer strokes become legs, arms, tree trunks and ground lines.

It can be observed that figures, trees and other objects do not actually look as they appear to our eyes. Remember that children relate their ideas in a less complex fashion and in relation to *their* experiences. To a child, however, these first representations of reality are giant steps in his thinking!

The most typical method in which children represent their ideas about things is through the use of simple geometric forms. These forms, a direct outgrowth of the child's former scribbling strokes, become the symbols which represent his understanding

From scribbles come these earliest symbols for man.

The child explores and finds his way beyond the symbol for man, thus extending his ability to reason and invent.

As the child gains control over his art tools and materials, he continues to invent different ways of making visual symbols to tell his thoughts. In this manner, he clarifies his personal ideas through art.

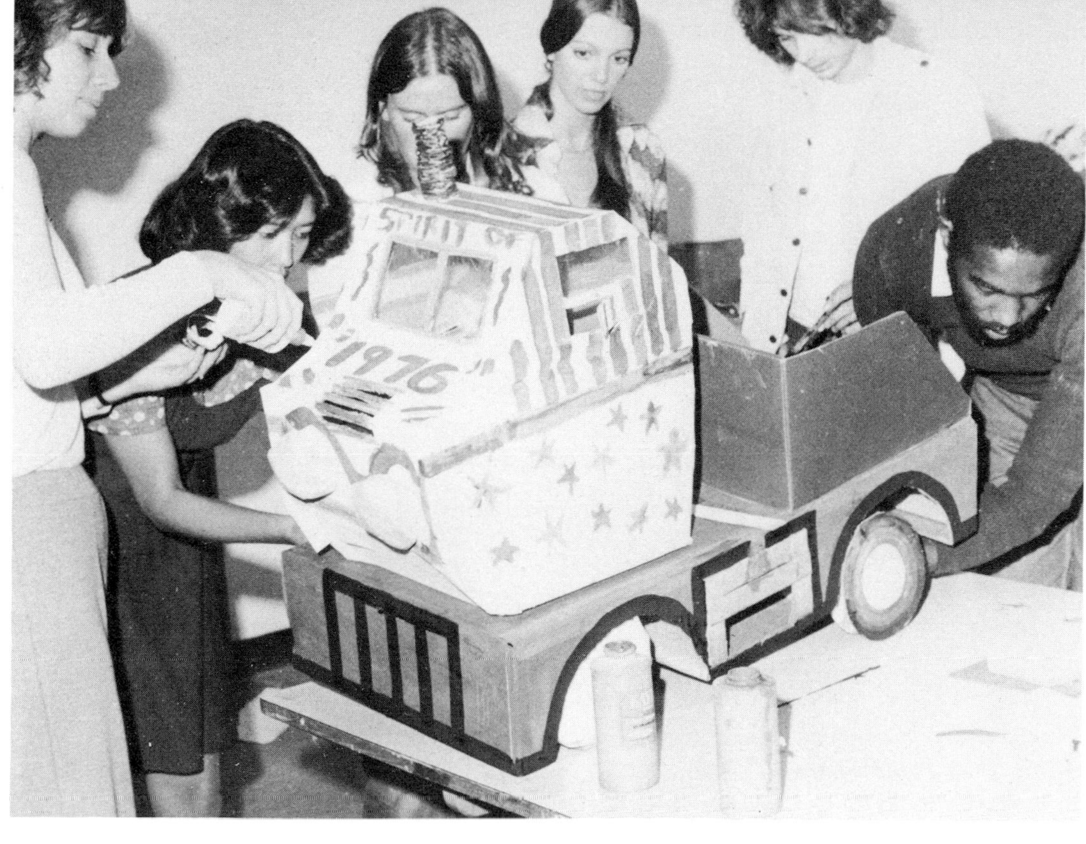

Whenever the student needs direction, the teacher guides the student towards increasing his perceptions about procedures and his skills in various art media.

of the world he experiences. The child's pictures are certainly not "correct" or in "proportion" or even "realistic" when compared with our grown-up standards! But children are not miniature adults, thus, their pictures are extremely real to their child-like manner of thinking. Learning about art is comparable to learning basic word formations. They have to begin with a basic alphabet and work from there. When children are provided with opportunities to practice their art, they soon learn to solidify concepts of their world. They develop confidence in their thinking and observational abilities during the later phases of this symbol stage (roughly second and third grade). Their pictures show an increased addition of details, greater control, and a significant increase in art skills.

For teachers who work with this age group, here are some characteristics which should appear in children's pictures.

Identifying Characteristics of the Symbol Stage

1. Children always exaggerate the parts of their pictures which are most important to them.
2. Children usually draw the sky at the top.
3. Objects in the picture are usually drawn on a ground line on the lower part of the paper.
4. Figures will all tend to look somewhat alike. This indicates a conceptual understanding rather than a visual observation of the figure.
5. Children sometimes omit details of objects which they did not think about during their drawing experience.

Here are some suggestions to help children at this stage of development:

1. Stimulate the child to utilize his idea-factory by providing stories, films and challenging discussions of animals, plants and people in action.
2. Make your own enthusiasms spill over so he will get excited and catch the spark.
3. Lead the child in his thinking to the point where he can pursue an idea independently.
4. Encourage the child to be original and inventive and to always do his own work.
5. Do not be overly critical, for mistakes are part of learning.

Art Materials for Children 4 to 8 Years Old

The most suitable materials for this stage of art development include:

1. Powdered poster paints mixed to a creamy consistency.
2. Both large and small brushes (round, flat bristle or sable).
3. Crayons of assorted colors and sizes.
4. Colored papers of assorted colors and sizes.
5. Clay, salt ceramic, or other modeling material.
6. Colored chalks.
7. Scrap materials for collage and material pictures.
8. Paint containers, smock, sponges, etc.
9. Newsprint, manila, white drawing paper, 12″ x 18″ to 24″ x 36″.
10. Glue, scissors and paste.
11. Tempera markers.
12. White glue.
13. Paris craft.
14. Papier mache.
15. Printmaking materials.

Although the foregoing supplies are basic to a child's art development, the teacher will discover other possible materials.

Summary: Symbol or Schematic Stage

The naming of scribblings may grow out of random marks the child has made on paper, but when the symbol appears it is a controlled shape that is drawn by the child. The producing of a specific recognizable symbol in a child's drawing to which he has given meaning is a very deliberate controlled act. It is the child revealing a significant fact, event, or experience from his life and mind. The symbols produced tell us what impressed that particular child at the time the symbol was made. The child will develop symbols for most things he contacts in his environment, such as dogs, houses, flowers, and toys, but most of all he will draw the symbol for people.

At first symbols appear isolated in a child's drawing and are not related to other symbols in the same drawing. It appears that the child is very intent on drawing one symbol at a time and only later relates two symbols to each other to convey an idea he wants to communicate. This is then followed by relating one or more symbols to base line or the ground. This is the third major step the child takes in his artistic unfolding, the first major step being the naming of scribbling and the second major step the creation of a recognizable symbol.

When these symbols are being created by each individual child, misdirected criticism can destroy a child's desire to relate his exciting ideas and emotions through symbols. The adult, whether parent, teacher, or friend, needs to understand the way the child uses symbols during this important stage.

Children have a certain "logic" in the way they depict and relate their symbols. At first symbols for human beings may all look alike except they are each a different color to give meaning to different individuals within the drawing. The most important figure symbol is often "ME" and is made larger than the rest of the figure symbols. These are all logical ways the child has to depict and give value to objects through his emotions. The adult also needs to know that the sky is at the top of the page, the grass or ground is at the bottom, with air in between, and that in that airspace the child will put people, dogs, houses, flowers, trees, etc. As he develops, his space concept will be expressed with other logical space concepts such as x-ray drawings, fold-over drawings, and others. They are all a part of moving towards a more realistic space concept.

Children do not at first relate the color of an object in their drawings to the way they see it. The color-object relationship will appear later. During the beginning symbol stage the child's need to concentrate on making symbols is more important than what color the object really is.

At the end of the symbol stage the child has definite schemas to convey meaning to his ideas. He can deal with constructing a work of art, and he can become involved in the artistic process much like the studio-artist model.

Realistic Stage of Art Development: Ages 8 to 12

This stage is generally thought of as the last outpost for childish pictures and the beginning frontier for a newfound "realistic" approach to drawing. Although children at this level (4th, 5th, 6th and 7th grades) still retain that uncritical blissfulness of childhood fantasy, their thinking has undergone a dramatic change. They are suddenly boy or girl, alive and bursting with a new social consciousness. The concept symbols which satisfied their earlier art works no longer suffice to represent figures, animals or objects. The child also discovers in his drawings that the sky meets the horizon, and that objects can overlap each other, thus creating spatial effects.

In observing pictures done by children in the "realistic stage," notice that the sky touches the horizon. Observe the more "realistic" approach to the figure. Notice also the increase of details in specific objects. Figures are more in proportion, with less exaggeration. Definite sex differences are apparent, such as pants or dresses. There may even be attempts to shade parts of the picture or otherwise to indicate atmospheric effects. Often there is an awareness of artistic principles such as repetition of shapes and definite spatial effects.

Identifying Characteristics of the Realistic Stage

1. Children at this stage make figures which more closely resemble reality.
2. They overlap objects in their pictures to create a sense of depth.
3. They make distant objects smaller.
4. There is a definite feeling for design qualities such as repetition, color harmonies and texturing.
5. Pictures include many more details than before.

Here are some suggestions to help children who are at this stage of their artistic development:

1. Provide the children with an opportunity to experiment, explore and discover what materials can do.
2. Always stress skillful handling of materials.
3. Begin teaching basic art elements such as shape, line, texture and color. Be sure to keep it at the children's level of understanding.
4. Introduce beginning concepts of perspective or ways to represent objects in space.
5. Stress the importance of personal expression of ideas in making pictures.

Art Materials for Children: Ages 8 to 12

Here are materials that are most suitable for children at this stage of their art development:

PAINTING:
- watercolor paints in the tray or tube
- soft brushes of various sizes, sponge
- poster paint

DRAWING:
- charcoal
- white, pastel, butcher, colored papers
- pencils (felt tips, pastel; scoring pencils are excellent!)
- chalks
- pens and markers of all sorts

MODELING:
- clay
- salt ceramic
- papier-mâché
- Paris craft

PRINTMAKING:
- gadget printing, potatoes, cardboard, spools, inner tubes, etc.
- linoleum
- silk screen

COLLAGE:
- cloth
- papers of various sorts and sizes
- strings, yarns

CONSTRUCTION AND THREE-DIMENSION:
- toothpicks
- cardboard
- tagboard
- construction papers
- wires
- woods
- weaving and stitchery yarns, cloth, string, needles, feet.

Summary: Realistic Stage

In the realistic stage hair has to look like hair, an eye like an eye, and the figure has to have realistic proportions to be acceptable to the child at this time in his development. The parts have to look right in relation to the whole. Colors are as they are seen and as a result are oftentimes not as bright as they were in the symbol stage. Visual space begins to dominate in picture making. The realistic figures are rather small on the page and things

Drawings made "before and after" a motivation show the effectiveness of arousing strong feelings that are involved in the act of "Stubbing My Toe."

Before

After

A strong motivation enables the child to imagine and relive experiences outside of himself. His ability to identify with other people, situations or things thus helps him to redefine the nature of his own creativeness.

in the distance are smaller than things are up close. Objects in the distance lack detail and are not as bright colorwise. Shading is attempted in order to make things look real. A concentration of details tells what is the most important part of the picture. Objects can overlap and extend off the page. The entire object does not have to be shown. Words appear to help explain what is being communicated in the artwork.

At this age there can be a great mixture of both the schematic stage and realistic stages in one grade level. Some children will need to refer more to objects they wish to draw. Sketching from the model and the landscape is now more typical than at earlier stages. More complex materials can now be handled. The child is beginning to practice criticism in relation to his own work and the work of others. This vital capacity needs to be cultivated so that as the child matures he will be able to continue making more mature critical judgments.

Evaluating Children's Art Growth

How can a teacher be certain, after providing children with a number of art experiences, that some tangible growth has taken place? Actually there are a number of definite characteristics to look for. Some of these characteristics can be found in the finished art work, in the young artists themselves.

One of the most satisfactory procedures in evaluating your art program is to collect the children's art works. Parents of a young child will be able to save all his work. Teachers should try to save representative samples at intervals during the month. These can be returned at the close of the semester or school year. Keep each child's work in a separate folder and place the date on each picture. This will facilitate comparisons between early and later art works.

Listed are some specific characteristics which indicate art growth. These characteristics can be used as a progress guide in evaluating children's art development.

Basic Check Points in Evaluating Children's Art Growth As Seen in Children's Pictures

A. Age: 2-4
Grade: Preschool or kindergarten
Stage: *Scribbling*
Signs of Art Growth:

1. Does the child follow typical scribbling sequences as described in this chapter?
2. Does the child enjoy scribbling?
3. Are the scribbles vigorous and forceful?
(This indicates emotional and physical growth.)
4. Are the lines distributed over the entire paper?
(This indicates emotional and aesthetic growth.)
5. Does the child work independently?
(This means he is more creative.)
6. Can the child control his motions?
(This indicates muscular coordination.)
7. Do the lines change in intensity and direction?
(This indicates flexibility.)
8. Does the child concentrate when he scribbles?

Danger Signals:

1. Does the child only repeat marks on the same paper?
2. Does the child ask the teacher to draw for him?
3. Does the child interrupt his scribbles frequently?
4. Does the child try to imitate other children and grown-ups?

B. Age: 4-8
Grade: Kindergarten through 3rd grade
Stage: *Symbol*
Signs of Art Growth:

1. Does the child draw simple, geometric figures?
2. Does he exaggerate important parts?

Each individual approaches new media in different ways. Some manipulate the material first while others may express ideas right from the start. Materials suggest ideas and ideas suggest materials. It is not important that one always precede the other.

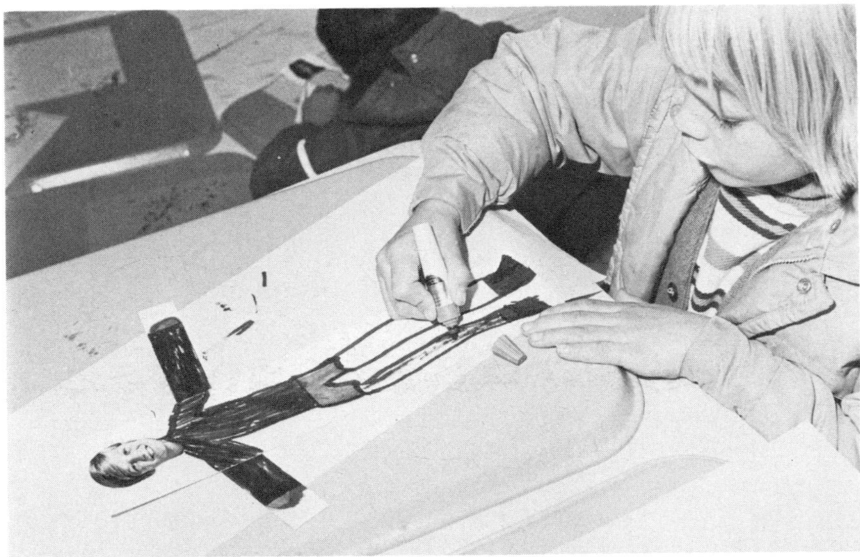

Signs of Artistic Growth

Does the child exaggerate important parts and things?

Does the child draw simple, geometric figures?

Is the drawing distributed over the whole paper?

Is the base line or ground line included?

Do objects appear in proportion?

Are objects overlapped?

Are there indications of perspective?

Do the figures look more like real people?

Does the child include many details in the drawing?

Does the child show growth by using deviations in his space concepts such as using the x-ray view, mixed plane and elevation and the bent base line?

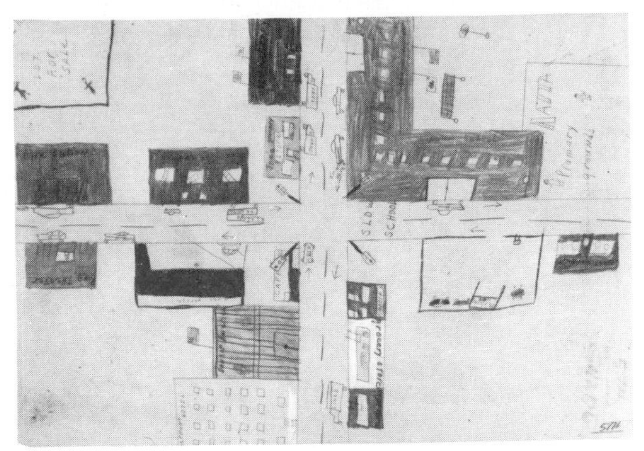
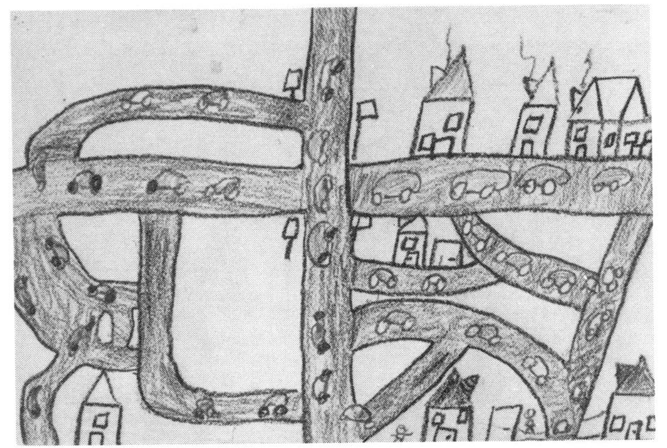

SCRABLE

Bodily action and awareness of environment emerge more fully in the child's beginning realism stage. Details of clothing, hair, and facial features are treated more completely. Overlapping of shapes foretells of a perspective readiness to come.

3. Do his drawings indicate many details? (nostrils, eyelashes, fingers, toes, etc.)
4. Is there evidence of improvement in his images for figures, trees, houses, flowers and animals?
5. Is the drawing distributed over the whole paper?
6. Does the child employ decoration in his work?
7. Is there evidence of balance?
8. Does the child use many colors?
9. Does he use more than one value of the same color?
10. Are distant objects drawn smaller?
11. Does the child work carefully?
12. Does he finish his work?
13. Does the work indicate original ideas?
14. Is the child imaginative?
15. Does the child indicate textures by making contrasting surface treatments?

Danger Signals:

1. Does the child say, "I can't"?
2. Is the drawing full of patterns and rigid stereotypes (stick figures, v-shaped birds, etc.)?
3. Does the child draw only one object such as airplanes, horses or houses etc.?
4. Does the child make "warmed-over" pictures?
5. Is the work lacking in details and freshness?
6. Does the child like to copy?

C. Age: 8-12
GRADE: 4th-7th
STAGE: *Realistic*

Signs of Art Growth:

1. Does the child include a horizon line in his picture?
2. Does the child include shading?
3. Do the figures look more like real people?
4. Does he include many details in his drawings?
5. Does the child make distinctions between boys and girls in his work?
6. Does the child show decorative elements in his pictures?
7. Is there a sense of balance and rhythm?
8. Is there evidence of experimentation with the medium?
9. Is the work inventive?
10. Does the child relate colors to each other?
11. Are there indications of perspective?
12. Does he overlap objects?
13. Do objects appear in visual proportion?

Danger Signals:

1. Do his pictures still contain symbolic geometric figures?
2. Does the child imitate others?
3. Does the child desire to copy or trace?
4. Are stick figures or patterns included in the pictures?
5. Does the child show lack of enthusiasm while he is drawing?
6. Does the child continually repeat the same object?

Signs of Art Growth as Observed in Children's Thinking, Attitudes and Actions

Of course not all signs of art growth can be detected through evaluating children's pictures. Often growth is taking place, but instead of showing up immediately in their pictures, it may be evident in their thinking, attitudes and actions. Here are some questions for detecting signs of art growth.

1. Are the children confident and eager to express ideas in art materials?
2. Do the children notice color in things around them?
3. Do they notice the way things feel to their touch?
4. Do they discuss ideas related to art?
5. Do they express more of their own ideas about things?
6. Are the children more inventive in their thinking?

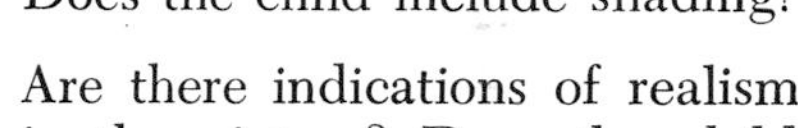

Does the child include shading?

Are there indications of realism in the picture? Does the child show decorative work in his pictures?

Is there a sense of balance and rhythm?

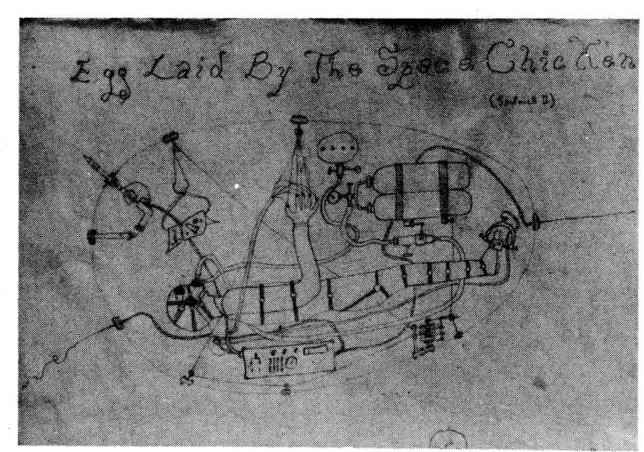

7. Do they work on their art for longer periods of time?
8. Are the children more flexible in their own work?

Check Points for the Teacher

Good art teaching is most dependent on the strength of those who teach it. At the classroom level this includes both teachers and parents. Here are some suggestions to help those who are beginning to teach art to children:

SUGGESTED DO'S

1. Encourage the child always to do his own work.
2. Exhibit all the children's work. Do not favor the "talented ones."
3. Teach the child to be independent.
4. Encourage the children to be original and inventive.
5. Encourage the children always to finish their work.
6. Encourage the children to talk about their work.
7. Provide ample time and opportunity to engage in art.
8. Encourage children to be observant and aware.
9. Teach children to care for materials.
10. Teach children to concentrate on their thinking and feeling.
11. Encourage children to be imaginative.
12. Encourage children to experiment with materials.
13. Utilize visual aids to strengthen your teaching.
14. Always motivate with specific objectives in mind.
15. Encourage the child to think in new directions.

SUGGESTED DON'TS

1. Do not teach indoctrinary techniques which force all children to do the exact same thing.
2. Do not use pattern books, dittos or hectographed materials.
3. Do not express fears about attempting original work.
4. Do not create the notion that art is busy work or "playtime."
5. Do not give children art materials and tell them to make "anything they would like." Very few are "self-motivated."
6. Do not use imitative methods such as copying, tracing.
7. Do not impose adult standards on the child.
8. Do not expect children always to do beautiful pictures.
9. Do not compare children's art work.
10. Do not be overly critical of children's art work. Mistakes are a necessary part of learning.
11. Do not discriminate by favoring certain children.
12. Do not use the same materials repeatedly.
13. Do not use only one size paper.
14. Do not limit art lessons to occasional fill-ins on the schedule.

Tips for Parents and Teachers to Use in Cultivating Creative Traits in Children at All Stages of Artistic Development

Teach children to be *originators.* In whatever manner the child expresses ideas or works through problems, we must encourage him to be unique and unusual. His thoughts should reflect a strictly personal and individual manner of arriving at problem solutions. While he can develop new ideas from listening to others, he should never imitate or copy another person's work.

Teach children to be *idea-trackers.* This trait signifies an ability to think of many possibilities when solving a particular problem and a faculty for keeping the ideas coming until the most suitable one is chosen. Always encourage a child to by-pass the first idea and to consider many others in exploring a given situation. Teach him to be dissatisfied with the ordinary and commonplace solution. Teach him to search for his strongest ways to tell what he knows.

Teach children to be *imagination-stormers* curious about things and situations which at first glance seem mysterious, unknown or puzzling. Encourage him to be inquisitive and imaginative. Teach him to search for answers without being afraid to plunge forward into uncharted territory.

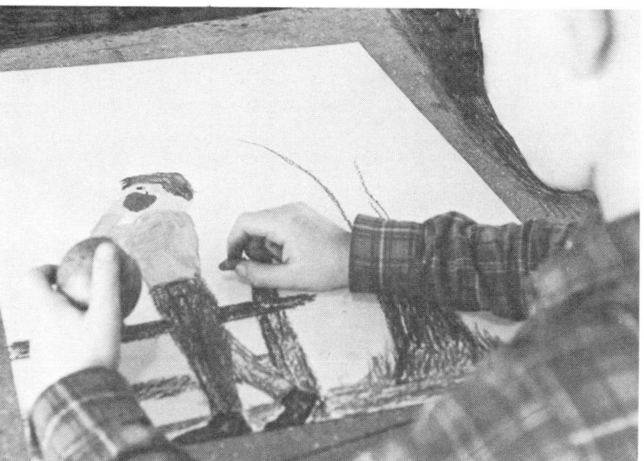

A strong motivation that clarifies ideas will intensify the working process.

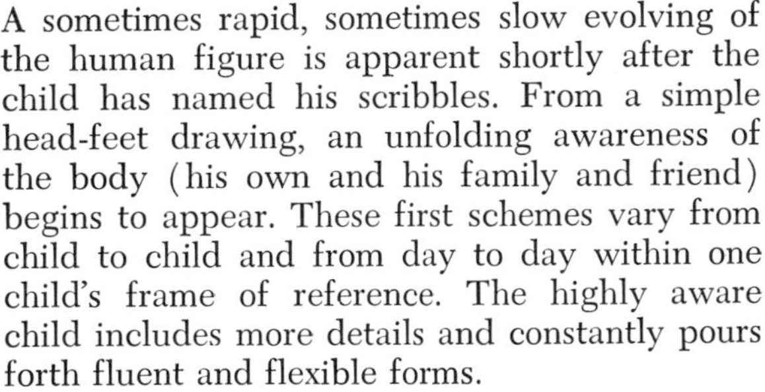

A sometimes rapid, sometimes slow evolving of the human figure is apparent shortly after the child has named his scribbles. From a simple head-feet drawing, an unfolding awareness of the body (his own and his family and friend) begins to appear. These first schemes vary from child to child and from day to day within one child's frame of reference. The highly aware child includes more details and constantly pours forth fluent and flexible forms.

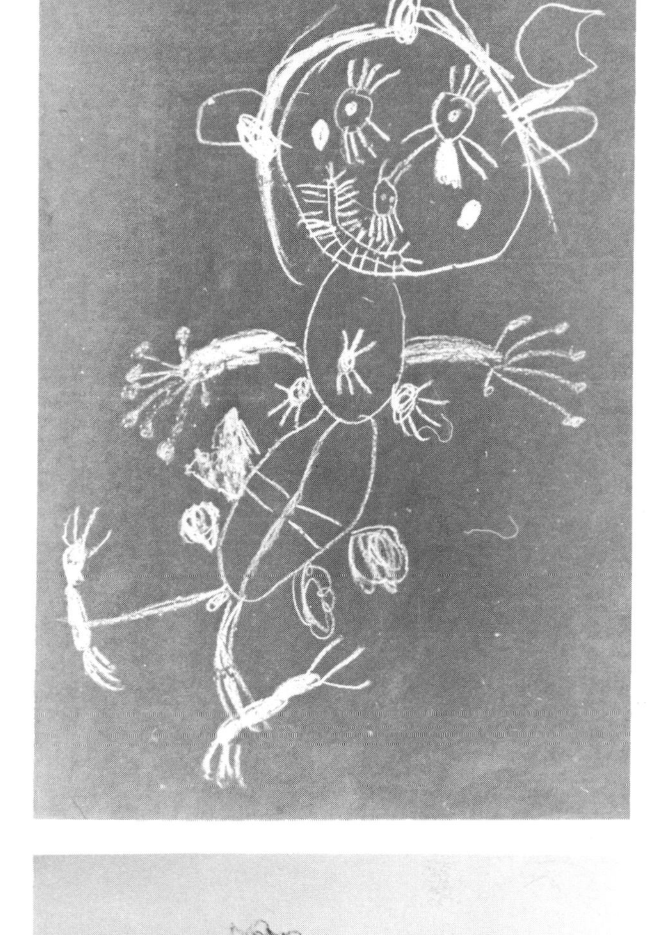

The drawings on pages 70 to 72 represent a child's development in figure drawing from typical head-feet drawings of a child of four to realistic figures of a twelve year old child.

Motivations should include many types of experiences. Texture can be felt by both sight and touch.

Teach children to be *independent,* able to work independently and to stand on his own feet in meeting situations. Encourage him to take the initiative when working alone or with a group. Encourage him to rely on his own judgments and to be unafraid of differing with others.

Teach children to be *expressive* and *flexible,* outgoing and free in expressing his opinions or feelings concerning his relationships with others. Encourage him to inquire and ask questions without fear of seeming ridiculous. Encourage him to be understanding and gentle with others, yet to be firm in his own convictions. Encourage him to laugh when he is happy and to cry when he is sad.

A child should be *perceptually alert.* This means learning to utilize all of his sensory equipment to gain awareness and knowledge of his world. Teach him to be observant when he looks, to listen for what his ears can tell him, and to feel the surface quality of things. He will become more sensitive to all he can take in by remaining open and aware in his responses to different experiences. This means helping him to become more of himself more of the time.

Developing these traits is fundamental in structuring the child's mental foundations. They become the fuel of his mind. Recognizing and cultivating traits of this nature offer to the parent a new focus for helping a child to grow intelligently.

Summary of Stages

For a greater detailed discussion of some of the past and present theories on child art see McFee,[7] Lowenfeld,[8] Harris,[9] *Child Art, The Beginnings of Self-Affirmation,*[10] recent issues of *Studies in Art Education,*[11] and the *Report of the Commission on Art Education.*[12] Anyone who wishes to become an elementary teacher or administrator should be well acquainted with child art theories.

It should be clearly stated that the stages and grade levels given in this chapter were presented to give a general overview of how child art begins and continues through the sixth grade. It should also be stated that there is no *one pattern* or way in which all children develop in artistic expression. Their work in art is an outgrowth of "deep-seated psychological patterns"[13] which reflects their own personalities in relation to their cultural surroundings.

Art is a necessary means for a child to use to externalize a deeply felt inward experience. Through art the child extends and deepens experiences and once externalized in an art product the child is free to analyze them. The creative process in art carries the child through three stages in his elementary school years and he needs adult support at each stage. During the scribble stage he needs acts of approval, art materials, and a place where he is free to work. Throughout the symbol stage he needs encouragement to express ideas through stimulating verbal discussions, skills in the use of materials, ways to evaluate his work and that of others, and a deeper commitment to learning about his art heritage. When the child reaches the realistic stage he will need help in developing visual skills of expression since he will have a more critical attitude toward his work and at this time he will need help in developing art techniques with art materials. He will need to be guided to works of art and assisted in ways to probe and understand their meaning. And finally he will have to learn to play the role of art critic, as a producer and consumer of art.

Ways to Involvement

The following are some suggested exercises which will create a greater understanding in depth of the materials presented in this chapter.

1. Collect a series of linear drawings by
   a. 2-year-old child
   b. 2 1/2-year-old child
   c. 3-year-old child

d. 3 1/2-year-old child
e. 4-year-old child

Write the age on the back of each drawing. Try to arrange them from disordered scribbling to naming of scribbling without looking at the information on the back.

2. Collect several drawings from a five- or six-year-old child. See if you can notice the way he changes the symbol he uses.

3. Collect ten drawings of the human figure from ten different children between the ages of six and seven to see how many different symbols are used for nose, mouth and eyes.

4. Collect several drawings from a second- and third-grade classroom. Check the use of the space symbol. How many have used a deviation from the "base line"? What are the different deviations used in the drawings which you collected?

5. Collect drawings of the human figure from kindergarten and first and second grades. At what age does the costume appear as a part of the figure symbol? Is color related to the object? In what parts of the human symbol does the child relate visual color?

6. Collect several drawings or paintings involving an environmental setting from the fourth, fifth and sixth grades. Check to see how many in each grade have done the following:

Overlapped objects?
Made distant objects smaller?
Made sky meet the ground?
Changed the value of a color?

References

[1]Howard Gardner, *The Arts and Human Development, A Psychological Study of the Artistic Process,* New York: John Wiley and Sons, 1973.

[2]———, "Unfolding or Teaching: On the Optimal Training of Artistic Skills," in *The Arts, Human Development, and Education,* edited by Elliot W. Eisner, Berkeley, Calif.: McCutchan Publishing Corp., 1976, pp. 99-110.

[3]Kenneth M. Lansing, "The Research of Jean Piaget and its Implications for Art Education in the Elementary School," *Studies in Art Education* 7:33-43, spring, 1966.

[4]*Ibid.*

[5]Constance K. Kamii and Norma L. Radin, "A Framework for a Preschool Curriculum Based on Some Piagetian Concepts," *The Journal of Creative Behavior* 1:314-324, July, 1967.

[6]*Ibid.*

[7]June King McFee, *Preparation for Art,* Belmont, Calif.: Wadsworth Publishing Co., Inc., 1970.

[8]Vicktor Lowenfeld, *The Nature of Creative Activity,* New York: Harcourt, Brace & World, Inc., 1939.

[9]Dale Harris, *Children's Drawings as Measures of Intellectual Maturity,* New York: Harcourt, Brace & World, Inc., 1963.

[10]Hilda Lewis, ed., *Child Art: The Beginnings of Self-Affirmation,* San Francisco: Diablo Press, 1966.

[11]*Studies in Art Education,* A Journal of Issues and Research in Art Education, National Art Education Association.

[12]Jerome J. Hausman, ed., *Report of the Commission on Art Education,* National Art Education Association, 1965.

[13]H. A. Witkin, et al., *Psychological Differentiation,* Studies of Development, New York: John Wiley & Sons, Inc., 1962.

Additional References

Alschuler, Rose H. and Laberta Hattwick, *A Study of Painting and Personality of Young Children* 2 vols., Chicago: University of Chicago Press, 1947.

Anderson, Warren H., *Art Learning Situations for Elementary Education,* Belmont, Calif: Wadsworth Publishing Co., Inc., 1965.

Art Education: Elementary, National Art Education Association, Washington, D.C., 1972.

Art for the Preprimary Child, National Art Education Association, Washington, D.C., 1972.

Bland, Jane Cooper, *Art of The Young Child,* New York Museum of Modern Art, 1960.

Cole, Natalie Robinson, *Children's Art From Deep Down Inside,* New York: The John Day Company, Inc., 1966, 210 pp.

Conrad, George, *The Process of Art Education in the Elementary School,* Englewood Cliffs, N. J.: Prentice-Hall, Inc., 1964, 296 pp.

de Francesco, Italo L., *Art Education: Its Means and Ends,* New York: Harper & Row, Publishers, 1958.

Eisner, Elliot W. and David W. Ecker, *Readings in Art Education,* Waltham, Mass.: Blaisdell Publishing Co., 1966, 468 pp.

Eisner, Elliot W., *Educating Artistic Vision,* New York: The Macmillan Publishing Co., Inc., 1972.

Eng, Helga, *The Psychology of Children's Drawings from the First Strokes to Coloured Drawing*, London: Paul, Trench, Truber, 1931.

Erdt, Margaret Hamilton, *Teaching Art in the Elementary School*, rev. ed., New York: Holt, Rinehart & Winston, Inc., 1962.

Gaitskell, Charles, and Hurwitz, Al, *Children and Their Art, Methods for the Elementary School*, second edition, New York: Harcourt, Brace and World, Inc., 1970.

Hess, Robert P., *et al. The Use of Art in Compensatory Education Projects: An Inventory*, Chicago: University of Chicago Press, 1966, 112 pp.

Hoover, F. Louis, *Art Activities for the Very Young*, Worcester, Mass.: Davis Publications, Inc., 1961, 77 pp.

Jefferson, Blanche, *Teaching Art to Children* 2nd ed., Boston: Allyn & Bacon, Inc., 1963.

Kellog, Rhoda, *Analyzing Children's Art*, Palo Alto, California: National Press Books, 1969.

Lansing, Kenneth M., *Art, Artists, and Art Education*, New York: McGraw-Hill, Inc., 1969.

Lark-Horovitz, Lewis and Luca, *Understanding Children's Art for Better Teaching*, Columbus, Ohio: Charles E. Merrill Publishing Company, 1967.

La Tronico, Elaine, "Scylla, Charybdis, and the Art Teacher," *National Education Association Journal*, December, 1961, pp. 30-31.

Linderman, Earl, "Child Art: The Wellspring of Life," *National Catholic Kindergarten Review*, Winter-December, 1963.

———, "Child Art and the Teacher," *Grade Teacher*, April, 1962.

Linderman, Earl W. and Linderman, Marlene M., *Crafts for the Classroom*, New York: Macmillan Co., 1977.

Linderman, Marlene, *Art in the Elementary School*, Dubuque, Iowa: Wm. C. Brown Company Publishers, 1974.

Lindstrom, Miriam, *Children's Art*, Berkeley: University of California Press, 1957.

Lowenfeld, Viktor, *The Nature of Creative Activity*, New York: Harcourt, Brace & World, Inc., 1939.

———, *Your Child and His Art*, New York: The Macmillan Company, 1955.

Merritt, Helen, *Guiding Free Expression in Children's Art*, New York: Holt, Rinehart & Winston, 1964.

———, *Creative and Mental Growth*, New York: The Macmillan Company, 1960.

McIlvain, Dorothy S., *Art for Primary Grades*, New York: G. P. Putnams' Sons, 1961.

Rueschhoff, Phil, and Swarts, Evelyn, *Teaching Art in the Elementary School*, New York: The Ronald Press Co., 1969.

Schaefer-Simmern, Henry, *The Unfolding of Artistic Activity*, Berkeley: University of California Press, 1948.

Wachowiak, Frank, *Emphasis Art*, 3d ed., New York: T. Y. Crowell, 1977.

Verbal motivations can bring about a deeper personal investigation. A richer experience leads to actualization of the self.

Chapter 4

When we as adults take the time to observe and to study children, and to extend our own understanding of the countless ways in which young people grow and develop, the creative achievement of youth will be increased. How can we as adults stimulate this growth? We need to provide abundant creative opportunities. A child's surroundings—his world of man-made things—his world of God-made things: people, plants, animals, the sun, moon and stars—all provide infinite exploratory possibilities which will help him develop the sensitivity and the imagination so important in living. Children need to be helped to see, to feel, to listen and to think, for out of these abilities comes the power to relate and to interpret the world around them.

Arne W. Randall and
Ruth Elsie Halvorsen
from *Painting in the Classroom,*
Worcester, Massachusetts:
Davis Publications, 1962, p. 5

Motivation: Winding up the Mainspring of Art

Art education practices for the past two decades have been firmly founded on the philosophy that children have the innate capacity to transform their primary means of knowing, that is their experiences of feeling, thinking, and perceiving, into their own unique art forms. In attempting to retain and foster this precious human gift of discovery through art, leading art education authorities have emphasized the importance and value of motivations as the basic means of evoking art responses from children.

Beginnings of motivations in art as they are understood today had their roots in the teachings of Franz Cizek in Austria at the turn of the century and later in the teachings of Natalie Cole in the United States. More recent authors, including Lowenfeld, Brittain, Mendelowitz, Keiler, Mattil, Jefferson, Gaitskell, Horwitz, and others, continue to emphasize in their art education philosophy the responsibility of parents and teachers in providing motivations for children's art productions.

These writers have dealt with motivations as the main thrust in teaching art to children, and their central concern is that of dealing with the interaction of the child with his environment. The final result of any motivation, whether it comes from (1) viewing an object in detail, (2) recalling past experiences, (3) having empathy, (4) becoming aesthetically involved with an art object, (5) delving into one's art heritage, (6) creating from the imagination, or (7) being stimulated through the use of art materials, will culminate in an inner intensity which the child transforms into a visually exciting art product.

A child's pursuit of art emerges from primary sensitivities, concrete experiences, and intuitive and aesthetic feelings. The articulate process of transforming those perceptions into his personalized art forms can come about through a strong self-motivation, or the teacher can help motivate the child to put in order his personalized detailed impressions.

In responding to a motivation, the child is challenged to reflect, to relate, and to form his ideas. He is encouraged to be inventive, imaginative, and original. He is guided in exercising self-judgment and self-discipline as he chooses and as he limits and controls the internal images he is forming.

How Can Motivations Help Children in Their Art Production?

1. They can help a child give shape to his experiences from the depth of his feelings so that he is more capable of putting them into visual forms.
2. They can help children share moods, emotions, and feelings whether they are verbal or just felt silently. Sigmund Freud once stated that in all fundamental issues of life, the final decision we make is best left to our feelings.
3. They can help a child to visualize from his inner sources, especially for the young child.
4. They can help children learn to use their "hunches" in creating solutions to art problems.
5. They can be dynamic inquiries into human behaviors that can lead to a greater awareness of one's self and one's environment.
6. They can help children "open" up to the intuitive side of their minds or the "right side" of the brain, which can jump gaps in information and can more successfully deal with the uncertainty in art production and creativity.
7. They can assist children in creative art expression when we motivate them to use their imagination.
8. They can help a child to visually perceive an object or work of art by looking for such visual elements as color, texture, shape, etc.
9. They can assist the child's artistic development as it unfolds to find new ways for him to visualize his ever-changing perceptions, emotions, and feelings. After a child has visualized his perceptions, emotions, or feelings into mental images they can then be drawn on paper, modeled in clay, carved in wood, or executed in whatever material the child selects.

A recent National Art Education Association publication, *Art Education: Elementary,* listed some eight ways art is taught in the United States. Motivations can be effectively designed and used with any of the approaches suggested, such as the child centered approach, artist as model approach, and the perceptual approach.

During a motivation the teacher or parent acts as nurse and helps the child give birth to an idea. Once the idea is born the child will need additional help to work out the idea in detail. Here, once again, the skillful help of the teacher is necessary to help the newly born idea grow and mature. With children, as with all creative persons, the birth of the idea comes differently to each child and the growth of that idea will only mature with the right nutrients supplied by the attending teacher or parent.

"I don't know what to draw."
"I don't have any ideas."
"I can't do it."

How many of us have heard children make comments of this sort during the art lesson? What do we say to children that will stimulate in them a desire to tell their ideas and experiences with art materials? Do we simply pass out the paper and tell them to "go to work"? It is probable that a procedure of this sort would only encourage statements like those mentioned.

We usually cannot expect children to sit down with art materials and pour forth a multitude of ideas. Very young children are still fascinated by art materials and living things in general; however, many school-age youngsters have already developed stop signs in their thinking. As children grown older, these stop signs may become considerably more frequent with all sorts of S-shaped curves to surpass, thus slowing down a clear view of the thinking road ahead.

If a teacher instructs a child to do a drawing or painting without providing him with any prior stimulation, there is a strong chance that he will make a generalized picture which does not say very much as a personal expressive statement. Pictures of this sort (which some children repeat over and over again) are the result of "warmed-over" ideas which the child has done in the past. He falls back on them when he has not been motivated by his personal experiences to say something challenging in terms of his present awareness. A typical example of the warmed-over picture is the tree-house-sun-tulip picture often seen at the primary level, and the palm tree-desert island setting-sun-ocean picture of older students. These pictures and their prototypes are frequently found hanging at the easels, the results of a "turn" at painting.

Children need direction and strong challenge in their art thinking. They need to get excited about their ideas. In order to recreate an experience through art media, the child needs to recall the experience vividly. He must be stirred sufficiently that he has a desire to communicate his thoughts in visual terms. In this respect, he needs to develop somewhat the eye of the artist. The true artist is always full of ideas. He is able to select from his stockpile of thoughts the ideas most suitable to express a specific intent. In addition, he is able to tell his ideas in *original* and *inventive* ways. The artist is both a *thinker* and a *craftsman*, able to unite *art skill* and *idea skill* into a personal technique for telling what he knows and feels about things in his world. Similarly, our objective in working with children deals with how to stimulate *their* art thinking and develop *their* art skills in saying things with art materials. Here is where motivation comes in!

Ways to Motivate Children in the Production of Their Art Products

Motivation refers to a teacher's or parent's ability to arouse and stimulate a child's thinking so that he will discover ways to communicate his ideas in visual forms. It is also a method by which we can help children think through ideas, relive their experiences, or create new images from their own personal sources.

Visual-aid, firsthand, material, and sensory experiences support the verbal discussion during a motivation. Verbal discussion alone usually produces only memory drawings and does not enrich visual concepts. The young child's drawing may very well be a weak memory drawing because he has not learned how to use his sensory experiences to enrich his visual thinking (concepts).

The verbal discussion should always be the basic means for challenging the child's thinking during and/or after he has participated in one of the following experiences.

Visual-Aid Experiences

This type of experience occurs when the teacher or parent uses films, slides or other illustrative material to stimulate visual observation. If a film is used, the procedure might go something like this: The teacher must first select the film, basing his choice on its relatively short length, its concentration of intended details and its photographic properties. Emotional factors might also be considered. For example, the film *Spider Engineers* deals with a creature somewhat repugnant to many people; thus an emotional re-

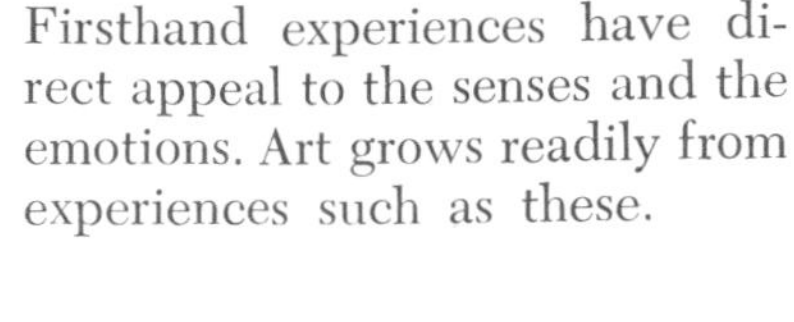

Firsthand experiences have direct appeal to the senses and the emotions. Art grows readily from experiences such as these.

The joy or frustration of self-discovery is difficult to measure from the appearance of the person. The reaction can be measured better through the growth evidenced in art processes or art products.

Becoming involved with materials can be through direct contact or rather detached intellectual contemplation before creative action begins.

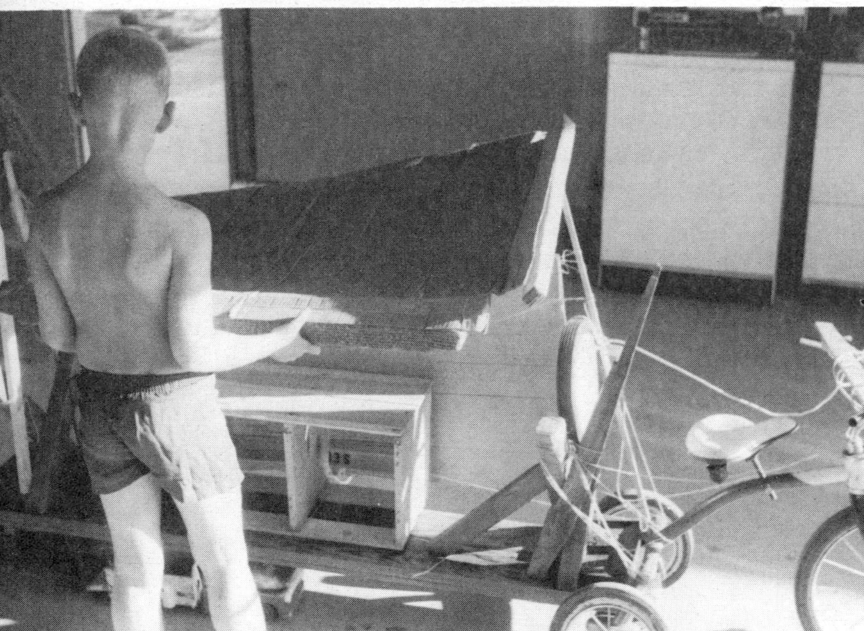

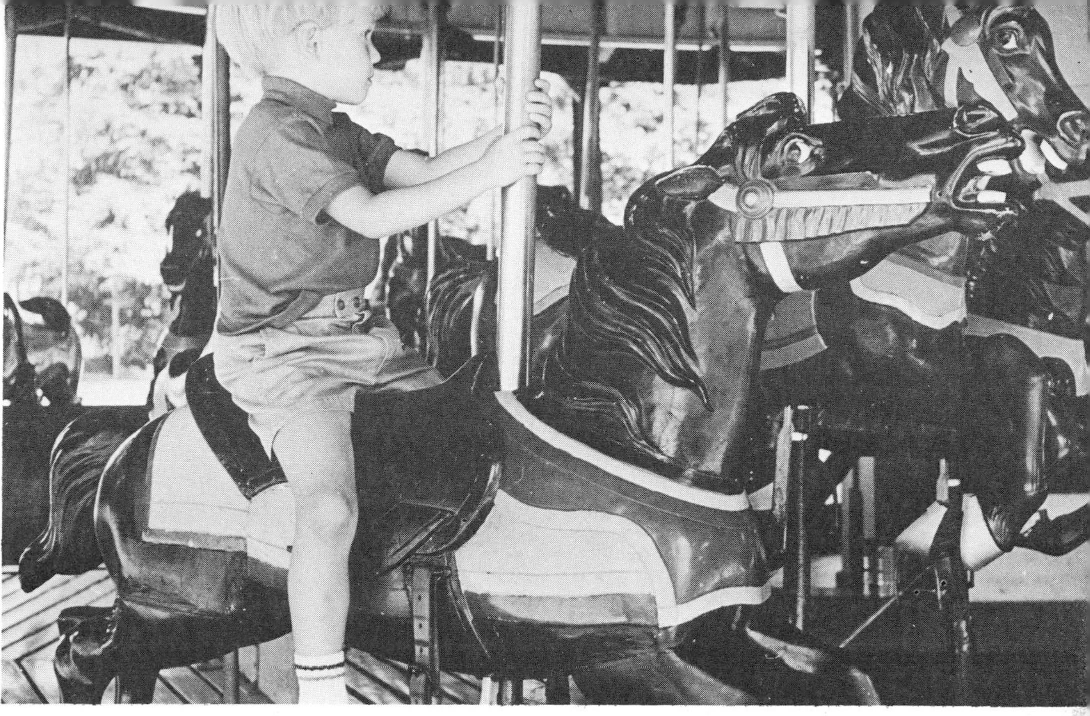

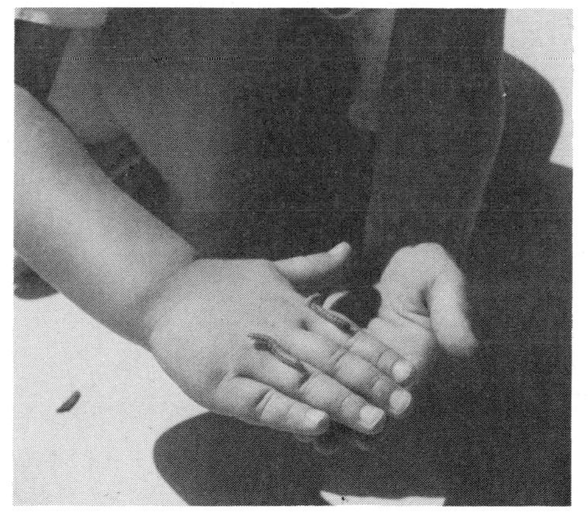

Motivations stem from a diversity of experiences. The thrill of riding, the scent of a rose, the excitement of a carnival ride, the tickle of a caterpillar, the tenderness of a hug—all combine to enrich personal aesthetic experiences.

sponse is quite likely. When such a film has been selected and shown, the teacher might introduce the verbal discussion with such questions as:

How would it feel to have eight legs?

How would it feel to be stuck with the spider's hyponeedle?

How would it feel to be caught in his sticky web?

How would it feel to be pulled down into a dark hole and eaten?

When sufficient discussion has stimulated thinking, the children use art materials to develop their own ideas evolving from the particular film. Art materials should always be prepared ahead of time and be available for instant use at the peak of readiness. A positive factor in using films to help motivate is that they strengthen mental images by allowing the child to focus on the details of a particular experience. Films are also invaluable in that the camera can slow down such rapid actions as birds in flight, or speed up the entire growth sequence of plants, things which the naked eye cannot witness. Thus the film enables us to see details, an important factor in artistic and creative thinking.

Firsthand Experiences. This means providing the children with actual experiences involving live animals, flowers, people, or going to various places and events. It refers to opportunities in which children can observe, question and investigate on-the-spot characteristics of specific things. Such experiences include going to the zoo, the farm, bringing animals to class, walking through a greenhouse, visiting a bakery, a factory and so forth. In such activities, the teacher or parent must do more than lead the child to the object. He must encourage the child to make discoveries into the nature of the object. The teacher must lead the child along the path of inquiry to the point where *he will make the discoveries for himself.* This is done by utilizing a questioning type approach. For example, a teacher may surmise that the students need to strengthen their concepts of horses. In terms of a firsthand experience, here are some questions to lead the child into avenues of search and exploration:

Is the horse very large? How large? Is he larger than yourself?
What color is he? Is he the same color all over?
Can you see his muscles?
Does he have eyelashes? Do his eyes look like your eyes?
How does the hair grow to form his mane?
How long is his tail?
How does he bend his neck?
Who has ever ridden on a horse? Did you bounce up and down?
Can a horse run fast?
Who has ever touched a horse? What does he feel like?
Did you ever imagine that you were a horse?

Questions of this nature direct the child's thinking to specific details about horses. As the questions are asked, the child will search for visual images. In this manner, the child is able to *crystallize* his images pertaining to the experience with a horse. He should now be ready to reflect some of these images in his art expression.

Material Experiences. This refers to experimentation, search and investigation as the child works directly in the art materials without previous stimulation. If, for instance, a child were working with clay, he would be more apt to discover possibilities and ideas by actually experimenting with it before he started to make an object. If he were experimenting with paint on a surface, the manipulation of the pigment would often suggest possibilities for investigation. In these instances it is possible for the material to be the major factor in motivating the child. The experimentation could be interspersed with questions such as:

What happens when two colors run together?
How can we make the color green?
What happens when you wet the paper first?

Let us try an ink line over our water colors.
Can you make coils with the clay?
How can you texture the surface?
What can you discover about this material?

Of course all questions should be oriented to a specific grade level. At all times the teacher should guide the children and yet be ready to let *them* take the reins as soon as they can see new possibilities in the material.

Sensory Experiences. Sensory experience refers to the manner in which we perceive or "take in" outside information through the senses. We can increase our intake of information about the world around us by increasing our capacity for utilizing our senses. For our purposes this refers to visual sensitivity or learning to observe with our eyes; auditive sensitivity or learning to listen; tactile sensitivity or learning how things feel to our touch; and olfactory sensitivity or the ability to learn about things through our sense of smell.

The method of teaching children to examine and observe is not too difficult. Basically, a good general approach is to direct their attention to an object by asking a series of questions. Your questions can be organized in such a manner that they have to search for the answer. Your questioning will become a guide for them to make their own discoveries. In this way, they find the answer rather than having you tell them. It would be much easier for the child if you supplied him with all the correct answers, but so much more challenging and valuable to him if he must make the discoveries! Do not be afraid to be persistent. (And remember to be enthusiastic!)

Discovering Visuals. See Chapter 2, page 23 for other examples of learning to look at and see details in our environment. Remember we look at the individual parts of an object and we look for the elements of art, color, line, shape, texture, and form.

For an exercise in visual observation, the teacher could instruct each child to collect some flowers and bring them to class. The children could then examine their flowers very closely to see what they could discover. Here are some questions to ask:

What is the flower's name?
Can you count the petals? How many?
What is the shape of the petals?
Can you find the seed pockets?
What color is your flower?
Have you ever seen this color before? Where?
How tall is the stem?
How long is the stamen?
Where is the pollen located?

Discovering Sounds

While vision seems to be the most common method by which learning takes place, there are also other important means to learning which are often neglected. The growth of creative awareness, and ultimately the artistic mind, *also* depends on those other avenues of sensory learning, for they tell us things which vision cannot capture. One such avenue is the development of our listening ability. This refers to the manner in which we are able to inquire into the nature of different sounds.

Sounds can be endless in variety. The most familiar are musical sounds, such as those we hear from recordings and musical instruments. However, for greater clarity of understanding, let us group sounds into four different categories so we can study them more easily. The four groups of sounds include:

1. musical sounds
2. sounds in nature
3. man-made sounds
4. unusual and imaginative sounds

1. Musical Sounds: We think of musical sounds as those which are made by voices singing or instruments being played

Odd-ball or unusual materials provide a less conventional means for the adult to experiment without immediately focusing on an idea.

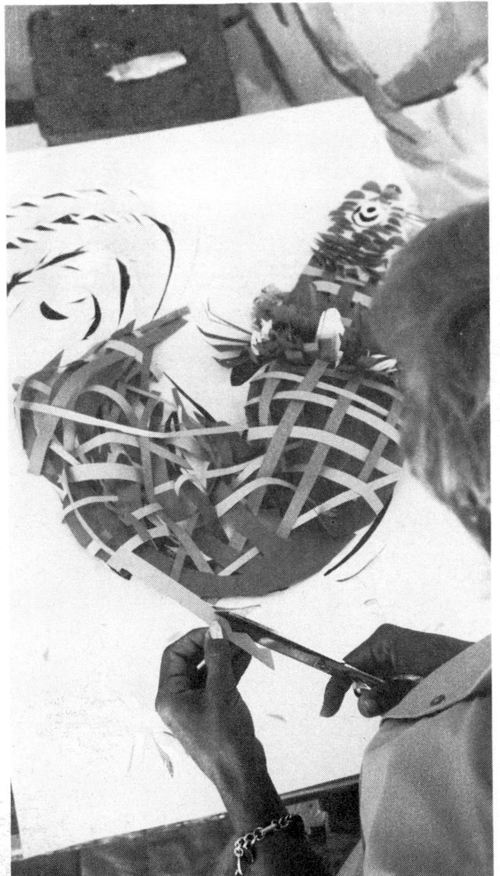

Does the grass whisper?

Have you ever invented a sound machine?

in a rhythmical sequence. You can help children become more aware of differences and similarities of rhythm, tone, pitch and quality in such musical instruments as:

drums	guitars
trumpets	bass fiddles
trombones	pianos
violins	clarinets

and many other instruments you learn about

2. Sounds in Nature: There are countless numbers of sounds in nature which are both beautiful and rhythmical to hear if we learn to listen and become aware of them. These sounds tell us of beauty, rhythm, and a higher order of things of which man is a part. You can help children become more aware and sensitive to such sounds as:

wind rustling through the trees
the water of a brook
the snap of a twig
rain on a windowpane
the hum of insects
the flapping of a bird's wings
the crackle of burning wood
the sound of thunder
the stillness of a peaceful glen
and many other sounds you learn about

3. Man-made Sounds: There are many sounds in our every-day environment which are both pleasing and stimulating to listen to. Children can lend richness to their experience when they learn to become more aware of the sound of things. Sounds stimulate the mind. Who has not heard a familiar sound and felt warmed by the past association it presented? Some of the sounds that children can listen for include:

the whine of a saw cutting through wood
the heartbeat of a tractor digging into soil
the crunch of an apple between the teeth
the whistle of a passenger train in the night
fog horns sounding across the bay
the whirr of a trolly cable
the rhythm of the subway car
the streak of a jet through the sky
a garden sprinkler rotating endlessly
a car crossing a gravel driveway
a clothesline pulley turning around
horseshoes hitting the pipe
bacon frying on the stove
the sound of many footsteps on the pavement
the creak of a porch swing
the whiz of a fishing line
and many other sounds you learn about

4. Unusual and Imaginative Sounds: Sometimes we hear sounds which startle us because they are unrecognizable or not familiar. Sounds such as these cause us to imagine things which may not exist, for they seem to be mysterious and puzzling. Sounds such as these may:

be explosive in character
have an unusual beat or rhythm
seem to occur far-off in the distance
be muffled or vague
be scratchy or tearing
have many high and low tones combined
have unusual frequencies
be very soft and delicate
be very high pitched
seem like many things put together

In a hearing experience, the objective would be to increase our ability to listen. One method to use would be to collect as many different kinds of objects as possible, for example, nails, hinges, glassware, dishes, twigs, sandpaper, cloth, metals, sponges, plastic objects and whatever else is available. Next place a cardboard screen in front of the associated objects in order to conceal their identity. Stand behind the screened objects and create various sounds by hitting, rubbing, tapping, rolling and shaking the objects. Encourage the children to listen closely, and then attempt recognition of the sounds they hear. Again, the teacher should ask questions that will direct their thinking toward an increased awareness in responding to sounds. For example:

Can you recognize the sound?
Do you enjoy hearing these sounds?
What does this sound remind you of?
Is this a musical sound?
Which sounds are soft?
Which sounds are mellow?
Which sound are rhythmical?
How do you feel when you hear a certain sound?

An exercise for the children would be to have them collect several objects in a box and encourage them to construct their own sound box by fastening, hanging and positioning various materials inside of the box.

Discovering Textures

In a *tactile experience*, the objective is to encourage an awareness of differences and similarities in the "feel" of objects. The variety is endless. For example:

What is the difference between the feel of wood and stone?
Which is smoother, an egg or a glass?
What things are rough? slippery? soft?
Which is softer, fur or cotton? Which is warmer?
What things feel sandy? fuzzy? fluffy?
What things feel moist? wet? dry?
What things feel cool to the touch?

An exercise for tactile sensitivity would be to have the children collect differently textured objects and bring them to class. Some possibilities include papers, spools, beans, rope, cotton, pebbles, corrugated cardboard, cloth, buttons, steel wool and burlap. Have them also bring a lidded container, such as a shoe box. Let them construct their own "feeling boxes" by gluing, fastening, suspending and positioning objects that have interesting textural qualities inside the boxes. After the inside is complete, have each child cut an opening in one of the sides so the hand can reach in and explore the textures. Experiences of this nature direct the child's imagery toward tactile considerations.

Discovering Smells

In *olfactory experiences*, the objective is to increase an awareness of differences and similarities in smell. One method of stimulating this awareness is to collect various scents and put them into small bottles. Solid pieces can be crumbled with a hammer and then dropped into bottles. In this manner an entire collection of various scents can be acquired and stored for comparison. Some possibilities for scents include pine, mint, hay, clover, sawdust, flowers, dried foods, spices, perfumes and powders. When a sufficient variety of scents has been collected, encourage the children to recognize and to develop images based on specific smells. Ask questions such as:

Which smells are pleasant?
Which smells are not pleasant?
What does the smell remind us of?
Where are such smells located?
Which one smells sweet?
Which smell is sour?
Which smell is sharp?
Which smell is mellow?
What does wet wood smell like?
Do all things have smells?

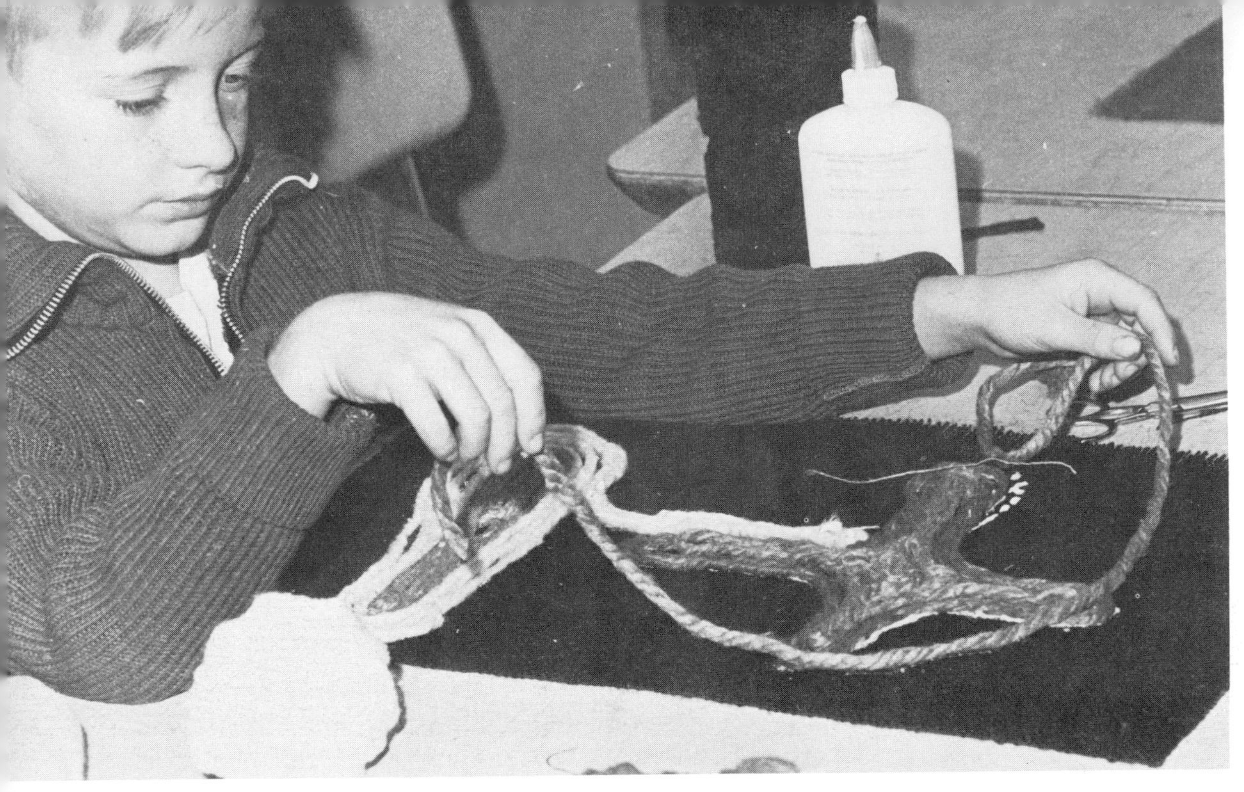

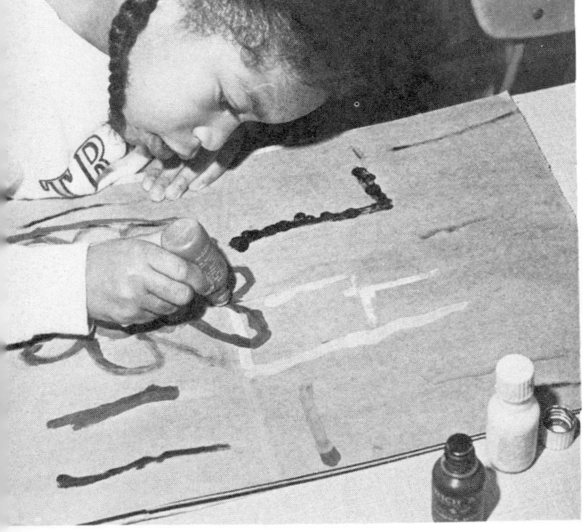

Skill and involvement of the self are essential aspects of art development.

Tactile sensations lead to images not perceived by the eye. The individual's awareness of differences and similarities is increased through perceiving how things feel and look.

What does a rose smell like? grass? soil?
Does the forest have a smell?
Did you ever smell a hayfield?
did you ever smell the pines in the forest?
How does grass smell after a rain?
What do flowers smell like?
Do they all smell the same?
What does a candy factory smell like?
Did you ever smell food in a bakery?
Did you ever smell a flower shop?
Did you ever smell a butcher shop?
Have you ever smelled smoke?
What other things can you find to smell?

Motivations which deal with sensory experiences are necessary for the development of a child's creative awareness. Children who are perceptually aware are more likely to inquire, explore and express their relationships as growing, purposeful beings. In terms of their art expression they are more ably equipped to say and tell ideas which are original and inventive.

Discovering Tastes

The objective in the tasting experience is to give the child another source to enrich his creative awareness potential. The emphasis within this area is related mainly to understanding and appreciating differences in the taste of foods. Adventures in tasting can center around the kitchen, or occur in various commerical establishments. Here are some questions that will aid you in these explorations with children:

We learn to taste
How does a potato taste?
Does it taste the same as a carrot?
What is the difference?
What is the difference between a tomato and a lemon?
Does bread taste the same as cake?
What do olives taste like?
Did you ever taste a dill pickle?
Did you ever taste crabmeat?
Do nuts taste different from each other?
What does corn taste like?
Does water have a taste?
What is the difference between a peach and an apple?

Of course, there will be a wonderful time for tasting at the family meal. For example, what do the following foods taste like:

Spaghetti and meatballs	Bacon and eggs
Macaroni and cheese	Smoked salmon
Beef stew	French fried potatoes
Chop suey	Candied sweet potatoes
Hungarian goulash	and many others

Visiting different restaurants offers a chance to learn about more unusual foods, such as Sukiyaki, Tacos, Wienerschnitzel, lobster and seafoods, and so forth.

Children can be more readily moved to express ideas, images, or feelings through verbal discussion, provided they have had a rich background of sensory experiences. The child is less likely to say "I can't or don't know what I want to draw," if he has had a wealth of detailed firsthand experiences. With the help of the teacher, through verbal interchange, the child can develop the skill to transform materials into his own personal art forms.

Children should be encouraged to always include their own human feelings as an intergral component of these three basic motivational classifications. Visual skills of observation gained through sensory experiences and discoveries coupled with strong emotional feelings are basic to creative expression. Increased skill in the use of art media can be gained while practicing artistic, intellectual and imaginative skills.

The human qualities that are fundamental to child art are those kinds of feelings and ideas that children have and express to each other through their art work.

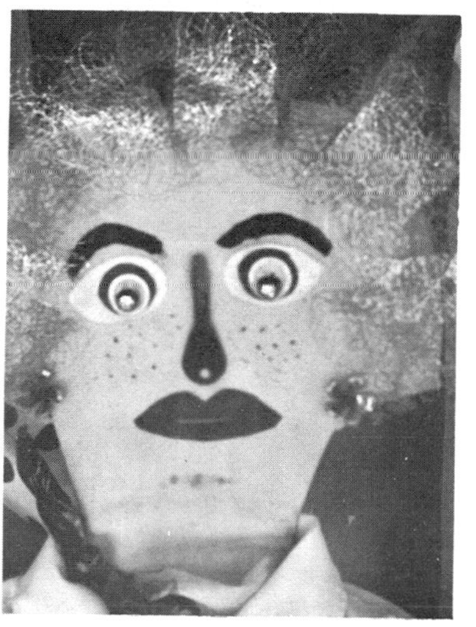

Individuals should be stimulated by motivations of a less conventional nature in order to break down established barriers which previously stalled inventive thinking.

Sensory and emotional experiences are integral parts of all art motivations, as are skills with materials and skills in making aesthetic judgments about the work created.

Basic Motivational Categories

For purposes of clarification, and to simplify art program planning, art motivations can be grouped under one of the following three major classifications:

1. *Artistic motivations*
2. *Intellectual motivations*
3. *Imaginative motivations*

Artistic Motivations. This refers to all art motivations which have as their goals the development of perceptual awareness, increased aesthetic sensitivity and skills with art media. Emphasis within this area should stress the *development of skills in using art media, learning to design and becoming responsive to the aesthetics of natural and man-made forms.* Artistic motivations can be introduced as early as the kindergarten level, but it should be in keeping with the learning level and thinking of the child. It is never too early to begin making children aware of colors, textures, shapes, and lines. Here is a sample approach in working with children of primary school age:

> *(Paints, brushes and pertinent materials have been distributed and the children are ready to go.) As part of our art learning time today, who knows one of the colors in front of him? There's a hand! Good. We all know yellow . . . red . . . blue . . . What do you suppose would happen if we mixed red and yellow together? Let's try it . . . Who has discovered? Let's each of us mix two colors together and see what we can discover. We might even make something that is this color. Let's see if we can mix colors right on our paper as we paint . . .*

Artistic motivations do not always have to deal directly with art materials as such. Discovering beauty in natural and man-made forms is a way to learn about art. For example, the teacher can encourage children to become more aware of aesthetic qualities by leading them to observe and discover the *shape* of things. Have them collect various stones, leaves, shells and other available objects. Point out the possible differences and similarities in shapes. Some stones are long, some short, some lumpy, some angular, some sharply curved and some very unusual in shape. Encourage the children to discover for themselves and to discuss what they have learned.

At the intermediate level some ideas for artistic motivations could include:

Experimenting with watercolors	Exploring textures
Learning about perspective	Discovering colors
Learning how to design	Drawing the figure
The elements of art	Drawing landscapes
Discovering what the brush can do	Drawing trees

Here is a sample artistic motivation for drawing the figure at the intermediate grade levels:

Learning to Draw Figures

Materials. Large sheets of paper, 18" x 24" or larger, crayons, brushes, charcoal, pencils.

Sample Artistic Motivation. Learning to draw people means that you must be very observant and willing to practice your art skills. What are some of the ways which can help us improve our figure drawing? Yes, using each other as models is a very good way. You could also use a large mirror if you wanted to draw yourself. When you look at others or at yourself you must look carefully to see how the head is bent, what the legs are doing, which way the body is leaning, and all the actions that our figure is making. When we have observed carefully, we can draw what we remember about the pose we were in. When you draw figures in action, do not worry about erasing. You can make many sketching lines in your pictures, and then darken the ones

which you feel are most correct. Some points to remember and look for when you are posing are:

1. Your body bends at the waist. Where else? It also bends at elbows, wrists, knees, neck and ankles.
2. Some poses to take might include bending over, stretching upward, getting ready to run, climbing a ladder. How many more can you think of?

Now we are ready to try our first pose and then to draw what we have observed and remembered.

Intellectual Motivations. This refers to all art motivations that have as their aim the development and enrichment of children's concepts for natural and man-made objects. In this respect, art materials become a tool in which intellectually understood concepts can be strengthened. That is, in order for a child to draw or paint his ideas, he has to rethink what he has just experienced. This causes him to refocus his mental images on the ideas which have stimulated a particular mode of thought. Basically, *intellectual motivations emphasize the acquisition and development of factual knowledge* 1. as it pertains to himself, to others, or to objects in question. *Knowledge is not a by-product of art expression, but it is a necessary prerequisite.* 2. Unless a child learns specific facts concerning people, animals, birds, flowers and so forth, he will not be able to say very much about them in his art. If for instance, the teacher asks a child to draw a picture of a bird the child is unlikely to say very much about birds unless he has learned specific information concerning them. The teacher can be assured of a much richer concept in terms of pictures, if the child's thinking is directed to factual information concerning birds. This could be accomplished by bringing a live bird to class, showing a good film or taking a trip to the zoo. Here is a sample motivation using an intellectually oriented discussion:

Learning About Characteristics of Birds

Materials. Paints, brushes or crayons, paper 18″ x 24″.

Sample Intellectual Motivation. For our art learning time this morning, I am looking for someone who can tell the class what he knows about birds. There is a hand. Bobby knows something, Rosie knows . . . Good! Already, many of you know something about birds. Yes, they can fly. Yes, they have two legs, feathers, wings, a beak. (At this point, you could introduce some live birds, or a film, or many illustrative pictures, or provide a firsthand experience by going to a pet shop or zoo.) As the children observe and examine the birds, the questions could become *much more* specific and detailed, such as:

How do birds move their wings to fly?
What shape are the feathers?
Are they all the same size?
What are the legs like?
Are they jointed?
How does the bird hold himself on a twig?
Are all birds the same color?
How does a bird bend to eat a worm?
What is the bird's mouth like?
Can birds talk?
Would you like to be a bird?
How would you feel up high on a tree limb?
Did you ever touch a bird? Do they feel like a kitten?
Do birds have different types of beaks? Why?

These questions should not be asked in rapid-fire sequence but should be interspersed throughout the stimulation time. When the children have learned some facts concerning birds, it is then possible to provide them with an opportunity to draw or paint what they have learned.

Here are some additional topics for intellectual motivations:

FIGURE: Learning what eyes are like
How the mouth chews
What ears can do
Where the body bends
How we run
All about fingers

INSECTS: Grasshoppers (How do they hop?)
Ants (How many eyes? Do they chew?)
Crickets (How do they sing?)
Bees (How do they collect nectar?)
Butterflies (Where do they come from?)

ANIMALS: Cows (udders, hoofs, horns, stomach)
Horses (Do they have teeth?)
Dogs (Is their fur soft?)
Cats (How do they arch their backs?)
Rats (Are they really sneaky?)
Bats (Do they have eyes?)

PLANTS: Learning about trees (leaves, bark, roots)
How flowers are different
How do grapes grow?
What makes corn-on-the-cob?
How do vegetables grow?

Any object can be suitable for an intellectual motivation. We want to teach children to perceive the details of these things. We also want them to relate themselves in some way to the items. Intellectual motivations serve two purposes: 1. They strengthen factual knowledge of things, 2. they establish relationships between child and thing. For instance, learning details of what birds are like is factual. "Feeding the chickens," "talking to the myna bird," or "flying south" pertain to how the child establishes relationships with birds. Both types of experiences are necessary if a child is to express his ideas in an aesthetic manner. Art skill cannot develop if the child has never developed the necessary mental imagery.

Imaginative Motivations. Imaginative motivations are concerned with the development of a child's imagination, inventiveness and originality. Within this motivational area, *creative thinking* has an opportunity to grow. In *imaginative motivations, the main emphasis is on developing uniqueness of idea.* These motivations should stress individual idea skills and unusual solutions to problems.

What we should look for in this motivational category are ideas which are less conventional and less bound to routine thinking. In this respect, teachers and parents must learn to accept from children all ideas which may seem *oddball* or different from the standard. In fact, *oddball* is exactly the term we want to start using in this particular approach. That is, we are looking for motivations which in themselves will stimulate a variety of new possibilities for art problem solutions. The *oddball approach* can enable us to break through conventional patterns and rules and can thus encourage a uniquely new type of fundamental thinking. Ideas which might have seemed silly and ridiculous now have an opportunity to fit into motivations and experiences which employ *oddball* methods for stimulating creative methods of using art materials. In this respect, the individual is less defensive and more apt to be flexible during the working process.

Here are some suggestions for stimulating thinking in an imaginative vein. Many of these ideas are strictly *oddball* in approach:

Inventing a nonsense machine
Turning into an insect
If you were the tallest person on earth
If you were invisible
Replacing your head with something else
Growing wings
Swallowing things whole
Turning into a monster
Shrinking to microscopic size
Becoming the last person on earth

We are concerned here with what happens to increase a person's inventiveness through exploring such unusual directions. Listed is a sample problem relating to an *oddball* or nonsense machine:

Inventing a Nonsense Machine

Sample Imaginative Motivation. All of us have seen and know what regular machines can do. Some wrap packages, others shape rockets, auto parts and silverware. Machines can do many, many things. I am thinking of some very special machines. These machines do nothing useful or practical. In fact, they are quite silly. I call one an automatic pea-picker. Another is a self-operating hair comber, and another is an automatic pickpocket. It is exciting to imagine ideas like this, and it helps us think in less conventional ways. If you were going to construct a machine that did nothing useful, what would you think of? These questions will help get you started on an idea:

Can you wind it up?
Will there be a trigger release of some sort?
Will you operate it by hand?
Will there be a surprise element involved?
How will you make the wheels and pulleys turn?
Do you have to think of balance?
Will there be levers, gears and pulleys?
Will all the wheels turn at the same time?
Can you crank it?

Perhaps we should collect a number of scrap items first and then develop our ideas from what we find. Here is a list of materials that might prove helpful to you. Add as many more as you can find:

string	paper
rubberbands	beads
toy wheels	sticks
gears	spools
old tinkertoy and erector set parts	wire
thumbtacks	nails
glass	nuts and bolts
stones	washers
glue	and many more things you discover

Check Points on Improving Art Motivations

The most important phase of any art lesson is the art motivation. A good motivation can stimulate children's thinking and set the stage for wonderful experiences with art media. There are several points to consider in learning to present a strong motivation. Here are some suggestions when presenting art motivations to children:

1. Practice by giving art motivations to children.
2. Be dramatic! Blanche Jefferson[2] says that when you dramatize children love it and catch the spirit quickly.
3. Be enthusiastic and eager to experience ideas.
4. Always start a motivation with an interesting introduction.
5. Outline objectives clearly. Know what to include in art motivations. Motivations and their structural content as well as use of provocative visual-building words is thoroughly put forth in *A Child's Pursuit of Art, 110 Motivations for Drawing and Modeling*, by Herberholz and Herberholz.[3]
6. Utilize sufficient visual material to strengthen the presentation.
7. Do not overwork the motivation by prolonging it until the children are restless. Stop at the high point.
8. Be alive and alert to each motivational situation.
9. Be sure to give the children an understanding of procedures for working with materials.
10. Ask questions that lead the children into discussion and search for their own ideas.[4]

An increased awareness of the body is a necessary preliminary in drawing the schema or human figure during the beginning realism stage. This awareness has its roots in body feelings and kinesthetic and visual observation of sizes, shapes and bodily parts. The child relates these cognitive and affective areas in arriving at his own schematic representations.

Summary

In summarizing the aspects of a good motivation—whether it is artistic, intellectual, or imaginative—the main component of a motivation is that it must contain a structure. Structure is used here to mean that the teacher has clearly in mind the content of the art task. After considering the ability of the child to handle perceptual information, the teacher will sometimes be very specific and limiting in the motivation, and at other times very general and stimulating to the imagination. A word of caution: don't try to teach everything about art in each art lesson. The teacher must set specific goals for students and then structure the motivations to reach these goals. It is also understood that the teacher will relate to the specific environment (subculture) in which the students live. The motivations will have to be structured to meet their individual habits of perception in order to modify behavior through art tasks. Motivations should stress aspects of discovery or inquiry on the part of the student in gaining the knowledge necessary to articulate his feelings into an art product. For specific examples of many approaches to a variety of motivations for use in the elementary classroom see, *A Child's Pursuit of Art, 110 Motivations for Drawing, Painting, and Modeling.*

To motivate is to confront someone or oneself with what Piaget[5] calls "knowledge" or what Holt[6] terms "intelligence." To be open and to take in everything one can through the senses is not merely perceiving nature and making a copy of it. To "know" an object is to modify and transform it into an interiorized feeling or form. The motivation process in the classroom is a creative act in which each child relates to his own unique style of artistic creation.

A motivation is the teacher's strategy in facilitating behavior change in the student. In structuring a motivation for an art task the teacher should:

provide opportunities for the child to perceive something and see that he perceives it accurately;

help the child recall visual percepts and feelings and organize them into art products by stimulating the child's recall and helping him arrive at personal and unique interpretations;

provide tools and materials that will help the student transform or interpret the aroused concepts into a tangible product or act;

provide means for the child to evaluate his product in relation to his cultural heritage and aesthetic judgment.

A series of structured motivations for elementary school children will provide for:

1. a greater perceptual awareness
2. a heightened aesthetic sensitivity
3. an increase in art skills with tools and materials
4. an increase in visual concepts
5. an increase in expressive art skills
6. an increase in the imaginative use of visual concepts[7]

Ways to Involvement

1. Write a detailed specific motivation for each of the three basic motivational categories on page 90.
2. Write and administer a motivation that has a strong emotional appeal in relation to the self. Compare the results obtained from the motivation with a schema for the human figure drawn previously by the same child. Has the motivation caused the child to deviate from his schema by omitting, changing or enlarging some parts?
3. Select a topic and write a motivation that will help the child become conscious of the total drawing area.
4. Write a detailed motivation for each of the following deviations from the base line: a. base line, b. x-ray, c. space-time, d. foldover, e. mixture of plane and elevation.
5. Select a topic and write a detailed motivation which would be appropriate for the "beginning realism stage" with em-

phasis on development of visual knowledge about a particular event, experience or object.

References

[1]Blanche Jefferson, *Teaching Art to Children* 2nd ed., Boston: Allyn & Bacon, Inc., 1963.

[2]Donald and Barbara Herberholz, *A Child's Pursuit of Art: 110 Motivations for Drawing, Painting, and Modeling,* Dubuque, Iowa: Wm. C. Brown Company Publishers, 1967.

[3]Earl W. Linderman, *Invitation to Vision: Ideas and Imaginations for Art,* Dubuque, Iowa: Wm. C. Brown Company Publishers, 1967.

[4]Frank G. Jenning, *"Jean Piaget: Notes on Learning," Saturday Review,* May, 20, 1967, pp. 81-83.

[5]John Holt, *How Children Fail,* New York: Dell Publishing Co., Inc., 1964.

[6]Opal Oleson and Haste, W. Reid, "Art in the School," Ch. 2, *Art Education in the Elementary School,* National Art Education Association, 1967.

[7]Robert E. Ornstein, *The Psychology of Consciousness,* New York: Pelican Books, 1975.

Additional References

Bannon, Laura, *Mind Your Child's Art,* New York: Pelligrini and Cudahy, 1952.

Bloom, Benjamin, *Taxonomy of Educational Objectives, Handbook I, Cognitive Domain,* New York: David McKay Co., Inc., 1960.

Bruner, Jerome, *The Process of Education,* New York: Vintage Books, 1960.

Carter, Bruce, "Artistic Development and Auditory Sensitivity: An Initial Study," *Research in Art Education* vol. 14, Eastern Art Association, May, 1957.

Cole, Natalie Robinson, *The Arts in the Classroom,* New York: The John Day Company, Inc., 1940.

D'Amico, Victor and Frances Wilson, *Art for the Family,* New York: Museum of Modern Art, 1956.

Herberholz, Barbara, "Christmas Motivation," *School Arts,* November, 1959.

Herberholz, Donald, "An Experimental Study to Determine the Effect of Modeling on the Drawing of the Human Figure by Second Grade Children," *National Art Education Association Yearbook,* 1957.

———, "Imagination Makes the Difference," *School Arts,* February, 1962.

———, "Stimulation by Film," *School Arts* 62:25-26, December, 1962.

Keiler, Manfred, *Art in the Schoolroom,* Lincoln: University of Nebraska Press, 1955.

———, "Some Thoughts on Motivation," *Everyday Art* 37:12-17, fall, 1958.

———, "Motivation versus Stimulation," *Art Education, Journal of the National Art Education Association* 411:6-74, December, 1959.

Linderman, Earl W., *Invitation to Vision,* Dubuque, Iowa: Wm. C. Brown Company Publishers, 1967.

———, "Figure Drawing as a Personal Style," *School Arts,* October, 1962.

———, "Idea-Tracking in the Classroom Teacher," *Art Education, Journal of the National Art Education Association,* January, 1963.

McMullan, Mary, "The Key to Action," *School Arts* 63:5-7, March, 1964.

McVitty, Lawrence, "An Experimental Study on Various Methods in Art Motivation at the Fifth Grade Level," *National Art Education Association Yearbook,* 1956.

Snow, Aida Cannarsa, *Growing With Children Through Art,* New York: Reinhold Publishing Corp., 1965, 152 pp., 200 illus.

Sproul, Adelaide, *With A Free Hand,* New York: Reinhold Publishing Corp., 144 pp. (painting, drawing, graphics, ceramics and sculpture for children)

Viola, Wilhelm, *Child Art and Franz Cizek,* New York: Reynal & Company, Inc., 1936.

Film References

Art and You. A Stuart Roe Film. 11 min.
What Shall We Paint? A Lawrence Frank, Jr. Film. 11 min.
Masks. A Pegasus Film. 12 min.
Color Associations. 8mm film loops. Film Associates of Calif.
Mixing the Basic Colors. 8 mm film loops. Film Associates of Calif.
Value and Intensity. 8 mm film loops. Film Associates of Calif.
Basic Color Schemes. 8 mm film loops. Film Associates of Calif.
Color and Space. 8mm film loops. Film Associates of Calif.

G IS FOR GOAT GOAT
GOAT GOAT

When the artist is alive in any person, whatever his kind of work may be, he becomes an inventive, searching, daring, self-expressing creature. He becomes interesting to other people. He disturbs, upsets, enlightens, and he opens ways for a better understanding. Where those who are not artists are trying to close the book, he opens it, shows there are still more pages possible.

The world would stagnate without him, and the world would be beautiful with him; for he is interesting to himself and he is interesting to others. He does not have to be a painter or sculptor to be an artist. He can work in any medium. He simply has to find the gain in the work itself, not outside it.

Robert Henri
from *The Art Song*
Philadelphia: J. B. Lippincott Co., 1923, p. 5

Chapter 5

Selected Examples of In-Depth Explorations with Art Tools and Materials

The beginning of a work of art may come from one or many directions at once. These beginnings might include sensory perceptions, feelings, experiences, ideas, images in the mind, tools or materials. The initial phase might come from any combination of these or any one; or it might start with one and shift back and forth rather often. A tool and how to use it might start a train of thought that could be pursued for several weeks. The same might be true of an art material or any material in our environment that we find stimulating to our senses or feelings. Enumerating a list of tools that could be used to paint with often "opens up" many ideas for an art activity or art investigation. The following list of tools might be used to push or move paint around on a surface.

In-Depth Explorations with Painting Tools

The tool might be hard or soft, fat or thin, narrow or wide, long or short, rough or smooth. These words suggest many dimensions of tools which can be used to manipulate paint on a surface for an in-depth exploratory experience.

Have you ever tried to paint with:

- fingers
- sticks
- blocks of wood
- branches
- brushes:
  - bottle brush
  - house brush
  - paste brush
  - solder brush
  - soft hairs
  - hard bristle
  - rubberized bristle
- rope
- feathers
- rags
- rags tied to a stick
- sponges cut into many shapes
- toothpicks
- plastic dispenser bottles
- dish scrapers
- brayers

An individual's perceptual openness may not allow him at first to think of these tools as "brushes." They are not brushes, but they all serve as the idea of a brush; that is, they allow the person to put the paint on the painting surface and allow the paint to be moved around, to be spread thick or thin, to be textured, to be blended, or to be put into shapes and lines. The use of such tools as these in painting will do much to develop awareness as to what can be done with paint as well as to the investigation of tools. Combining different tools offers an almost endless number of experiments and experiences for the beginner and the mature artist.

We might also think of these tools in relation to a definite idea or expression of an experience. You might ask yourself what tool could be used to paint a picture that would create a feeling of lightness and airiness, or softness and delicateness, or freshness and crispness, or make a sparkling surface like wet grass. What tool would give the softness of fur, which one the roughness of rocks, which one would give powerful lines, angular shapes, and which one would give the splash of sloppy tracks on the paper? These are all things tools can do. There are many ways to use tools which we discover as we work with them. We should always try to have many experiences with each in order to develop not only a fluency and flexibility but also a *depth* of experience in a few of them. Which one will we discover to be our special tool?

When painting a tree, we might ask ourselves what tool could best be used to paint the roots that go deep into the earth? What tool could be used to paint the stretching up of the branches? What tool could best suggest the smooth or rough bark of the trunk? What tool could suggest the delicate bud or fragile blossom? What tool could be used to suggest the moving leaves in the wind of early summer? What tool could be used to indicate the snow heavy on the branches, or the strong contrast of light or dark on the branches after a rain, or sharp pine needles, or soft blossoms of the poplar in the spring? These are some suggested ways to think of trees in relation to tools. The selection of the proper tool or tools can lead to a more successful expression of an idea, perception or feeling.

In-Depth Explorations with Drawing Tools

Drawing tools are instruments used to inscribe or make marks on surfaces which can assist the child in the delineation of his art forms.

Have you ever tried to draw with:

- crayons
- pencils
- fingers
- chalk
- charcoal
- ink pens
- felt tip pens
- toothpicks
- bamboo
- bones
- straws
- feathers
- twigs
- soap
- soldering wire
- nails
- sticks

Depending on our background we may not be able to think of a thing to draw on with a bone, let alone what kind of a mark a bone would make or what could be done with solder in

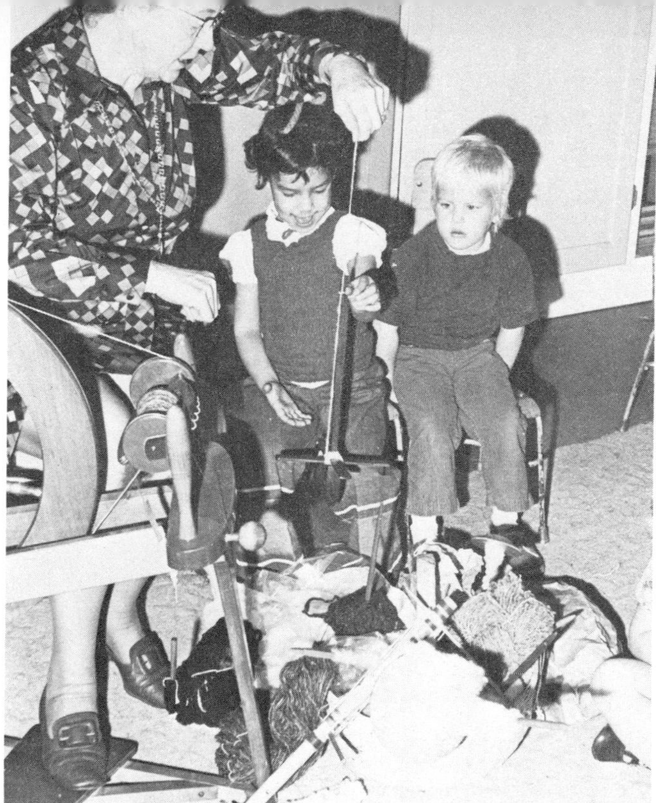

An essential aspect of art development is learning to use art materials in unique and unusual ways. Being open to the possibility of how tools can be used stimulates greater flexibility in their use.

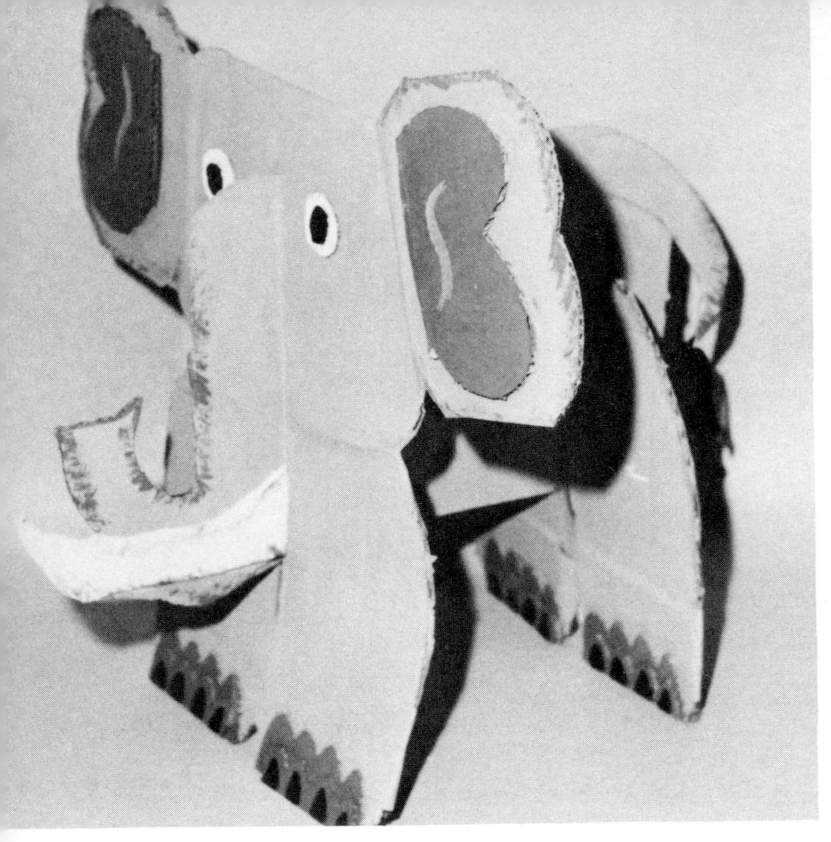

Each art material used has a quality unique in itself. Through search and experimentation, the individual learns to release such qualities within his art expression.

relation to drawing. A great number of these materials may seem "odd" at first and we may not be able to think of them as drawing instruments. It has been found that when a person has not experienced the tool previously that he is likely to approach it with more openness and therefore be more creative and inventive in its use.

Most people would have difficulty trying to think of a new way to use a pencil in drawing. It is generally used to make lines and shading. It has also been used by the average person to write with for a number of years, and as a result he is so familiar with it that he is "blinded" by past experiences in relation to its other possible uses. He tends to miss the silver-gray lines as well as the black ones. In contrast, the average person would be more alert to the possibilities of drawing with a tool to which he has not become "dulled." For instance, how would we draw with a toothpick, a twig, a feather, a pipe cleaner, or a nail? One might have to go through a line of thinking such as the following to discover the uses of these tools. Will I have to sharpen it, burn it, wet it, tie it together, hit it with another tool or break it before I can mark with it? Will I have to use a liquid with it? What kind of consistency should the liquid have? What kinds of surfaces will the tool mark on? Will specific materials or surfaces be more suitable for certain tools than others? This line of questioning about odd or unusual tools develops more possibilities for awareness. Conventional tools such as pencils, pens and brushes will be more difficult to use with flexibility, fluency or inventiveness.

In-Depth Explorations with Drawing and Painting Surfaces

The surface might be absorbent or nonabsorbent, shiny or dull, smooth or rough, hard or soft, wet or dry, flexible or non-flexible, thick or thin. These are some of the things to consider when selecting a material or surface on which to paint or draw.

Have you ever tried to paint or draw on:

- paper
  - newsprint
  - paper plates
  - paper bags
  - tissue paper
  - crepe paper
  - paper towels
  - cellophane
  - carbon
  - butcher
  - waxed paper
- wood
- stones
- glass
- cardboard
  - corrugated
  - pressed
- cloth
- saran wrap
- acetate
- aluminum foil
- masonite
- sidewalks or driveways
- backyard fences
- chalkboards
- hard soil
- sand

One can experiment with any combination of painting tools, drawing tools and surfaces on which they might be used. To experiment means to find out about how surfaces and tools interact with each other. It is assumed that through experimentation, many new facts, ideas and feelings about the tools and surfaces will be realized. The experiment should lead to a tentative conclusion and then another experiment and not be just a meaningless manipulation of materials. Through experimentation one should have a greater identity with the surfaces and tools and as a result be better able to predict their behavior.

Experience with tools and surfaces is very important to consider when thinking about an art activity. Children need not only stimulating ideas to work with but also stimulating tools and surfaces. They require materials and tools that permit exploration, arouse investigation, stimulate thinking, and are suitable for their stage of development. In fact, a child needs several lessons concerning the use of a tool or surface before he is ready to express ideas. Poor art expression often is due to lack of skill with the tool or surface. The older child will require more detailed instruction in the procedures of painting and drawing.

In-Depth Explorations with Unusual Drawing Tools and Surfaces

What ideas could you paint using a manila rope the size of your thumb and aluminum foil or corrugated cardboard as a painting surface?
Have you ever tried painting with watercolors on soft sugar pine?
Have you ever tried drawing with crayons on a weathered board from an old building or an old fence?
What tools could be used to draw or paint with on tissue paper?
Would you use a pencil, crayon, finger, stick, straw, feather, toothpick, bamboo, bone or nail to draw with in the hard earth? What could you use to color it with?
What tools could you use to make marks on glass? What liquids would adhere to glass? Could you mark through these liquids after they are dry?
When you think of branches as a painting tool do you think of one or many? Is it possible to make a tool of several smaller branches so that many marks could be made with one stroke?
What kind of marks could you make with a bar of soap? On what kind of surfaces would you be able to make these marks?
Could you draw a line with the tip of a feather?

In-Depth Explorations with Drawing and Painting Liquids

Liquids used in drawing or painting might be thought of as those that remain basically on the surface or those that stain or penetrate the surface to which they are applied. The liquids might be thought of as opaque or transparent.

Have you ever tried to paint with:

watercolors	food dyes	bleach
poster paints	liquid shoe polish	liquid wax
muddy water	melted crayons	glue
corn syrup	rubber cement	condensed milk
india ink	egg tempera	buttermilk
tea	rubber base enamels	
coffee	berry juices	

Exploring the combinations of painting and drawing tools, surfaces and liquids will give one an almost endless list of possible experiments. These explorations and experiments should not only lead one to an enriched understanding of unusual or *oddball* materials but should reopen the senses to conventional art materials.

In-Depth Exploration in Discovering Color and Texture

In combining tools and materials the teacher or child should have some experiences with color and textures. Most people are responsive to *color* and it is a good element to start with.

To discover color one might try:

- dropping colors onto a wet surface and allowing them to run together
- dripping melted crayons
- looking through a prism
- making a crayon etching
- looking at a color against a white background and removing it to see the afterimage
- using poster paint on black construction paper
- using sponge and overlay poster paint colors
- putting colors on a folded piece of paper and pressing it so the colors run
- dropping different colors of ink or food coloring into a glass of water
- placing tissues or cellophane over each other to create new colors

These are all ways that give quick results, are exciting to view, and can be accomplished by any age group.

To discover textures one might make crayon or brayer prints of different surfaces around the house and then use the textured paper for cutting and pasting a picture. Various textures can be

When the individual identifies completely with the material, the art product is produced. The process is then repeated again and again, and the individual matures aesthetically.

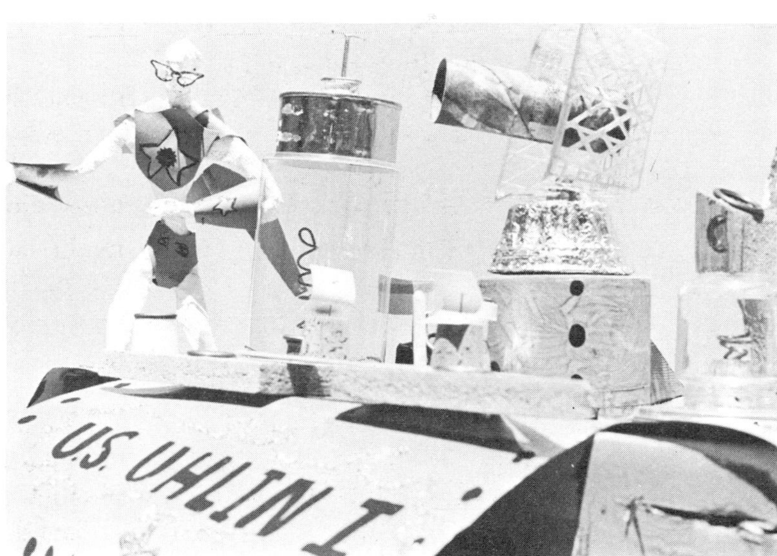

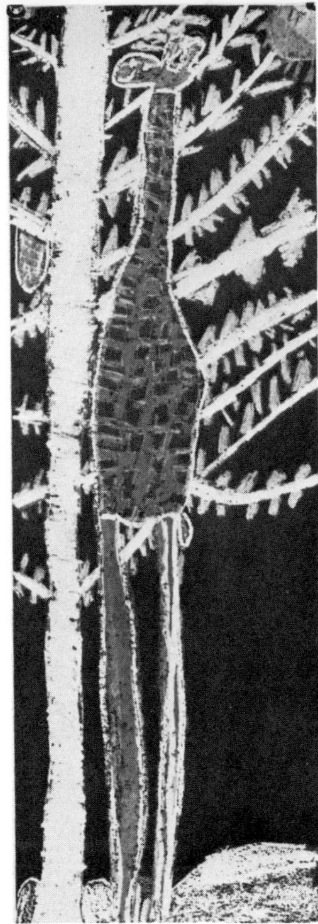

Concepts may evolve from many different materials. It is more the individual's awareness of the uniqueness of the material that enables him to discover its potential.

Traditional art materials combine gracefully with scraps and discarded items in the field of puppetry. Two important goals for the puppet maker should be the portrayal of facial expression and the inclusion of moving parts.

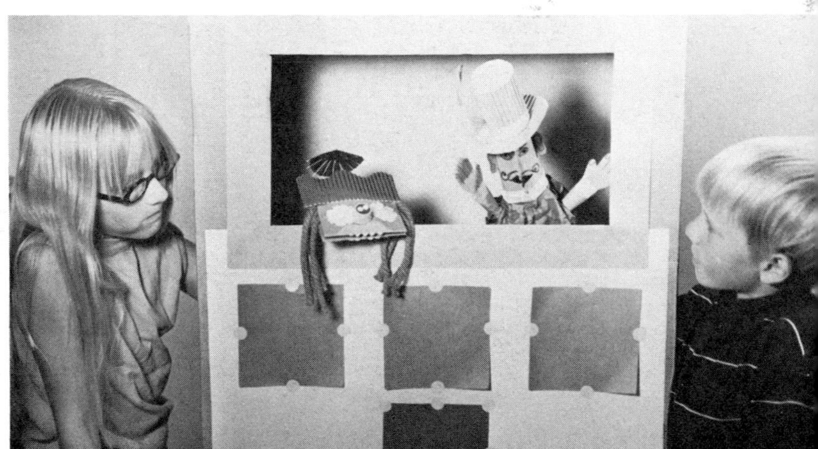

Rich detailing and mixed-in color make this doll from Ecuador an eloquent example of the possibilities inherent in pliable dough.

Baking dough gives children direct modelling experiences. This versatile material takes readily to texturing and is adapted to bas-relief and free standing forms. An hour in a slow oven bakes it to a golden tone. For recipe, see "Ways to Involvement" at the end of Chapter Five.

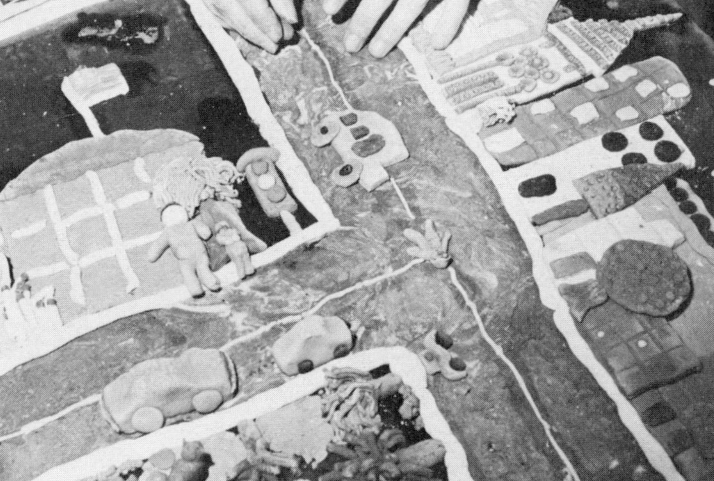

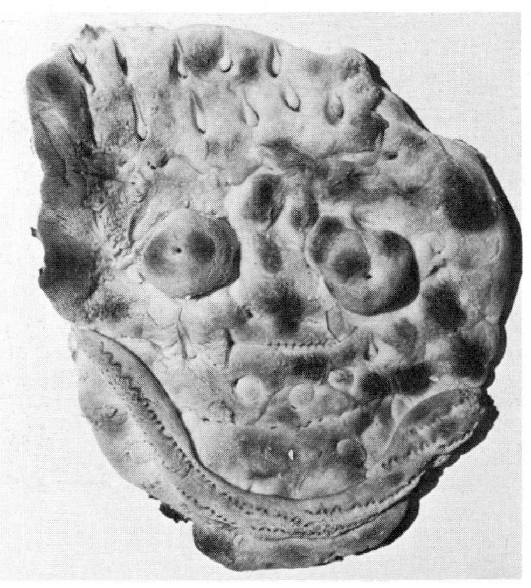

Linoleum, inner tubes, styrofoam meat trays, white glue, and construction paper are all simple direct materials to use in print-making. Texture and light and dark areas create strong patterns and contrast.

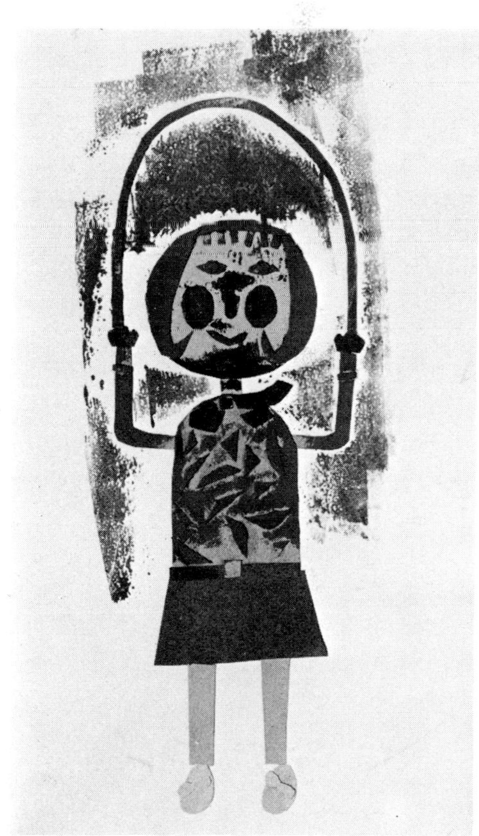

Cut construction paper can be bent, folded, torn, scored and then it can be glued, taped or tied. It can take many forms. Paint over it, gadget print on it, draw on it, glue other papers to it and glue string and yarn to it.

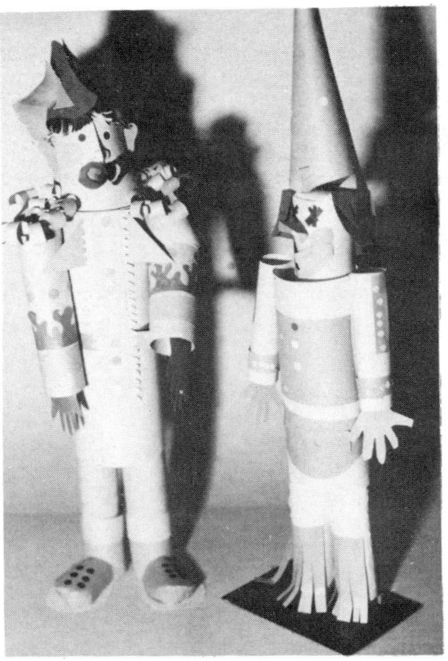

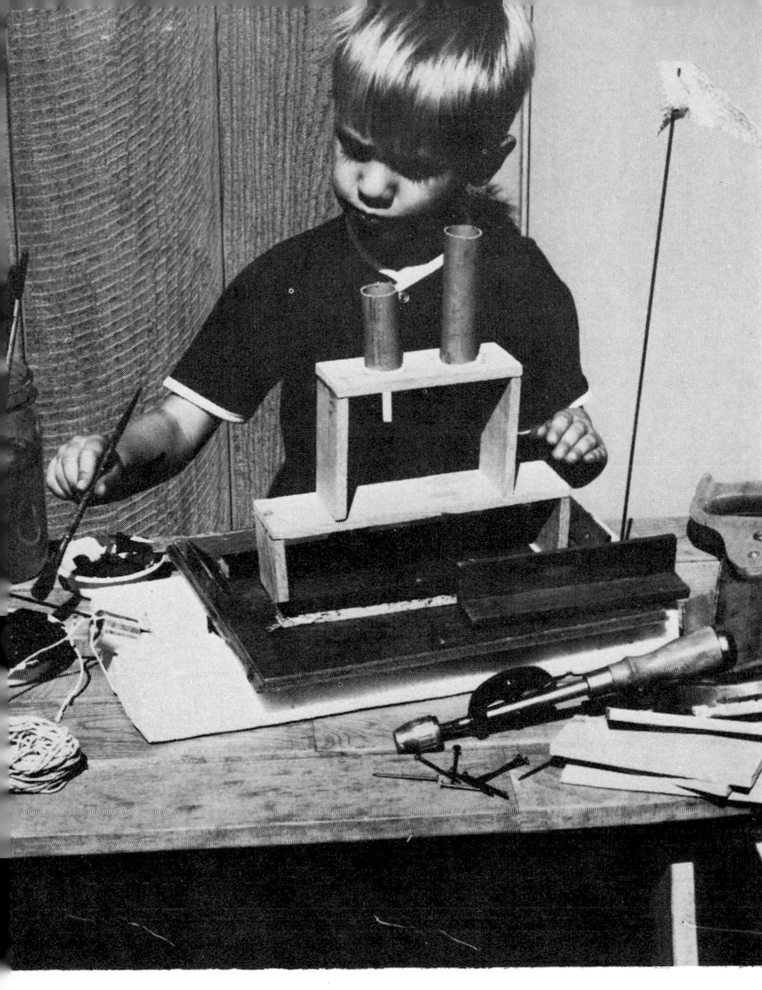

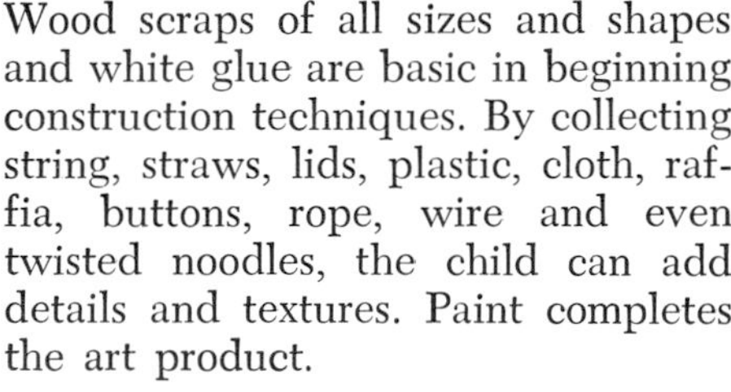

Wood scraps of all sizes and shapes and white glue are basic in beginning construction techniques. By collecting string, straws, lids, plastic, cloth, raffia, buttons, rope, wire and even twisted noodles, the child can add details and textures. Paint completes the art product.

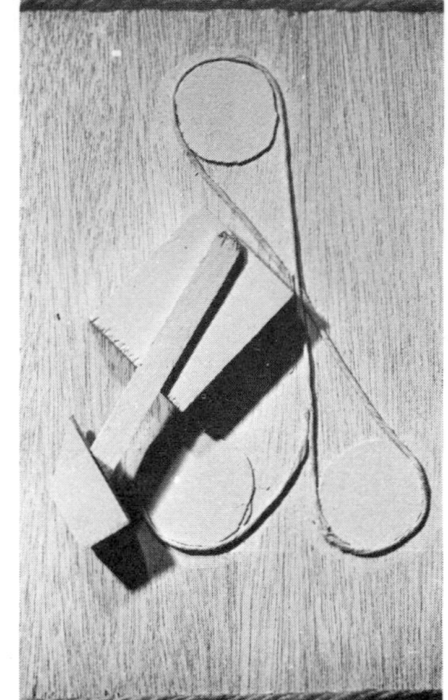

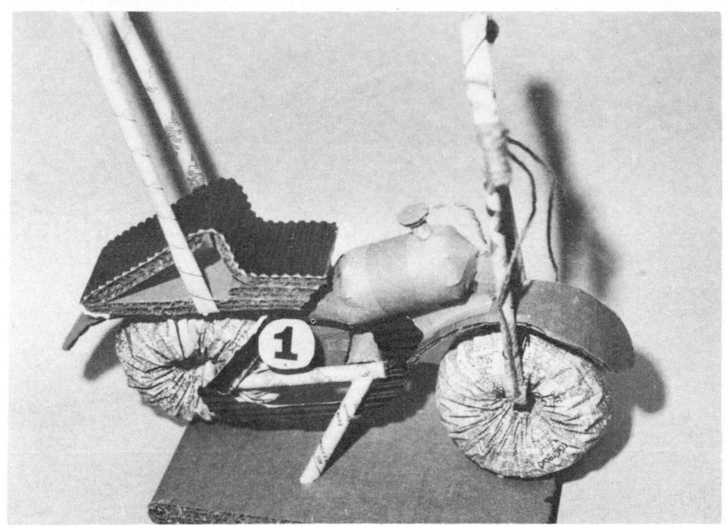

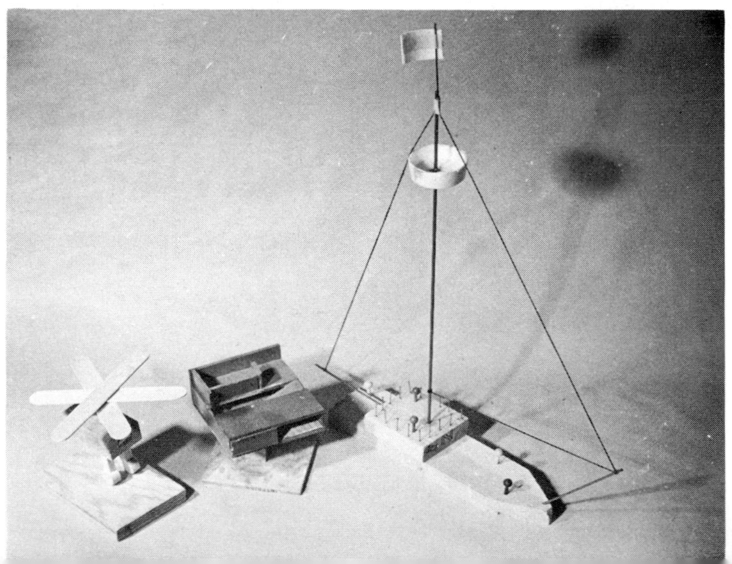

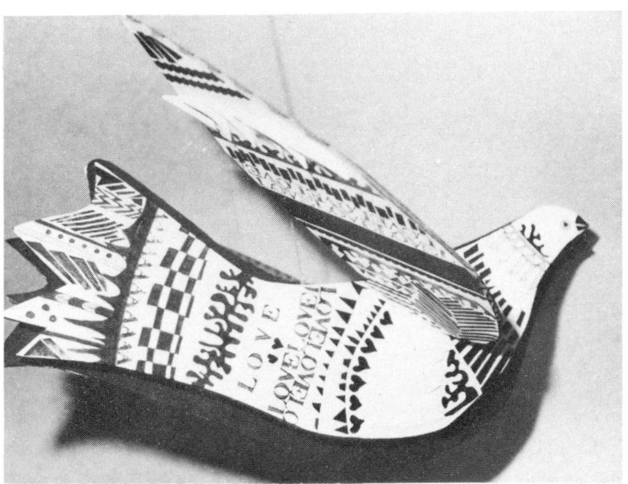

Assemblage constructions, flat or three-dimensional are derived from collections of cardboard boxes, mailing tubes, egg cartons, and plastic containers. Masking tape, white glue, a good assortment of scrap materials, and paint combine for a free flow of imaginative structures.

combined in a collage. (How many soft textures can we collect; how many smooth, shiny, rough, fuzzy?) Gadget prints and blottos help one discover the texture qualities of paint. Rubbing the side of the crayon on paper will bring out the texture of the paper. Printmaking brings out the textures one can make with a tool on linoleum or wood. The textures made with our fingers or a tool in clay can better be realized after the impression has been cast in plaster. Look through a reading glass or magnifying glass at textures. See how many different textures can be collected from a magazine. See how many similar textures can be found in real objects. All these will be ways to enrich our knowledge about the two- and three-dimensional textures of things that surround us every day.

What Skills Are Developed from In-Depth Explorations with Tools and Materials?

In-depth explorations provide learning experiences for children to develop skills necessary to transform ideas, images, or feelings into personal aesthetic art forms. These are:

1. skill in selecting tools to convey ideas, images, or feelings
2. skill in selecting materials to transform ideas, images, or feelings
3. skill in manipulating selected tool and material into a meaningful art form
4. skill in making aesthetic judgment about the art form created

How Do We Measure Artistic Skills That Are Produced from In-Depth Explorations With Tools and Materials?

When the teacher has considered the ideas presented in Chapter 1, provided for the awareness experiences suggested in Chapter 2, used a variety of motivations from Chapter 4, and provided in-depth explorations with tools and materials, he can use the Skills Evaluation Form to discover how the child's behavior has changed because of the art experience.

Measuring Artistic Skills as Expressed in Children's Art Productions

Name ______________________

Check the column which you consider most appropriate after observing a child of a particular age at work and after studying his art production.

Child has improved in:	CHECK ONE		
	little	some	much
1. skill in handling and controlling tools and materials and making them do what he wants them to do			
2. skill in experimenting with new combinations of materials*			
3. using his imagination more and in finding new ways of expressing his ideas*			
4. understanding his visual perceptions**			
5. working for a longer time without getting tired or losing interest in his idea			
6. developing a more sensitive use of line, value, texture and shape			
7. understanding pictorial use of space or perspective			
8. empathy for other people, as projected in his art			
9. projecting his *own* personal feelings in relation to his own experiences and in using individualized forms			
10. his willingness to try new ideas*			
11. "sticking to it" and finishing all assigned work			
12. understanding and using shading and value change in the use of color			
13. including more detail**			
14. mixing colors rather than using them as they come straight from the jar			
15. improving his composition and in sharpening his sense of design and arrangement			
16. mixing and trying out new colors, inventing new textures, and using a variety of shapes for the same object			

*"little" usually indicates need for more "open-ended" assignments by the teacher

**"little" usually indicates need for a more detailed visual perception of his immediate environment

Summary

In summary, learned artistic skills are a vital part of art experiences. Chapter 2 explains the creative process and perception models which the child uses to develop skills through the use of his senses. We also discussed how to give meaning to these perceptions or ideas resulting from these sensory perceptions. Empathy is also a necessary and vital part of communication in an art product. These three artistic skills—sensory perception, giving meaning to experience, and relating that human identity—are essential parts of art production and training for children. Chapter 4 explained the form and content of motivations needed to develop skills of artistic, intellectual, and imaginative expression.

As part of transforming these images, ideas, and feelings, the child also needs to develop skills with tools and materials. The ability to use materials and tools with skill develops through frequent use and instruction. The child will have to experience each tool and material numerous times before he can manage it with skill to produce a successful art product. He will need to develop the necessary skill in selecting the best tool or material to conform to or explore an idea, or vague image he has in mind. This skill can only develop through its repeated use. Yet at the same time we must keep in mind that sometimes the idea or image grows out of the material or use of the tool. In addition to the afore mentioned skills the child needs to develop aesthetic skills (see Chapter 6) as he works with tools, materials, and ideas to create his personal art form.

The selected examples of in-depth explorations presented in this chapter are intended to give the teacher some models to follow for providing additional in-depth experiences for art productions.

In-depth experiences with art tools and materials will be a part of the *artist model* the teacher will encourage in elementary school art. The teacher needs to direct in-depth explorations of art tools and materials as well as follow-up repeated use of tools and materials. The child needs to explore many art media to find those that work best for him in producing art works and he also needs in-depth experiences with those tools and materials that he finds most meaningful for him.

Ways to Involvement

1. Select one of the tools, other than a brush, and make a painting using poster paints. Create a mood or feeling by the selection of three colors for the painting. Make the painting on colored construction paper rather than white paper.
2. Make a drawing with one of the unusual tools given on page 102 and draw on one of the unusual surfaces given on page 102. Select a tool that will help you give character to the idea you have in mind.
3. Make a print by using either styrofoam meat trays or cut paper for your block.
4. Make a baking dough modeled figure. Mix 4 cups flour with 1 cup of salt. Add approximately 1 1/2 cups of warm water or just enough to make a pliable mixture that does not stick to your hands. Knead thoroughly for 5 minutes or until it is smooth. Make flat or standing forms, using toothpicks or wires or pipe cleaners to attach small parts. Moisten slightly when sticking small pieces together. Bake on baking sheet for about one hour at 350 degrees. Larger thicker pieces will require a longer time.
5. Make a salt ceramic figure either 1. in action or 2. in relation to another figure, either a human or an animal. Mix 1 cup of salt with 1/2 cup of corn starch. Add 3/4 cup of water and mix thoroughly. Place in a double boiler over heat. Stir for 2 or 3 minutes until it becomes a thick lump. Remove from pan and let it cool on a piece of foil. When it is cool enough to handle, knead. You may use this mixture over a wire armature or other suitable core. Dry figures may be painted with tempera or acrylics. Food color may be added to the water before it is cooked if a colored dough is desired.
6. Make a figure over a core using Pariscraft.
7. Have a child make a painting using Rich Art Colors in-

stead of brushes and liquid paints. For a set of six colors of these Tempra-Markers, send $2.50 to Rich Art Color Co., Inc., 31 West 21st St., New York 10, N. Y.

References

Here is a list of self-starting art activities, books, records, films and things that teachers should find stimulating enough to guide them to more creative ways of thinking. Through looking, listening, thinking and doing we can increase our knowledge about art.

Basketry

MEILACH, DONA Z., *A Modern Approach to Basketry with Fibers and Grasses,* New York: Crown Publishers, 1974.

THE NAVAJO SCHOOL OF INDIAN BASKETRY, *Indian Basket Weaving,* New York: Dover Publications, 1971.

TOD, OSMA GALLINGER, *Earth Basketry,* New York: Bonanza Books.

Ceramics

BALL, F. CARLTON and JANICE LOVOOS, *Making Pottery Without a Wheel,* New York: Reinhold Publishing Corp., 1965, 160 pp.

BERENSOHN, PAULUS, *Finding One's Way with Clay,* New York: Simon & Schuster, 1972.

HOFSTEAD, JOLYON, *Ceramics, Step-by-Step,* New York: Golden Press, 1967.

HOGAN, ELIZABETH, ed., *Ceramics, Techniques and Projects,* rev. ed., Menlo Park, Calif.: Lane Publishing Co., 1973.

NEUVILLE, CHRISTIANE, *Fun with Clay,* New York: Franklin Watts, 1974.

POST, HENRY and MICHAEL MCTWIGAN, *Clay Play Learning Games for Children,* Englewood Cliffs, N. J.: Prentice-Hall, 1973.

ROTTGER, ERNST, *Creative Clay Design,* New York: Reinhold Publishing Corp., 1963, 96 pp.

Collage, Construction, Wood

LALIBERTE, NORMAN and MAUREEN JONES, *Wooden Images,* New York: Reinhold Publishing Corp., 1966, 136 pp.

LORD, LOIS, *Collage and Construction in Elementary and Junior High Schools,* Worcester, Mass.: Davis Publications, Inc., 1958, 111 pp.

MEILACH, DONA and ELVIE TEN HOOR, *Collage and Found Art,* New York: Reinhold Publishing Corp., 1964, 68 pp.

ROTTGER, ERNST, *Creative Wood Design,* New York: Reinhold Publishing Corp., 1961, 96 pp.

Drawing and Painting

BETTS, VICTORIA, *Exploring Finger Paint,* Worcester, Mass.: Davis Publications, Inc., 1963.

COULIN, CLAUDIUS, *Fundamentals of Technical Drawing: For Draftsmen, Students, Designers, Architects,* New York: Reinhold Publishing Corp., 114 pp.

DAVIDSON, MORRIS, *Painting With Purpose,* Englewood Cliffs, N. J.: Prentice-Hall, Inc., 1964.

GREENBERG, PEARL, *Children's Experiences in Art: Drawing and Painting,* New York: Reinhold Publishing Corp., 1966, 144 pp.

HAYES, COLIN, *The Technique of Watercolor Painting,* New York: Reinhold Publishing Corp., 96 pp.

LALIBERTE, NORMAN and ALEX MOGELON, *Drawing with Ink, History and Techniques,* New York: Van Nostrand Reinhold, 1970.

———, *Drawing with Pencils, History and Techniques,* New York: Van Nostrand Reinhold, 1969.

LALIBERTE, NORMAN, ALEX MOGELON, and BEATRICE THOMPSON, *Pastel, Charcoal and Chalk Drawing,* New York: Van Nostrand Reinhold, 1973.

LINDERMAN, MARLENE, *Art in the Elementary School: Drawing, Painting, and Creating for the Classroom,* Dubuque, Ia.: Wm. C. Brown Company Publishers, 1974.

PETTERSON, HENRY and RAY GERRING, *Exploring With Paint,* New York: Reinhold Publishing Corp., 1964, 68 pp.

RANDALL, ARNE W., *Murals for Schools* rev. ed., Worcester, Mass.: Davis Publications, Inc., 1961, 112 pp.

ROTTGER, ERNST and DIETER KLANTE, *Creative Drawing: Point and Line,* New York: Reinhold Publishing Corp., 1963, 144 pp.

Graphics and Printmaking

ANDREWS, MICHAEL F., *Creative Printmaking,* Englewood Cliffs, N. J.: Prentice-Hall, Inc., 1964, text edition.

BROMMER, GERALD F., *Relief Printmaking,* Worcester, Mass.: Davis Pub., Inc., 1970.

Erickson, J. D., *Printmaking Without a Press,* New York: Reinhold Publishing Corp., 1966.
Garbaty, Norman, *Printmaking with a Spoon,* New York: Reinhold Publishing Co., 1960.
Green, Peter, *New Creative Printmaking,* New York: Watson-Guptill Publications, 1964, 120 pp.
Heller, Jules, *Printmaking Today,* 2d ed., New York: Holt, Rinehart & Winston, Inc., 1972.
Kampmann, Lothar, *Creating with Printing Materials,* New York: Van Nostrand Reinhold, 1969.
Meilach, Dona Z., *Printmaking,* New York: Pitman Publishing Corp., 1965.
Ota, Koshi, *Printing for Fun,* New York: McDowell, Oblensky, Inc., 1959.
Pattemore, Arnel, *Printmaking Activities for the Classroom,* Worcester, Mass.: Davis Pub., Inc., 1966.
Rasmusen, Henry, *Printmaking with Monotype,* Philadelphia: Chilton Book Company, 1960, 182 pp.
Schachner, Ervin, *Printmaking, Step by Step,* New York: Golden Press, 1970.
Weiss, Harvey, *Paper, Ink and Roller,* New York: Young Scott Books, 1958.

Metalwork and Jewelry

Brynner, Irean, *Modern Jewelry: Design and Technique,* New York: Reinhold Publishing Corp., 96 pp.
Dhamers, Robert and Howard A. Slatoff, *Simple Jewelry Making for the Classroom,* Palo Alto, Calif: Fearon, 1958.
Granstrom, K. E., *Creating Wtih Metal,* New York: Reinhold Publishing Corp., 96 pp.
Solberg, Ramona, *Inventive Jewelry-Making,* New York: Van Nostrand Reinhold Company, 1972, 128 pp.
Von Neumann, Robert, *The Design and Creation of Jewelry,* Philadelphia: Chilton Book Co., 1972, 271 pp.
Winebrenner, D. Kenneth, *Jewelry Making as an Art Expression,* Scranton, Pa.: International Textbook Co., 1955, 181 pp.

Mosaics

Levoos, Janice and Felice Paramore, *Modern Mosaic Techniques,* New York: Watson-Guptill Publications, 1967, 170 pp.
Sister Mary Magdalen, I. H. M., *Mosaics for Everyone,* Los Angeles: Brown Letter Shop, 1751 Hillhurst, 1958, 38 pp.

Paper

Betts, Victoria B., *Exploring Papier-Mache,* rev. ed., Worcester, Mass.: Davis Publications, Inc., 1966, 132 pp.
Fabri, Ralph, *Sculpture in Paper,* rev. ed., New York: Watson-Guptill Publications, 1976, 166 pp.
Johnson, Pauline, *Creating with Paper,* Seattle: University of Washington Press, 1966, 207 pp.
Rottger, Ernst, *Creative Paper Design,* New York: Reinhold Publishing Corp., 1961, 95 pp.

Puppets and Puppetry

Hopper, Grizella, *Puppet Making Through the Grades,* Worcester, Mass.: Davis Publications, Inc., 1966, 64 pp.
Lanchester, Waldo, *Hand Puppets and String Puppets,* Peoria, Ill.: C. A. Bennett Co., Inc., 1953, 44 pp.

Sculpture

Andrews, Michael F., *Sculpture and Ideas,* Englewood Cliffs, N. J.: Prentice-Hall, Inc., 1965.
Clarke, Geoffrey and Stroud Cornock, *A Sculptor's Manual,* New York: Reinhold Publishing Corp., 144 pp.
Hughes, Toni, *How to Make Shapes in Space,* New York: E. P. Dutton & Co., Inc., 1955, 217 pp.
Meilach, Dona, *Creating With Plaster,* Chicago: The Reilly & Lee Co., 1966, 74 pp.
———, *Soft Sculpture and Other Soft Art Forms,* New York: Crown Publishers, 1974.
Weiss, Harvey, *Clay, Wood and Wire,* New York: William R. Scott, Inc., 1956, 48 pp.

Textiles

Beetler, Ethel Jane, *Create With Yarn,* Scranton, Pa.: International Textbook Co., 1964, 196 pp.
Chamberlain, Marcia and Candace Crockett, *Beyond Weaving,* New York: Watson-Guptill, 1974.
Enthoven, Jacqueline, *Stitchery for Children: A Manual for Teachers, Parents, and Children,* New York: Reinhold Publishing Corp., 1968, 144 pp.
Hartung, Rolf, *Creative Textile Design: Thread and Fabric,* New York: Reinhold Publishing Corp., 1963, 96 pp.
———, *More Creative Textile Design: Color and Texture,* New York: Reinhold Publishing Corp., 1964, 96 pp.
Krevitsky, Nik, *Stitchery: Art and Craft,* New York: Reinhold Publishing Corp., 1973, 120 pp.
Laliberte, Norman and Sterling McIlhany, *Banners and Hangings: Design and Construction,* New York: Reinhold Publishing Corp., 1966, 92 pp.

Modelling in clay, salt ceramic, papier mache and Pariscraft involve children in three dimensions. Relating parts within a form promotes aesthetic growth. Sticks, toothpicks, wire, pipe cleaners aid in attaching arms and legs in materials other than clay. The finished product may be painted, or left natural. Ceramic pieces may or may not be glazed.

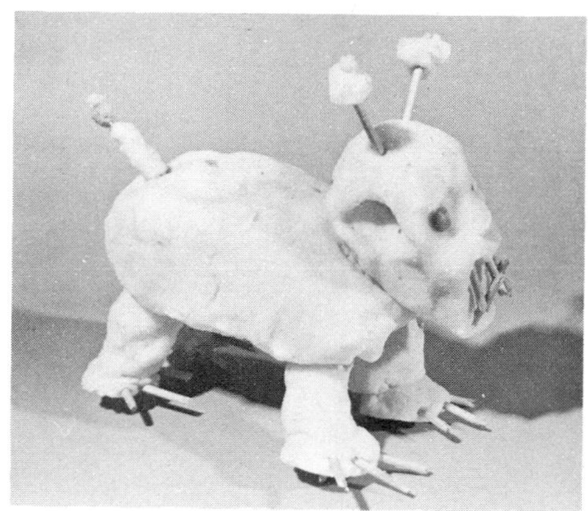

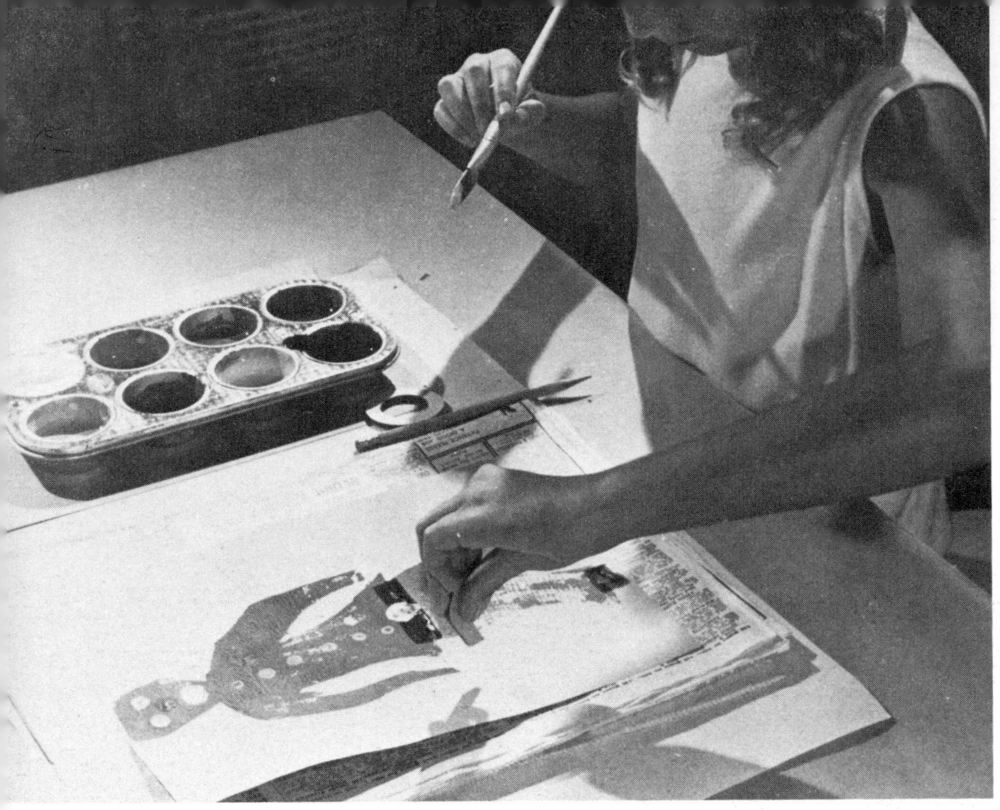

The skills developed in working with a variety of combinations of materials will increase the child's ability in divergent thinking habits.

Yellow brick road to the cafeteria by John Adams Jr. High, Santa Monica, California. Art teacher—Ann Goodwin

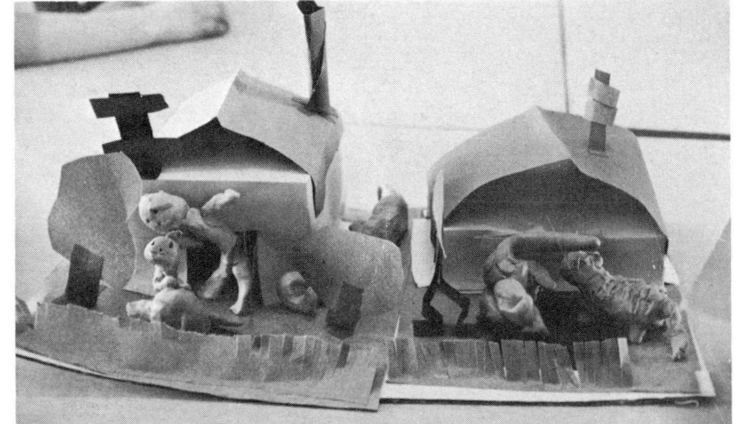

Rainey, Sarita, *Weaving Without a Loom,* Worcester, Mass.: Davis Publications, Inc., 1966, 132 pp.

Shaw, George R., *Knots: Useful and Ornamental,* 2d ed., New York: Macmillan Co., 1972.

Van Dommelen, Davis B., *Decorative Wall Hangings: Art With Fabric,* New York: Funk & Wagnalls, 1962, 178 pp.

Materials, Techniques and Processes

Accorsi, William, *Toy Sculpture,* New York: Reinhold Publishing Corp., 92 pp.

Bodor, John J., *Rubbing and Textures,* New York: Reinhold Publishing Corp., 112 pp.

Borglund, Erland and Jacob Flauensgaard, *Working In Plastic, Bone, Amber and Horn,* New York: Reinhold Publishing Corp., 96 pp.

Brett, Guy, *Kinetic Art: The Language of Movement,* New York: Reinhold Publishing Corp., 96 pp.

Brodatz, Phil and Dori Watson, *The Elements of Landscape: A Photographic Handbook for Artists,* New York: Reinhold Publishing Corp., 1966, 144 pp.

Laliberte, Norman and Alex Mogelon, *Silhouettes, Shadows, and Cutouts,* New York: Reinhold Publishing Corp., 112 pp.

McElwain, Charlotte, *Knitting With Stop and Go Needles: Basic and Fashion Stitches,* New York: Reinhold Publishing Corp., 144 pp.

Rosenberg, Lilli, *Children Make Murals and Sculpture: Experience in Community Art Projects,* New York: Reinhold Publishing Corp., 1968, 128 pp.

Sunset Editors, eds., *Children's Crafts: Fun and Creativity of Ages 5-12,* Menlo Park, Calif.: Lane Publishing Co., 1976.

Wankleman, Willard F., Philip Wigg, and Marietta Wigg, *A Handbook of Arts and Crafts for Elementary and Junior High School Teachers,* 4th ed., Dubuque, Ia.: Wm. C. Brown Company Publishers, 1978.

Wiseman, Ann, *Making Things: The Hand Book of Creative Discovery, Book 2,* Boston: Little, Brown & Co., 1975.

Film References

Art in Depth Series. Two color filmstrips, Part 1 (44 frames, color): drawing, painting, crayon engraving, tempera batik and printmaking; Part 2 (40 frames, color): oil pastel, collage, plaster reliefs, ceramics, and sculpture.

Batik. ACI, Films Incorporated, 35 West 45th Street, New York, New York.

Crayon, Clay, Water Color, Printmaking. ACI Productions, New York.

Discovering Color. 16 min. Film Associates of Calif.

Discovering Composition in Art. A Paul Burnford Production. 16 min. Film Associates of Calif.

Discovering Creative Pattern. A Paul Burnford Production in Association with Jack Stoops, Ed. D. 17 min. Film Associates of Calif.

Discovering Dark and Light. A Paul Burnford Production in Association with Jack Stoops, Ed. D. 18 min. Film Associates of Calif.

Discovering Form in Art. A Paul Burnford Production in Association with Jack Stoops, Ed. D. 21 min. Film Associates of Calif.

Discovering Harmony in Art. A Paul Burnford Production. 16 min. Film Associates of Calif.

Discovering Line. 17 min. Film Associates of Calif.

Discovering Perspective. 14 min. Film Associates of Calif.

Discovering Texture. 17 1/2 min. Film Associates of Calif.

Edible Art. 6 filmstrips/6 cassettes, teacher guide/recipes, modeled cookies, candy clay, bread sculpture, frosting paint, graham cracker construction, fruit and vegetable assemblage. ACI Media, Inc., 35 West 45th St., New York, N.Y. 10036.

Emphasis: Art. Three color filmstrips, part 1, 2, and 3. International Film Bureau Inc., 332 South Michigan Ave., Chicago, Illinois.

Exploring Puppet Making. Ten Super 8mm silent film loops. Color. "Bag Puppets," "Bag Puppets with Strings," "Sack and Cloth Puppets," "Flat Puppets," "Tubular Puppets," "Folded Paper Puppets," "Papier-Mache Puppets," "Puppets with Moving Parts," "Puppets with Strings," "Staging the Puppet Show." Bailey-Film Associates, 2211 Michigan Ave., Santa Monica, Calif.

Exploring Relief Printmaking. A Motivational Art Films Production. 12 min. Film Associates of Calif.

Introduction to Contour Drawing. 12 min. Film Associates of Calif.

Introduction to Drawing Materials. 16 min. Film Associates of Calif.

Introduction to Gesture Drawing. 12 1/2 min. Film Associates of Calif.

Making Relief Prints. Eight Super 8mm silent film loops. Color. "Found Objects," "Carving Soft Materials," "Styrofoam," "Monoprints," "Torn and Cut Paper," "Dried Glue," "Collograph," "Combining Techniques." Aim Instructional Media Services, Inc., P.O. Box 1010, Hollywood, Calif.

Macrame. ACI, Films Incorporated, 35 West 45th Street, New York, New York.

String. A kaleidoscope of creative weaving, knotting and macrame. Film Fair Communications, 10900 Ventura Boulevard, Hollywood, Calif.

Textile Touch. Introduction to macrame, rug-hooking and loom-weaving techniques. Oxford Films, 1136 North La Palmas, Hollywood, Calif.

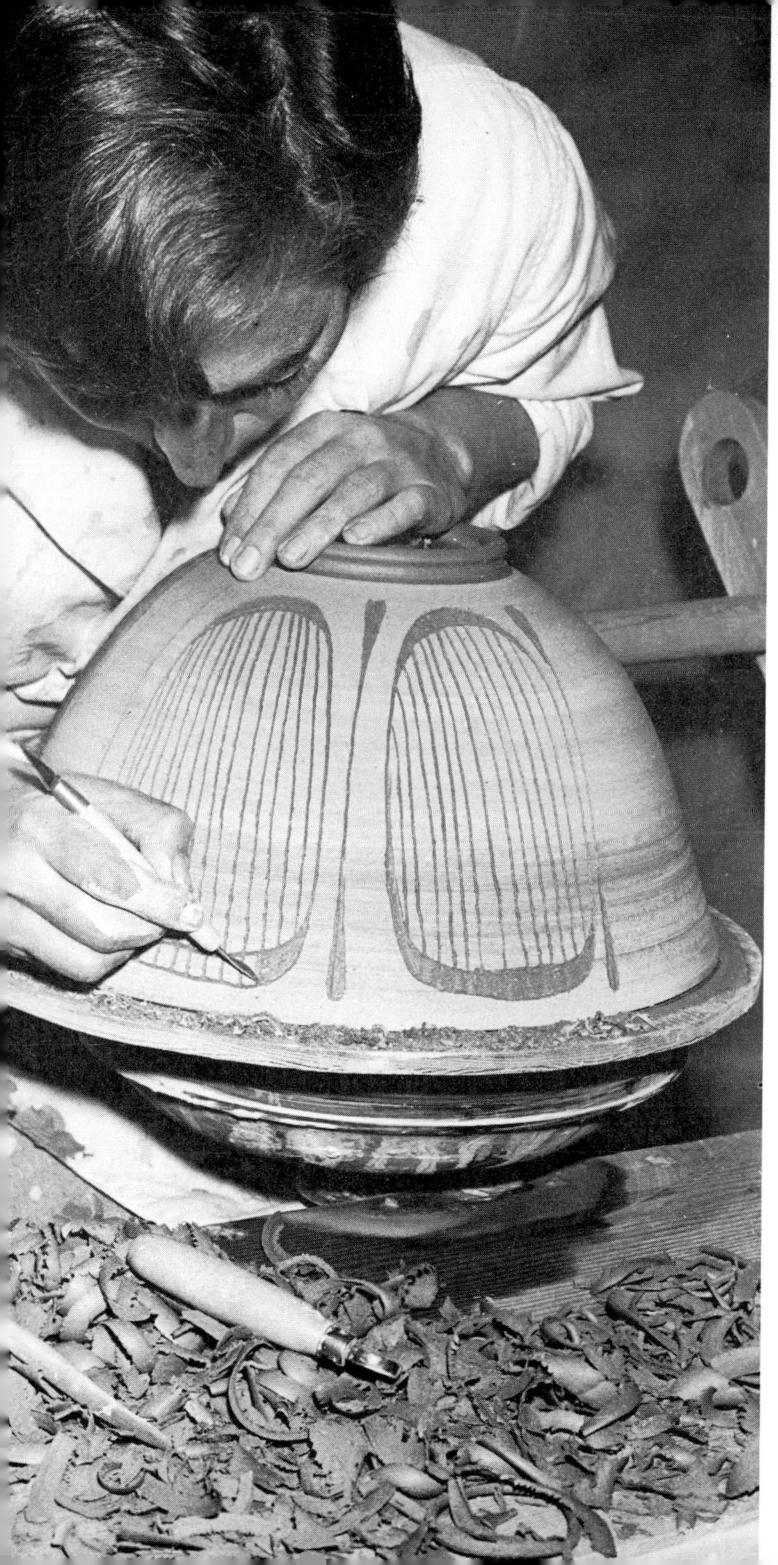

Artists use various materials to express ideas. They try to select materials which will best correspond to their mental images.

Chapter 6

Criticism is judgment, ideally as well as etymologically. Understanding of judgement is therefore the first condition for theory about the nature of criticism. Perceptions supply judgment with its material, whether the judgments pertain to physical nature, to politics or biography. The subject matter of perception is the only thing that makes the difference in the judgments which ensue. Control of the subject-matter of perception for ensuring proper data for judgment is the key to the enormous distinction between the judgments the savage passes on natural events and that of a Newton or an Einstein.

John Dewey, from *Art As Experience*,
New York: Minton, Balch & Company,
1934, page 298.

Developing Awareness for Aesthetic Judgment and Art Heritage

The development of art in American schools began under the influence of industry and has always been more concerned with the production of products than with a regard for why the product was made. This does not imply that the evaluation of products produced in arts classes was not considered, but the main emphasis was on the making of art works.[1] Concern for the critical and aesthetic judgment of art works was cursory or nonexistent. The study of art history was also neglected in school programs. Even today our continuing overriding emphasis on the making of art (studio model) neglects the art critic and art historian models.

Most children will grow up to pursue art as viewers rather than producers. In reference to our role of teacher as *art critic* (see Chapter 1), we need to indicate to children that the evaluation of art products involves definite skills in looking and in describing what they have seen.

How Does the Teacher Project the Model of Art Critic?

The teacher projects the model of art critic by bringing selected examples of art objects into the classroom and attempting to explain how she feels about them.[2] Some items which can be discussed about art objects include the following:

1. How can I look at a painting so that it will have meaning for me?
2. What can I look for in a painting that will help me get at this meaning?
3. What art terms do I need to know to relate this meaning?
4. What symbols do I need to know from the culture and art history in which it was created?
5. How can I put all these together and *read* the art object with excitement and a depth of understanding?

The critical processes of looking at and describing works of art that can be learned by elementary school children should consist of the following:[3]

1. *Describe the subject matter.* This includes identifying the work as a painting, sculpture, print, craft, etc. The description should also include the materials and techniques used, for example, *this is an oil painting, this is a stone carving.* Describe the subject of the painting or other work. Include all literal aspects such as figures, people, fruit, trees, animals, atmosphere, and those qualities which determine the appearance of reality or abstraction. Consider also whether the work is based on some event in history, mythology, or if it is an invention of the imagination.[4]

2. *Describe the art elements.* This includes identifying the qualities of line, shape, texture, color, Describe the kinds of lines used, the variety of shapes, the use of one or many textures, and the intensity and value used in color.

3. *Analyze the elements and principles of art.* Discuss how the lines, shapes, textures, and colors (art elements) are put together by the artist in the work. Consider also the compositional aspects of the work. This relates to how the artist put the work into a final arrangement. The principles of art are the means by which the artist assembles the art work. These include balance, harmony, rhythm, and proportion.[5]

4. *Interpret the art work.* This refers to the expressive qualities of an art object, such as moods, feelings, and emotions. Discuss how the artist has expressed a personally important emotional event from his life.

5. *Make the aesthetic judgment.* Verbalize the preceding four qualities and arrive at your interpretation of the aesthetic merit of the work.

The critical processes described can be learned by elementary school children in order to reinforce their role as *art critic model* of their own as well as other art works.

Teaching aesthetic awareness can be a stimulating adventure when children are encouraged freely to discuss and give their responses to art works. Reinforcing intuitive responses to art works by helping children to understand and articulate their feelings can heighten their aesthetic awareness. Learning to make aesthetic judgments increases one's ability to perceive natural and man-made objects, and increases one's ability to judge his own art works as well as historical works.

The authors believe that an intense, sensory awareness program as amplified in Chapter 2, and the critical learning skills expressed in this chapter will add a new dimension to art—that of children as *art critics.* Children will discover new depths of meaning in art when they have learned to look carefully before making aesthetic judgments.

Aesthetic Judgment Developers

The growth of aesthetic judgment as well as an historical language of art for students will occur when a variety of sequential activities are planned within and without the classroom situation. Aesthetic learning can take place continuously, for it utilizes the challenges established in the classroom by sensitive teachers, who also provoke aesthetic search in the greater environment that is part of the child's world. Aesthetic activities can incorporate news media, such as magazines and newspapers, films, television, books, events in the community, social experiences at home, vacation trips, and visits to stores, shops, and interesting places in the city or town. The teacher should prime the students to search for specific things rather than to generalize about art possibilities. For example, the student could be encouraged to search for subjects in various categories, such as insects, birds, fish, airplanes, automobiles, butterflies, plants, faces, costumes, abstract paintings, specific artist's works, watercolors, scientific inventions, and examples of weaving. Teachers need to help students crystallize what art can be. Here is a sample list of aesthetic judgment developers:

Find six examples of different spiders from books and magazines.

Bring ten examples of artists who work abstractly.

Seek out and write a paper on the sculptured faces of Mt. Rushmore.

Interview your parents on the question, "What is your definition of art?"

Find five good examples of artistic beauty in nature.

Select a picture of a painting or other work of art and tell why you like it.

Making aesthetic judgments is a function we all perform daily. We perform as an art critic at a certain level when we select the clothes we are to wear each day. It is the same aesthetic judgment we make when we look at works of art, only at a different level. We can increase our functional level of aesthetics by being more aware of the art principles that we use. Art should function as a part of life and not something to use on rare occasions.

Aesthetic judgment can be developed by dealing with everyday objects rather than just dealing with paintings in museums. We can encourage children to practice and exercise their aesthetic judgment each day. One can make and practice aesthetic judgment about how to arrange a vase of flowers, select one's clothing for the day, arrange food on a plate, or decorate a cake. Aesthetic judgment only develops through continuous use in our everyday activities. These all involve aesthetic judgments and they can be exciting to do and a pleasure to view when finished. These experiences help us integrate our lives and give us the necessary aesthetic satisfaction to improve our human condition. Aesthetic judgment with young children should be considered in a positive, joyful way and not as negative and faultfinding about their work.

We should make a specific effort to relate art judgment not only to fine arts but to our daily lives. The two are oftentimes considered as separate things. The transfer of aesthetic judgment will not take place by itself. It has to be nudged along and related for two reasons. One, if we make aesthetic judgments about our daily experiences, it will become "functional aesthetic" rather than "museum aesthetics." Too often we only use "aesthetics" as we enter the museum or art gallery and we put it away when we leave. The second reason is that art is a part of life and not something separate from it, that is, something we use occasionally. Art is central to daily living.

We tend to teach art as not related to daily living or to pattern it as something extra. Approximately 90 percent of our elementary-school children will never take art as a course in school again. If they go to college they may take an art history or art appreciation course. This means that they will have to obtain their aesthetic sensitivity during the elementary-school years. Our discussions of aesthetic judgment cannot be just limited to "museum art" or the art product when we deal with elementary children. We must involve children in using their aesthetic judgment to improve the quality of their environment and the quality of their daily life. Just as man needs daily bread, he needs daily aesthetics. It cannot be reserved for museum visits only. Judging museum art, gallery art and your own artwork is only one small aspect of aesthetic judgment.

Can a Work of Art Change Me?

Following are questions a child can answer to help discover ways he/she has reacted to a work of art. These and similar questions should be used over and over again by children when they look at objects they are making aesthetic judgments about until they are skilled in their use.

1. Do I enjoy looking at the whole art object?
2. Do I enjoy only parts of the art object?
3. Does it bring a particular emotion or feeling to mind?
4. Does the artwork make me think about things differently?
5. Does it make me want to see and enjoy other things?
6. Does it help me better understand myself or give me new information about myself?
7. Do I now have new ideas and feelings about art?
8. Do I think about or relate it to other things I know?

Judging Walk Through Works of Art

Which places in your town have artistic elements? To get started in your aesthetic search, here are some beginning places to investigate. Art is not found only in paintings that hang in museums. Walking into some restaurants, buildings, parks, antique shops is like walking through a work of art because some of these places are so beautiful. Even a cemetery can be an interesting place (especially at Halloween!). Art can be found in many places in one's environment. It's really up to each of us to discover the beautiful forms that are made by people or nature and arranged by sensitive hands just waiting to be discovered and shared!

Here are some works of art that the authors have walked through:

Old Town Train Depot, Sacramento, California
Ghiradelli Square, San Francisco, California
St. Mary's Cathedral, San Francisco, California
Squirrel's Nest, Lake Tahoe, California
Disneyland, Anaheim, California
Golden Gate Park, San Francisco, California
Zion National Park, Utah
Coastal rain forest, Oregon
Nut Tree Restaurant, Vacaville, California

There are artistic places in all areas of the country. See what you can discover to walk through in your hometown area!

More Walks Through Works of Art

Flower shops
Bakeries
Toy stores
Ice cream stores
Clock shops
Farmer's markets
Flea markets
Antique stores
Boat yards
Navy ships
Lumber mills
Used book shops

Aesthetic Judgment: A Finding Game

Aesthetic judgment can be developed through critical questions asked by the teacher and directed towards the artwork and how students relate to it. In this way the teacher helps the student develop his role as art critic. For the young child, questions can be those dealing with finding colors, shapes, or textures within a picture or how they feel about the artwork.

1. Find two contrasting colors and name them.
2. Find three shades of a color.
3. Find three similar shapes.
4. Find the two largest rectangles in the artwork.
5. How many different colors can you find and name?
6. How many different textures can you find?
7. How does it make you feel?

Let's Discuss Artworks

Discussing artworks done by artists, as well as your own art that is made in class, can help us to understand the processes involved in creating artistic imagery. Using the painting of a young man on page 143 titled "Young Mason Eating Dinner" by Bernhard Reinhold, a sample series of investigative questions might go like this:

What is this painting about?
What medium was used?
Is this young man really a mason or did the artist pose a model?
What does this painting tell of a particular culture?
What is the boy eating?
Did he make the wall he is sitting on?
Are there laces in his shoes?
How does he cut his hair?
What type of structure is he building?
What questions would you ask this boy if you could?
How long ago was this painting done?
What country was this done in?
How did the artist use the paint?
What can you notice in the painting that reveals something about the subject?
How old is the young man?
Is the painting peaceful?
Is the young man happy?
His sleeves and trousers are both rolled up. Do his clothes fit?
Are the stones heavy?
Can you see the ladder? Is he up high?
What food is lying on the newspaper?
Is the cloth on his lap an apron?
How did the artist organize the picture?
Is the painting balanced?
Does the painting have pleasing tonal values?
Would you like to paint a picture this way?
How has the artist utilized space?
Is the young man large enough in size in relation to the painting?
How does the artist achieve a feeling for depth?
Can you see the mountains in the background?
Does the space in the painting really go way back to the distant mountains?
Why did the artist place a building in the background to the right of the young man?
What did the artist think of in order to create this painting?
Can you find linear elements in the painting?
What shapes did he use?
Are there any textures?
How did he shade forms?
Can you find diagonal forms in the painting?

When we discuss artworks with students, it helps them to crystallize their thinking about art, for it actively engages their thinking about artistic forms. In order to grow in art awareness, we need to experience it.

The Organization of Study for Our Art Heritage

The first step is to organize a plan by which the vast subject of art heritage can be reduced into smaller, workable categories. Jot down on paper the various subject areas of art that come to mind. It does not matter where one begins since the launching of the program is the vital step. The information obtained can be adapted to a specific grade level. For example, here is a beginning plan for developing an initial art heritage study.

Step one, following, consists of selecting and listing the over-all general units intended for art study.

STEP ONE (General Classifications of Art Units)

Classification A: Fine Arts
- Unit I—Painting
- II—Sculpture
- III—Drawing
- IV—Printmaking

Classification B: Crafts
- Unit I—Weaving
- II—Ceramics
- III—Jewelry

Classification C: Design
- Unit I—Elements of design
- II—Fashion design
- III—Advertising design
- IV—Industrial design

Classification D: Architecture
- Unit I—Homes
- II—Commercial structures
- III—Landscapes and parks

From a general over-all subject plan such as this, it is possible to elaborate more fully. For instance, step two consists of selecting each of the foregoing units and then deciding which type of information and approach would best suit the needs of a particular class. Once the material has been organized for each specific subject unit, the next procedure would be to outline the material for future class presentation. From the general classifications and units presented in step one, a more detailed approach might be planned, something like step two.

STEP TWO (Unit Clarification)

Unit I—Painting

1. *Different types of artists*
   a. Realistic artists—tell us stories of everyday experiences
   b. Landscape artists—paint pictures of scenery
   c. Abstract artists—paint things in new ways
   d. Portrait artists—paint pictures of people
   e. Imaginative artists—tell us of make-believe events
2. *Materials of the artists*
   a. Watercolor paint
   b. Oil paint
   c. Brushes
   d. Varnish
   e. Casein
   f. Papers
   g. Turpentine
   h. Canvas

Each unit of the art program could be planned in a manner similar to the foregoing. In this way, vast amounts of information will not become unwieldy. Step three consists of further clarification in terms of the subject unit.

STEP THREE (Detailed Analysis)

Unit I—Painting (further breakdown on artists)

Realistic Artists

1. Definition of realistic artists. There are artists who like to tell us ideas of everyday life. Realistic artists paint pictures which tell us stories of people, animals, flowers, trees, trucks, trains, airplanes and many other everyday things.

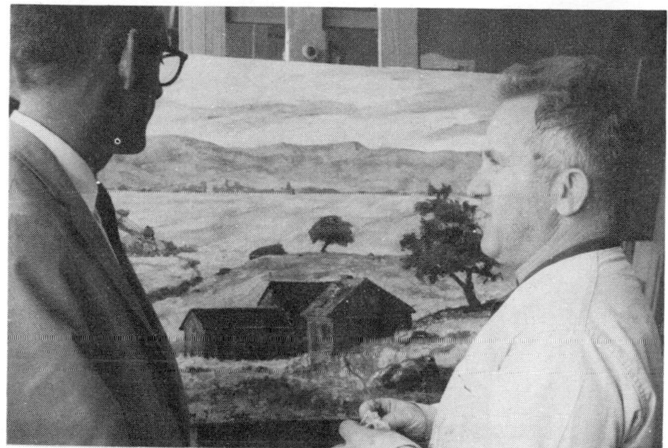

Art gallery directors and teachers can help us increase our understanding and appreciation of art. They do this by planned discussions and tours for groups as well as individual criticism of paintings.

Where can we find art sources in our community? Some sources include public galleries, private galleries, college art departments, and artist studios. Some galleries provide a rental service in which individuals can select fine, original art works for display in the home.

Barrios Gallery, Sacramento, California.

Crocker Art Gallery, Sacramento, California.

Art Fair, Downtown Mall, Sacramento, California.

"Arizona Kid," Charcoal, Earl Linderman.

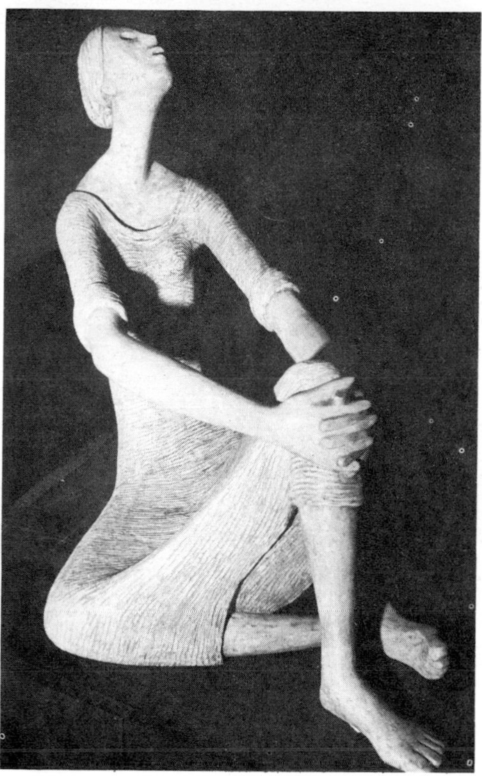

"Woman," sculpture, Georgiane Else.

"Waiting the Day," linoleum print, Don Uhlin.

Artists living today produce many styles which are personal to them. Artists throughout history have produced art in various styles.

"Medusa," stitchery, Jean Ray Laury.

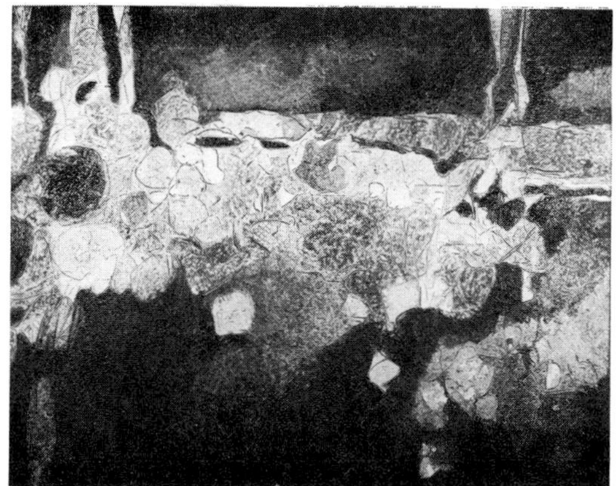

"Auburn Diggings," oil, David Dangelo.
Courtesy of artist.

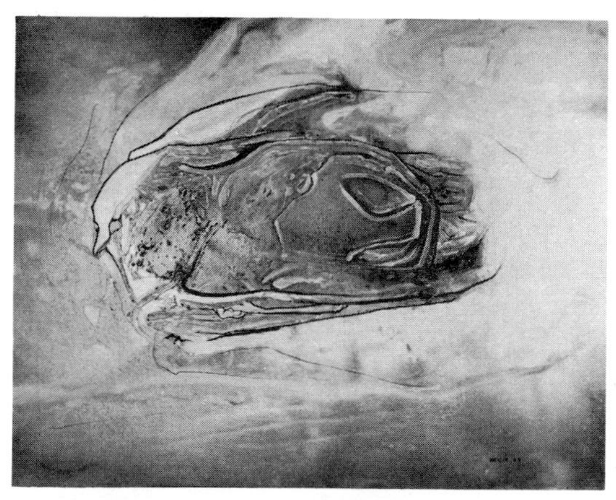

"Submerged Bird," oil, Don Reich.
Courtesy: E. B. Crocker Art Gallery, Sacramento, California

2. *American artists who have painted stories of everyday life*:

Edward Hopper	Andrew Wyeth
John Sloan	Thomas Benton
Albert Ryder	Grant Wood
Charles Burchfield	Phillip Evergood
Dong Kingman	Ben Shahn
George Bellows	Maurice Prendergast

3. *Artists from other countries who have painted stories of everyday life*:

Auguste Renoir	Georges Seurat
Claude Monet	Paul Cezanne
Francisco Goya	Honore Daumier
Maurice Utrillo	Camille Pissaro
Edgar Degas	

As the outline proceeds, each step along the way should become consistently more detailed in terms of the study unit. Each step should also be expanded in terms of what preceded it in the previous successive steps. The outline here is by no means complete or otherwise extensive, but it is presented to provide a beginning plan from which the teacher can begin to develop his own art program.

The truly talented and sincere artist is one who is hard working, dedicated and interested in the pursuit of specific objectives dealing with the art form. For example, artists can be placed into categories something like this:

1. Landscape artist: paints pictures of the landscape in watercolor or oil (Wyeth, Cezanne).
2. Seascape artist: chooses to paint pictures of the sea or waters of the world (Homer, Marin).
3. Social comment artist: chooses to make statements that reflect attitudes or events which have occurred, or are occurring in society (Shahn, Albright, Levine).
4. Portait artist: paints pictures of people (Rockwell, Picasso, Stuart).
5. Imaginative artist: paints pictures which deal with make-believe or personal interpretations of a subject or idea (Dali, Magritte).
6. Decorative artist: paints pictures of decorative themes. No subject intended necessarily. Emphasis here is on the pattern of colors, lines, textures and balance of art elements within the composition (Kandinski, Mondrian, Miro).
7. Figurative artist: paints pictures dealing with the figure in various settings (Degas, Renoir, Toulouse-Lautrec).
8. Abstract artist: paints things in new ways, using inventive harmonious solutions (Picasso, Davis, Braque).

No doubt, you would be able to establish more categories than these. Some artists fit within more than one category. Most artists after a time decide to narrow their pursuit of aesthetic form and explore one of these areas in depth. Most of their work can be found within a certain area.

Our Art Heritage: An Historical View

Studying the history of art in the elementary classroom will enable children to pursue aesthetically man's deepest emotions, artistic visions, and great ideas that are recorded in his visual forms. Man has always left a trace of his culture down through time and across centuries, and has therefore enriched the meaning of life through his expression in art forms. Man's art tells us of countless things which deal with both ideas and feelings—both fundamental to human expression and to all of life. A critical study of these art forms, both past and present should enable the student to *read* works of art as extensions of human situations so that he may gain insights into his own aesthetic as well as personal life. The teacher can help to unwrap the mystery of the masterpieces and show how to look at them as products of man. This can be done at any level if it is structured for understanding and not thought of as an elite mastery of higher ideals for the select few.

The subject of art history is so expansive that each teacher must decide what information is pertiment to her specific class. As the children gain more fluency in their "art language," the teacher will be able to approach art units of study in greater detail. In the beginning it might be wise to begin the history of art in simple but concise terms. Here are the major highlights of art as it has grown and influenced western art since the dawn of history. An approach such as this will provide a reference point and procedural plan.

Prehistoric Art
(40,000-5000 B.C).

Man's earliest attempts to represent his ideas and feelings in visual form have their origin in the predawn of history. The first evidence of prehistoric artistic endeavor was discovered on the roof of Altimira cave located near Santander on the northern coast of Spain. The cave of Altimira and many sister caves in both Spain and France yielded great discoveries of beautifully painted animals. There were deer, boar, bisons, elephants and many symbolic figures of man engaged in the hunt for survival, all painted by skilled artists who lived thousands of years ago. The artistry of these early people is evident not only in the cave paintings but in the simple stone and bone tools which they fashioned for utilitarian purposes. As seen from these earliest beginnings, man has indicated a special need to embellish his implements in order to create objects which contained elements of visual beauty as well as practicality.

Ancient Art
(4500-30 B.C.)

Ancient art extended through several cultures, some contemporary to each other in time. Many of these ancient civilizations occupied the area of the Mediterranean Sea, Middle East Asia, and extended as far as China and Japan. All told several of these societies left their mark on history, both in terms of recorded evidence of a people and as artistic achievement of an extremely magnificent stature. While it is almost impossible to pinpoint the entire picture of art at this time or to know precise dates, enough data has been and continues to be discovered to provide considerable insight into the artistic expression of these ancient peoples. The art forms of these ancient empires can be roughly chronicled in the following manner:

a. EGYPTIAN ART. Egyptian art encompassed three major kingdoms. They included the Old Kingdom, the Middle Kingdom and the Empire. The artistry of the Old Kingdom was created in direct relation to the philosophy which Egyptians of nobility held toward life. Basically they believed that existence on Earth was preparatory to life hereafter. As a result the all-powerful pharoahs, who represented diety figures on Earth, had tombs erected to glorify and protect their Earth bodies during the time when they would begin their heavenly journeys. These tombs contained the essence of Egyptian man's artistic achievements. The pyramids of Giza are the most dramatic architectural feats of this period. These magnificent tombs contained stone sculptures, elaborately painted wall reliefs which depicted everyday life, pottery, jewelry and many utilitarian remains contemporary to the time. The art of the Middle Kingdom and the Empire was characterized predominantly by elaborate temples erected in honor of the ruling emperors. The artistry of this age was present in these temples, in both architectural design and interior decoration. The artist was often directly involved with the architect and builders in the construction of such temples. The joint efforts of artist and architect are evident in the decorative colonnades and walled surfaces of the temples as well as the furniture and implements used in the interior of the structures. Sculptural forms were often united with structural support. The most famous of these temples were uncovered at Luxor and Karnak. During this period the Egyptians developed painting techniques to a highly proficient degree. Many of the other arts enjoyed great popularity during this period. Some of the most magnificent examples of metalwork, furniture design, pottery and glassware have been attributed to this splendid age.

b. SUMERIAN ART. Sumerian art existed as a cultural expression in an historical time that roughly parallels Egyptian achievements. This Middle East nation lacked stone or wood in any quantity, thus the chief building material consisted of sun-dried brick from clay. The Sumerians built temples and palaces also, although they did not seem to be as preoccupied with life in the next world as they were with the here-and-now. Their most notable achievement in the construction of their palaces was a colorful tower known as a *ziggurat*. For the most part, Sumerian art reflects a society filled with vigor and artistic power. Their artistic achievements are notably evident in the temple relief sculpture, metalwork and frescoed murals adorning the palace walls. The Sumerians developed a cuneiform system of writing, were accomplished builders (having explored the possibilities of the archway in architectural construction), and expanded their knowledge of glazed tiles for wall decoration.

c. ASSYRIAN ART. The main flow of Assyrian art was accomplished from 1000 to 600 B.C. The Assyrian state was located at the northern end of the Tigris-Euphrates Valley in Middle East Asia. Their art was a dynamic sort and depicted the militant and warlike nature of its people. Battle scenes, wounded animals and monster figures are characteristic images found in their sculptural pieces and wall paintings. Many of the Assyrian art forms suggest traces of Sumerian art but on a much grander scale. Unlike the more traditional Egyptians with their highly stylized approach to art and life, the Assyrians expressed life with brusqueness and vigor. The most significant of their art treasures is to be found in their architecturally magnificent palaces which housed many fine sculptures and wall paintings.

d. PERSIAN ART. Another ancient civilization which strongly influenced societies of this age was Persia. Some of the most exciting examples of woven and ceramic ware can be traced as far back as 5000 B.C. Persian rugs today reflect a style that continues to delight individuals around the world. Many of the art works of these earlier civilizations have been lost to us forever, and rarer still are the names of the artists from these forgotten times.

e. GREEK ART. The art of Greece began to flower around 600 B.C. The only remaining traces of their art in any quantity can be observed in their architectural and sculptural remains. Painting, although supposedly one of their most vital arts, has been all but lost to us. Their ceramic wares indicate that painting was commonly employed as part of their artistic expression. Greek art, as a style, influenced the entire world at one time or another. The Romans borrowed it almost entirely. During the Middle Ages both the Romanesque and Gothic cathedrals drew upon the Greek influence.[9] Our cities today clearly depict several architectural landmarks from this ancient civilization. Some of the Greek sculptors are known to us. The most influential included Phidias, Myron, Praxiteles, Polyclitus and Lysippus.

Art of the Middle Ages

(A.D. 300 to A.D. 1300)

This period of civilization is often referred to as the Dark Ages. Economic and social conditions were such that man had to devote the full measure of his time to the fight for survival. The church became the most important source of artistic achievement during this period. The monks in the various monasteries kept the glow of culture alive through their illuminated manuscripts which were finely decorated and painted. The *Book of Kells* from the eighth-century monastery of the same name contains excellent examples of the art work unique to this period. Most of the art of this time was painted flatly in a decorative style. Figures were represented in a symbolic manner to suggest divine images. Understandably the art of this time was closely akin to the religious beliefs which prevailed. Christianity and art grew hand in hand during this age, with the art forms reflecting the growing strength of the church. The flat handling of paint and the decorative style may have been influenced in part by a desire to discard the paganistic influences of Greece and Rome where realism and man were considered most vital.

Toward the end of the Middle Ages, particularly in the twelfth century, economic conditions improved to the point where old feudal systems began to deterioriate, thus paving the way for the growth of towns. Eventually, these towns became centers of learning, with the church providing a strong influential leadership. A style of art known as *gothic* developed, particularly in France and Germany, and is most evident today in the splendid cathedrals built to fit the needs of a deeply religious society. Unique innovations in architectural construction such as the flying buttress permitted the artist to employ vast amounts of stained glass for the wall surfaces. Consequently, the artist developed his artistic expression through the use of stained glass which was ultimately wedded to the cathedral structure in a functional bond.

The Renaissance in Italy

(A.D. 1300 to A.D. 1600)

The Renaissance, which means a new birth, was the result of a rediscovery of the classical art and ideas of Greece coupled with a revolt from the flat, decorative symbolic style of art prevalent during the Gothic period. It is perhaps one of the greatest periods in the world history of art development. Many of our present-day influences concerning art have their beginnings in the style of art that was developed during this time. Two of the most notable achievements in art which date from this period include the discovery of *perspective* (the illusion of depth on a two-dimensional surface) and *chiaroscuro* (the development of form through the use of light and dark). Both of these discoveries are key factors in the growth of a realistic style of art. Renaissance art is dotted with several great figures in painting and sculpture. The earliest to note was Giotto, who is said to have

"Christ Healing the Blind," School of Van Dyck.
Courtesy: E. B. Crocker Art Gallery, Sacramento, California

"Suits of Japanese Armor."
Courtesy: E. B. Crocker Art Gallery, Sacramento, California

"Young Mason Eating Dinner," Bernhard Reinhold.
Courtesy: E. B. Crocker Art Gallery, Sacramento, California

The artist is a spokesman in society. His reasons for painting specific ideas are closely related to his experiences and thinking.

Some artists may paint religious themes while other artists may be concerned with anatomical figures. Still others paint landscapes.

"Head of Bearded Man," drawing, Peter Paul Rubens.
Courtesy: E. B. Crocker Art Gallery, Sacramento, California

"Madonna and Child," polychromed wood, French, fourteenth century.
Courtesy: E. B. Crocker Art Gallery, Sacramento, California

"Three Trees," etching, Rembrandt.
Courtesy: E. B. Crocker Art Gallery, Sacramento, California

"Blind Hurdy Gurdy Player," oil, 17th Century Dutch.
Courtesy: E. B. Crocker Art Gallery, Sacramento, California

"Quiet Waters," etching, Lionel Barrymore.
Courtesy: E. B. Crocker Art Gallery, Sacramento, California

Sometimes paintings shock and disturb us. At other times they reflect our point of view. Art as a force can alert us to personal strife, social conditions, and other human problems past and present.

"St. Eustice," engraving, Albrecht Durer.
Courtesy: E. B. Crocker Art Gallery, Sacramento, California

"The Judas Kiss," German, sixteenth century.
Courtesy: E. B. Crocker Art Gallery, Sacramento, California

paved the pathway for those who came later. Giotto is respected as highly today as he probably was during his lifetime. The most noted artists of the Early Renaissance included such artists as Donatello (a sculptor), Masaccio, Fra Angelico, Botticelli, Fra Filippo Lippi and Pollaiuolo. The High Renaissance gave birth to such masters as Leonardo da Vinci, Michelangelo, Raphael, Tinteretto, Giorgione and Titian. Florence and Venice were great centers of art at this time.

In northern Europe, several Flemish and German artists contributed greatly to the painting and art of this period. The most noted artists included Jan van Eyck, Hieronymus Bosch, Pieter Breughel and Albrecht Durer.

Baroque Art

(A.D. 1600 to A.D. 1700)

Baroque art began in Rome in the first half of the sixteenth century. The Baroque artists developed a style of painting in which swirling figures and unusual compositions utilizing multicurved arrangements gave a feeling of superreality as well as romantic mysticism to their compositions. Baroque art extended from Italy to Flanders, Holland, France and Spain. In each of these countries certain outstanding artists emerged. These included Peter Paul Rubens, El Greco, Velazquez, Frans Hals, Rembrandt, Vermeer and Poussin.

Rococo Art

(A.D. 1700 to A.D. 1789)

Rococo art is usually considered a modification or domestication of the Baroque style. Its influence was felt in the entire western world. Rococo art was very decorative, gay, ornamental and free. It was in fact a reflection of times which were relatively free from major world catastrophies and upheavals. Rococo art was present in France, Italy, Holland and England. Although no great figures emerged during this flamboyant period in art, several artists made minor marks on the scene. These included Watteau and Fragonard in France, and Van Dyck, Holbein, Reynolds, Gainsborough and Hogarth in England. Rococo art was such a definite style that it was incorporated into everything possible from architecture, tapestries and teapot handles to furniture pieces and silverware. Its major influence ended about the time of the French Revolution in 1789.

Neoclassicism

Neoclassicism was the result in part of the French Revolution, whereby the new government wished their artistic voice to speak of good fortune to come. Rococo art, which spoke of the aristocracy, was buried and the new classical style began. The glory of Greece and Rome once again rose to the fore, and French artists adopted traditional styles in their search for a classical grace befitting the new regime. Strong emphasis was placed on technical skill and composition. Content was based on classical themes and heroic ideals. Human feeling became somewhat submerged due to the emphasis on style. Figures tend to be cold and intellectually treated. Paintings done during this period tend to have a sophisticated appearance, although technical rendition is superb. The most notable artists of this period include Jacques Louis David and Jean Auguste Dominique Ingres.

Romanticism

Romanticism was a revolt from the French Academy with its traditional classicism and imitative styles. It began around the time of the Salon of 1819. This type of painting style introduced human feelings back into the figures. The subjects tended to be highly exaggerated versions of life treated in a very idyllic manner. In France, Theodore Gericault and Eugene Delacroix were most influential in leading the Romantic movement in art. In America, Albert Ryder and George Inness painted in a manner that paralleled the Romantic manner.

Realism

Realism was a mid-nineteenth century form of art expression in which the subject was treated in a highly realistic manner. Realistic qualities in the paintings were achieved by using dramatic effects of light and dark and by exaggerating subjects for emphasis. These artists often painted social conditions which reflected economic struggles of the times. Some artists who could be included within this period include Honoré Daumier, Francisco Goya and Rembrandt van Rijn.

Impressionism

This art movement began in France about 1870 and was due in part in an interest of how natural light effects occur in nature. Artists

"Landscape near Rome," oil by Jan van Bloeman.
Courtesy: E. B. Crocker Art Gallery, Sacramento, California

"San Marco Piazza, Venice," oil, Franceso Battaglioli.
Courtesy: E. B. Crocker Art Gallery, Sacramento, California

"Gobelin's Tapestry," French, fifteenth century.
Courtesy: E. B. Crocker Art Gallery, Sacramento, California

Some paintings are flat and decorative. Some are symbolic. Some are highly realistic, emphasizing perspective and chiaroscuro to create atmospheric effects.

of this school tried to achieve with pigment on canvas the same effect as one would receive while viewing fields and landscapes if bright sunlight were present. The Impressionist painters succeeded in developing new ways of mixing pigments, of organizing space in relation to color and of intensifying their palette to a much greater degree than previously accepted standards permitted. Two very influential painters of this movement in art included Claude Monet and Auguste Renoir.

Post-Impressionism

Post-Impressionism, which began about 1880, was an attempt by several artists in France to extend beyond the then popular Impressionistic styles which certain artists had developed. The post-Impressionists were not entirely satisfied with the principles set down by the Impressionists and set out to prove or clarify them. While still retaining the spontaneity and freshness of the Impressionist style, the post-Impressionists developed many new styles and approaches to painting. Seurat and Cézanne approached the idea of painting by using scientific means. To this day Cézanne is considered the father of modern painting. Two other painters of this style included Vincent Van Gogh and Paul Gauguin.

Cubism

Cubism, which began in Paris shortly after the turn of the century, is considered the beginning of the abstract art movement. The most notable artists to explore and originate the Cubistic styles included Pablo Picasso and George Braque. Fernand Leger and Juan Gris also painted in the Cubistic manner. In developing the Cubistic style, the artist reduced the forms of the picture to simplified geometrical elements which included spheres, cylinders, rectangles and other irregular shapes. Cubism opened the door for artistic inventiveness and exploration that continues to influence contemporary art. It also marks the point where the artist begins to develop art forms for their own sake, thus narrowing the path of communication between the artist and the general public.[10]

Expressionism

Expressionism developed principally in Germany and France and was a reaction to conditions immediately surrounding World War I. It was an art form in which the artist expressed his own emotional reaction to a specific subject. Subject matter was usually based on depressing and violent themes which dwelt on the morbid side of life. Color was treated very subjectively with little attempt to relate it within a more natural relationship. Several artistic groups composed the Expressionist movement. In Germany, three successive groups included "The Bridge," "The Blue Riders" and "The New Objectivity." Several artists who contributed fine works within the Expressionist style include Kandinsky, Grosz, Kollowitz, Barlach, Ensor and Munch.

Surrealism

Surrealism developed shortly after World War I and was a reaction to conditions prevailing at the time. Surrealism was fathered by a smaller movement known as *Dada*, which was a protest against society and tradition. The ridiculous, the irrational and the bizarre were all stock in trade for both Dada and surrealism. While Dada flickered and vanished into the undercurrent of painting, surrealism picked up momentum on the strength of new findings in psychology by Freud and others. The subconscious and dream themes dominated Surrealist paintings. Highly realistic handling of content tended to give the viewer a deeper sense of reality. Among the painters connected in and around the Surrealist movement, the following artists gained prominence: Max Ernst, Kurt Schwitters, Paul Klee, Dali, Miro and Tanguy.

American Scene Painters

In America during the first half of the twentieth century, several artists have depicted the American scene each in an individual manner. The backyard, the small town, the rural scene, the commonplace and the ordinary became subject matter for these artists. While the reasons governing the types and styles of paintings varied from satirical reactions against cubism then popular in Europe to humor over homespun virtues, several artists made their mark on the American scene. They include John Sloan, Grant Wood, Charles Burchfield, Ben Shahn and Edward Hopper. Of this group, Ben Shahn stands out as one of America's contemporary painters of social conditions.

Abstract-Expressionism

Astract-Expressionism developed in the United States during the period 1950 to 1960. It was a movement that encouraged free experi-

"Owl"
by Donald W. Herberholz
Welded Metal Sculpture

"Academic Priest"
by Bruce Carter
Print

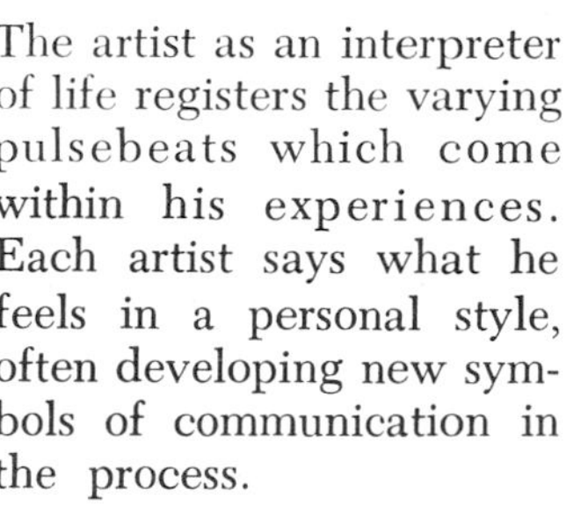

The artist as an interpreter of life registers the varying pulsebeats which come within his experiences. Each artist says what he feels in a personal style, often developing new symbols of communication in the process.

Courtesy of the artist

"Quiet Place"
by James Doerter
Watercolor

"Rooster"
by Paul Beckman
Print

"Aces and Eights"
by Earl Linderman
Charcoal

mentation and search by applying unorthodox methods of painting a picture. In many instances, paintings of this movement were done by dripping, throwing, splashing and literally scrubbing the pigment into the canvas. A representative image of an object was not a necessary intention. Paintings of this school reflected the inner expression of the artist in emotional form. The leading exponents of abstract expressionism include Jackson Pollack, Franz Kline, Hans Hoffman and Willem de Kooning.

Pop Art

Short for popular art, it has been one of the major trends since the early 1960's. This art uses images from mass advertising, comic strips, and ordinary objects such as pop bottles, soup cans, etc., presented in distortions or exaggerations of size but always recognizable.

Claes Oldenburg—Stove and painted plaster food; sculptor who also uses plastic and ceramics.
Jasper Johns—The American flag painting; also does targets.
Andy Warhol—takes photos and produces multiple portraits using the silk screen process.
James Rosenquist—16 foot long painting "Silver Skies."
George Segal—life size plaster sculpture.
Roy Lichenstein—comic strip characters.
Tom Wesselman—Great American Nudes, a series in which he uses collage materials, paints, glues, and photographs.
Marisol—wood sculpture.
Robert Rauschenberg
Wayne Thiebaud—Cut Meringues.
Mel Ramos—takes slides, puts them together, blows them up; does girls from magazines.
Robert Indiana—uses advertising images.
Nicholas Krushenick—successful; bright bold colors and black outlines.

Optical Art

Op artists experiment with precise shapes, wiggly lines, concentric lines, and moire patterns in their concern with unusual visual effects. The optical illusion is defined as a visual experience in which a discrepancy exists between what we see and what is there.

To develop and understand art history and art terms does not mean neglecting any aspect of a strong and deep personal involvement. Such an understanding should enrich rather than hinder the child's own expressive work. The knowledge of art gained through discussion of works of art and the student's own work should assist his expressive development. Through this added dimension to this knowledge, the child can become more involved with art techniques. He will thus have gained greater freedom to express his own ideas with greater aesthetic quality.

The overview example used here is that of the *history of western art,* and it is intended as only one example of how a classroom teacher can organize large bodies of information into bite-size chunks that children can digest. Other major art history movements could be handled in a somewhat similar manner. For example:

The Art of Mexico[6]

Pre History: 1700-100 B.C.
The Classic Era: 100 B.C.-900 A.D.
The New Civilizations: 900-1300
The Aztecs: 1300-1525
The Colonial Era: 1525-1810
Independence and Growth of Freedom: 1810-1954
Reform, Democracy, Dictatorship: 1854-1910
Revolution and Progress: 1910-1940
Contemporary Art: 1940-Present

Some great art periods will not be approached in this historical manner but rather from viewing the major art forms produced, or centering on the arts of a particular area of a country or a certain group of people. The art history of the native Americans or Indians could be told by the contributions of the different tribes or by following the development of their major art forms, such as baskets, pottery, masks, etc.

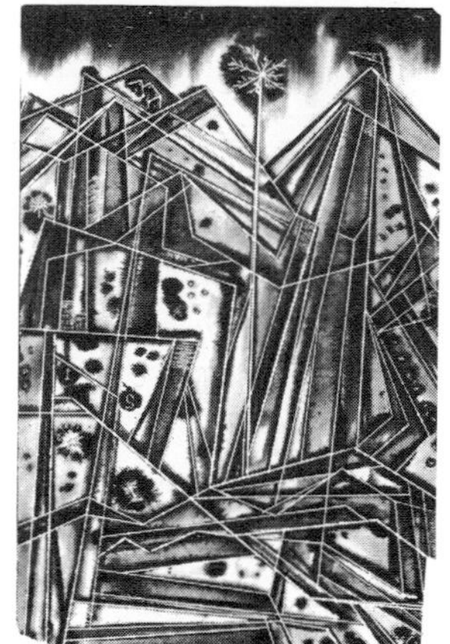

"City of Hope," water color, William Kasza.
Courtesy of artist.

Sculpture in wood, Harlan Hoffa.
Courtesy of artist.

"Tower Bridge," water color, Setsuo Kirinoe.
Courtesy: E. B. Crocker Art Gallery, Sacramento, California

Artists work in various styles. When the ideas of artist and viewer coincide, aesthetic understanding takes place.

Welded metal sculpture by Ray Fink.

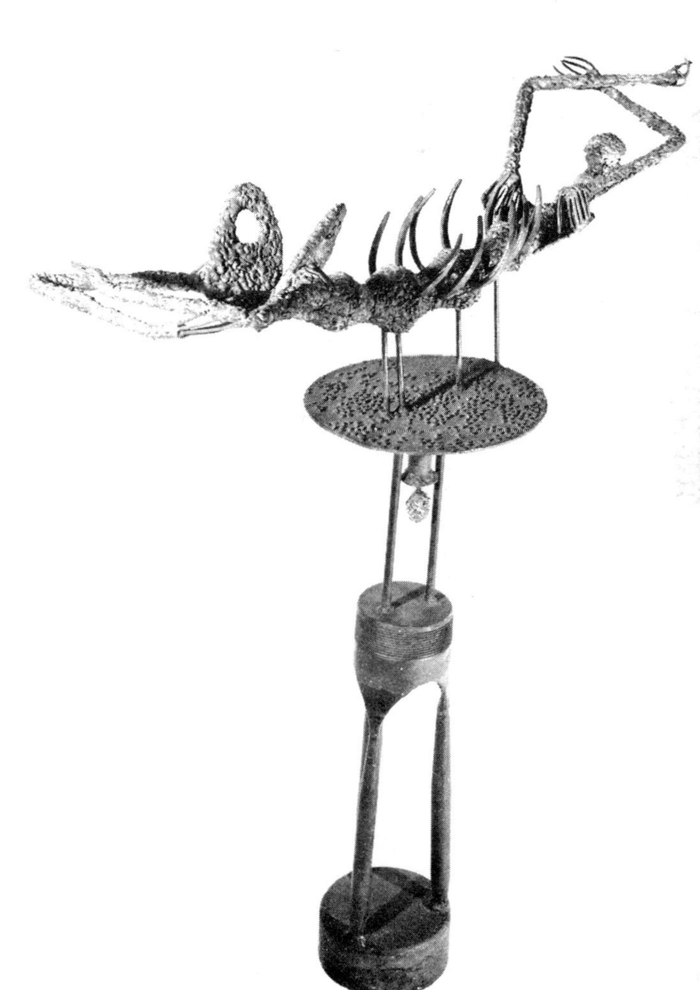

"River Scene," chalk drawing, Robert Else.

"Fighting Bird," water color, wax and ink, Marlene Linderman.

Another approach would be to start with different ethnic (subcultural) groups within your school system, city, county, or state and consider each of the unique art forms produced by each group. This could be done both from a contemporary and historical point of view.

The aforementioned groupings are suggestions as to how the elementary teacher can organize units in the study of art heritage. (Also see "Organizing Art Learning Experiences" within this chapter.)

Art Terms that Enrich Aesthetic Judgment

In any art program there are many terms which must be defined in order to develop a language of art. Once this language has been learned, communication between individuals is enriched. Listed are some typical art terms which teachers and children can learn. When the children have become familiar with these terms, many more can be added to the list. These can be readily included in the children's art notebook.

Art Terms

ABSTRACT: Simplified version, usually not representational.

ACCENT: Specific areas within a composition which are given greater emphasis by the use of more intense tone, size change, or other means which exaggerate these specific parts.

AESTHETIC: A term referring to the fine arts or to art forms in which the "beautiful" or artistic qualities of forms are given consideration.

ANALAGOUS COLORS: Colors which are closely related to each other, and in which a common hue can be found for example, blue, blue-violet, violet.

ARMATURE: Framework made of wire or wood and used to support the structure of a form in clay work, papier mâché, or other modeling techniques.

ASSEMBLAGE: An arrangement created by combining a variety of two- and three-dimensional materials such as pieces of cloth, wood, small objects, photographs.

ASYMMETRICAL BALANCE (informal balance): Unequal distribution of art elements resulting in a visually pleasing balance.

BALANCE: A visual impression of equilibrium between all interactive parts in any art work.

BAROQUE: An art movement of the seventeenth century; utilizing a decorative surface treatment of artistic space.

BATIK: A method of designing fabrics by dipping or brushing hot wax onto the cloth. The process is repeated for each color used. The wax is removed by boiling or ironing.

BAUHAUS: An artistic research center founded in Germany by Walter Gropius, for the training of architects, artists and industrial designers. It strived to integrate art, science and technology into new visual wholes.

BRAYER: Rubber or gelatin roller used in printing to spread ink evenly over a surface.

BURIN: A pointed steel tool used for cutting a metal plate for printmaking.

BUTCHER PAPER: Glossy paper which usually comes in large rolls suitable for mural work.

CALLIGRAPHY: Refers to the use of line in varying widths and rhythms as commonly used in brush lettering.

CANVAS: A coarse, heavy cloth of hemp, linen or cotton used as a surface for oil painting.

CARTOON: A preliminary drawing for a painting or mural.

CARVING: The act of designing by cutting away parts of a surface, such as stone or wood.

CASEIN: A paint medium containing a milk base; often used as tempera paint; mixes with water. The medium is more permanent than ordinary tempera paint.

CERAMICS: A term standing for objects made from clay and then fired.

Cloisonne Enamel: Surface design in enamel in which bent wire is secured to a background. The spaces, or cloisons between the wire are filled with vitreous enamels of various colors. The process is Byzantine in origin.

Collage: An arrangement of various materials such as cloth, wood, paper and various scraps pasted into a visually pleasing art form. The method used in pasting.

Color: Usually thought of as the hues found in a spectrum in which wavelengths of light are diffused into the various colors by their reflection against surfaces.

Complementary Colors: Refers to colors which are opposite each other on a standard color wheel, for example, red and green, orange and blue.

Composition: The arrangement and organization of parts into a unified whole in which all parts unite to form a new total relationship.

Contour: The outer surface of an object or figure, usually bounded by a line, change of color, or change of texture.

Dadaism: A French term meaning "hobby horse" and representing an art movement that originated during World War I.

Design: The skillful ordering and building of artistic thoughts into visual expressions with art media.

Etching: A method of engraving a design on a copper zinc plate by means of acid. From this plate a print is made.

Form: The finished product as it appears after the art elements have been arranged and completed.

Free-Form: A shape which has no fixed or rigid boundaries.

Fresco: Painting done on moist plaster in which the pigments become incorporated with the plaster.

Gouache: Refers to opaque water colors.

Harmony: Occurs when all of the art elements have been organized into a visually pleasing relationship.

Illustration: Refers to an art product in which the story content is clearly evident.

Intensity: Refers to the amount of pigment in a color. Bright colors contain considerable amounts of pigment.

Kiln: A furnace used for drying, hardening or firing clay products. Ceramic kilns are used in the firing of bisqueware and glazed pottery. Enamel kilns are used in firing enamelware.

Line: The path made by a moving point. It can vary in width, direction and length.

Lithography: Refers to the printing of an image on a surface material using a stone plate and a grease pencil.

Lost Wax Process: Method of casting objects in metal which have been made from clay or other plastic materials.

Mass: The combination of several forms within an art work to form a larger body.

Mat: A heavy border of paper or cardboard used to frame a drawing or painting.

Media: The art materials to be used. (plural of medium)

Medieval: The Middle Ages in history during which the Romanesque and Gothic styles of architecture were developed, the period between the third and fourteenth centuries A. D.

Mobile: A hanging, three-dimensional design which has moving parts.

Montage: A form of *collage* in which photographs are combined to create an art product.

Mosaic: A technique of imbedding colored stone, metal, glass or enamel in a surface of stucco or plaster. It is Byzantine in origin and was associated with early Christian art.

Mount: To place, paste or attach on a suitable support or backing. It enriches the visual appearance of an art work.

Oil Paint: Pigment in linseed, poppy or nut oil.

Pastel: Ground pigment that is combined with gum arabic and used in solid form. Colors are often tinted in appearance.

Perspective: The art of creating an illusion of depth on a two-dimensional surface. A visual method of drawing objects as they appear to our eye.

PICTURE PLANE: Refers to the surface on which the artist makes his drawing, painting or design.

PIETA: Refers to a religious painting or sculpture which represents the Virgin mourning Christ.

POINTILLISM: A technique of applying paint in small dots, or points to the canvas in order to effect an optical mixing.

PORCELAIN: A high-fire whitish smooth clay used in ceramics. Often has translucent properties.

POSTER PAINT: Opaque paint, in dry or liquid form, suitable for classroom use.

PRIMARY COLORS: These are thought of as the basic colors. They are red, yellow and blue.

PROPORTION: May refer to size relationship within an art work, or may refer to quantities of tone or color.

RELIEF: In sculpture, the exposure of certain parts away from a base or foundation.

RENAISSANCE: The great rebirth in art learning during the fifteenth and sixteenth centuries. It was a period when self-discovery and individual growth was held in high esteem. The glories and beauties of Greece were restudied.

RHYTHM: A regulated flow of colors, lines, textures or other art elements to achieve a pleasing effect.

SCULPTURE: The term describes the forming, modeling, carving, constructing, assembling of forms in wood, stone, ivory, clay and metal in the round or in relief.

SERIGRAPHY: Refers to designing and printing using the silk-screen process to reproduce art works.

SHAPE: Can be geometric or free-form in dimension and is defined by a line or color area.

SPECTRUM: A band of colors deprived from wavelengths of light when seen through a prism or other reflective material.

STILL LIFE: Any combination of objects, such as fruits, books, vases, that the artist arranges for use as subject matter.

STYLE: Individual way or manner of using art materials to form highly distinctive personal images.

SYMBOL: Something which stands for or represents the actual image or idea.

TACTILE: Refers to the sense of touch.

TEMPERA: See *poster paint.*

TERRA-COTTA: A fine quality of ceramic clay used for sculpture, vases, tiles, etc; characteristic color is brownish red.

TEXTURE: The visual or surface feel of an object to our touch or vision.

THROWING: In pottery, the act of shaping a vase or bowl on the potter's wheel.

TRIPTYCH: Three-part panels traditionally depicting a single painted religious scene.

VALUE: Refers to the lightness or darkness of a color.

VITREOUS: Refers to high-fire ceramic ware such as porcelain. This material is glassy and nonporous.

WARP: The threads used to warp a loom. These threads run lengthwise.

WASH: A watered-down pigment which causes a transparent effect when used over other lines or colors.

WEDGE: To cut and pound clay in order to prepare it for work in ceramics. This removes the air bubbles.

WEFT (WOOF): The thread used in weaving across the warp.

Have the children add more terms to this list.

Organizing Art Learning Experiences: Strategies, Models and Teaching Aids

Strategies

Setting the stage for artistic vision in seeing and experiencing life richly should begin early, and especially at the kindergarten level. Here are several get-started suggestions to help the classroom teacher begin an art program for children:

1. Plan at least one period each week in which to present art lessons to the class. Take time to plan each lesson, and consider what your artistic objectives will be. Chapters 1 and 2 will be helpful in this respect.

2. Plan at least one period every two weeks for discussing fine, original works of art. This could include paintings, sculpture, printmaking, ceramics, jewelry, weaving, and many other art media. Using the format discussed in Chapter 6, encourage the children to discuss what and how they feel about the artworks.

3. Develop an art-aesthetic corner where children can be encouraged to bring in beautiful objects and pictures they discover at home. Provide some time for the children to discuss their discoveries, which might range from snow-white daisies to a handful of nicely shaped pebbles.

4. Provide an exhibit space where original art works can be attractively displayed. Very often local art collectors will be happy to loan interesting art objects. Other sources include art galleries, high school and college art departments, and private collections of art teachers.

5. Bring guest artists to the classroom for discussion and demonstration of how they develop their art works.

6. Encourage the children to start a file collection of beautiful and interesting pictures. Classifications might range from "artists we learned about" to "exciting ideas we discovered through pictures."

7. Plan several trips a year for taking the children to an art gallery, antique shop, anthropology museum, or other discovery place for art. Make each trip a planned experience in which the children look for specific objectives rather than wander aimlessly from room to room.

8. Have each child make an "art learning" notebook. Information and knowledge of what they learn about art can be added to the notebook. The notebook can be divided into several parts, including 1) art terms, 2) art history, 3) art judgment, 4) art materials, and 5) art discoveries.

9. The elementary teacher can help children to verbalize their aesthetic feelings by developing an *Art-Talk Time* in which teacher and children talk about any form of beauty they can think of, for example, reflections on a rainy day, a television program, thunder in the sky, pictures in books, an art picture that a student made, the taste of beef stew on a winter day. . . .This approach will assist the class in thinking about aesthetic possibilities in every day perceptual discoveries as well as works of art.

Models

A Working Model For Teaching Art History In The Classroom

If you would like to teach some fundamentally significant history of art in understandable form to K-8, remember that you can begin at any point in space, time, or history. It's not necessary to be a superpowered art history expert to teach art as a subject to your class. All you need to do is read the specific area of your choice a few days before you teach it. You might even learn about the specific subject at the same time as the students. The following is an interesting place to begin in the yesterdays of life.

The Bayeux Tapestry

A great place to begin the study of art in history might be the time in which William the Conqueror, Duke of Normandy, France, stormed across the English channel in the year 1066 A.D. and did battle with King Harold I of England. The Bayeux Tapestry was created to commemorate the events surrounding this history-making battle in which William became the next King of England. His half-brother Odo, Bishop of the Cathedral of Bayeux, France, probably commissioned the monumental work.

The tapestry, which is really an embroidery composed of wool threads sewn on a linen background, is 231 feet in length, 231 feet of pure linen (three fourths of the length of a football field!). The most fascinating thing of all regarding this work is that it has survived for over 900 years, including the year 1792 when French revolutionaries yanked it out of the cathedral of Bayeux and used it as a wagon cover. Fortunately, it was rescued. The tapestry today hangs in a glass covered case especially built to display it, in the Bishop's Palace museum across from the cathedral of Bayeux in Bayeux, France. It is the single most important remaining piece of art to survive the latter part of what is known as the Middle Ages. It reveals that expert craftmen existed in the eleventh century. Many exquisite pieces of embroidery were created during this period of time, but they have all vanished into dust. Many of the finer examples were melted down to retrieve the gold and silver threads which were part of the works. Here are some interesting facts concerning the Bayeux Tapestry:

It was probably improperly labeled a tapestry instead of an embroidery when a clerk inventoried the holdings of the Cathedral of Bayeux in 1476.

Sewn into the 231 foot embroidery are 626 human figures, 190 horses or mules, 35 hounds or dogs, 506 other various animals, 37 ships, 33 buildings, 37 trees. The ships are Viking type.

At the time in which the tapestry was created, the city of London had a population of 15,000. And all of England had no more population than 1,000,000.

This embroidery would have been a formidable task to undertake in any age. Although in the town of Hastings, England, in 1966, the folks did just that. They made a new tapestry to commemorate all the events since 1066 to the present age. I wonder how long it took to make the second one? It took about ten years to make the first one.

During the Middle Ages, there were many schools of embroidery. Both men and women sewed. Also, there was no painting on canvas, as this developed later during the Renaissance. What painting was going on was of illuminated manuscripts done in the workshops of the churches. These shops were known as scriptoriums. We have the monks to thank for many of these beautiful pieces.

William the I of Normandy sailed with an army of 7,000 men, across the channel to invade England on October 14, 1066. How 7,000 men ever crossed that channel in longships with their square sail is a mystery.

The following books will provide considerable information on the Bayeux Tapestry and will help in planning a lesson at any level, regarding this great work of art:

DENNY, NORMAN and FILMER-SAKEY, JOSEPHINE, *The Bayeux Tapestry*, London: Collins Co., 1966.

STENTON, SIR FRANK, *The Bayeux Tapestry*, New York: Garden City Books, 1957.

One final footnote regarding the time of the Bayeux Tapestry: When the Black Plague (bubonic plague) struck Europe and England in 1348-49, over half of the craftsmen died, along with the population in general. As a result, the great embroidery and weaving shops that had existed had to change their way of working, because there was such a shortage of skilled labor in the form of expert craftsmen and craftswomen.

A Working Model For Teaching Design Concepts In Art

Design is actually the manner in which a person puts the art elements together in order to create an art product. Good design means that an art product is pleasing to one's eye in viewing it. Good design means that chaos is at a minimum, and aesthetic order is in operation. In teaching design concepts to students, the following considerations will be helpful (Remember to adapt to your particular grade level from K-8):

Define what is meant by design. For example, design is the creation of aesthetic order of the art elements into an art work. The art elements consist of line, shape, texture, color, space, form. All objects have these elements present in some degree. For example, a line that incloses itself becomes a shape. The art elements exist in people, houses, trees, land, mechanical things, everything. The design elements are really the way in which we see an object. Putting these elements together into a pleasing relationship is the challenge of art. It has challenged great artists down through the centuries. Even when we understand what good design is, the challenge to create an art piece remains. Artists don't come up with winning art products each time around. Like ordinary people, they also make plenty of unsatisfying results. But this doesn't stop them.

Copper Breast Plate Bra, Grace Hampton
Photo: Steve Terwilliger

"Exuberance," oil on canvas, Hans Hofmann
Courtesy: Gift of Seymour H. Knox, Albright-Knox Art Gallery, Buffalo, New York

They simply forge on to results which are more pleasing to their own personal standard for art.

Take each art element and try to find it in the environment. For example, the element line can be found in spider webs, vines, railroad tracks, telephone lines, fabrics, wood grains, fences, television aerials, wheel spokes, supporting beams and posts, billboard lettering, grain fields, grasses, radio towers, seed puffs, bridges, street markings, decorative wall units, wet tire marks, flower stems, petals, tree trunks, branches, pins and needles, strings, ropes, and wires. Have the students make their own list of linear elements that they observe in their environment. Take a line trip, and have your class record what they discover.

After the students have made a list of linear examples from their observations, talk about what lines do. Line in its pure form is an artistic device originated by man to help provide him with a method for giving meaning to his world of shape, form, and design. Lines can be at least three kinds:

a. They can serve as contour or structure in describing form.
b. They can be expressive, as in communication of ideas.
c. They can be aesthetic quality.

Lines which are *structural* enclose shapes to form outlines as in drawing. Structural lines exist in architecture when the skeleton of a building is erected. Lines can be *expressive*. If the aesthetic qualty of a line were reduced to its barest common denominator, we would perceive such a line without sensitivity. It would tend to be uniform in thickness and length, and would function as a vehicle for transmitting messages or ideas, devoid of personal feeling. Lines of this nature are often suited to technical drawings, blueprints, and the printed page which functions largely as communication. Lines which are artistic provide us with added feeling. When lines become more than signature lines, they can provoke an emotional response within us. For example, *curving lines* can suggest softness and grace, as seen in dancers, while other lines can suggest vigor and forcefulness, as in a thunderstorm. In drawing a curved line on a surface, we may find ourselves identifying with the curved lines of our environment. We might think of ballet dancers, children and babies, women, the edges of white clouds, billowy pillows, marshmallows, or powder puffs. (Add more of your own here. . . .)

Horizontal lines generally suggest things which are restful, slow, moving, drifting, spacious and quiet: our bodies when we sleep, the distant horizon, a table top, a flowing river, a still lake, a highway stretching across the plain, or a landing strip.

Vertical lines suggest strength, stability and poise. The images which come to mind when viewing vertical lines include our bodies when standing erect, trees, supporting members and posts of buildings, telephone poles, church steeples, and spires.

Diagonal lines suggest motion, rapid flight, action, and speed. Diagonal lines remind us of our bodies when we run, jump, dive. They also suggest hills, mountains, leaning structures, explosions, lightning, and rockets.

Aesthetic lines are those which we try to put into our pictures by taking all of the above information and then making very, very sensitively drawn art lines. An artistically (aesthetically) drawn line should be pleasing to behold. Encourage students to draw lines which are full of variety. Lines can be timid, aggressive, returning, extravagant, explosive, subtle, striking, or delicate. Lines can expand, contract, curve, or change direction. They can be swiftly flowing and smooth, or scratchy and lumpy. They can be shredded, sticky, hairy, or fibrous. They can be transparent, or opaque. They can be technically precise when made by an instrument, or willowy when made by a tool such as a feather. Often, the tool used will determine the type of lines which can be created. A brush line will be quite different from lines which are made with a pencil or pen (refer to Chapter 5). Discover how different tools will give different types of lines. Try using bamboo pens, dried twigs, feathers, rubber gloves, erasers, corks, felt tip pens, soap, pointed instruments, sponges, dipped string, edges of cardboard, cement, and glue. Add more of your own. A good book on design to help you get started is *Elements of Design* by Donald M. Anderson.

Heroes In Art Can Be Models For Children

In this age of nonheroes, we believe that it is extremely important to encourage children to develop heroes for various subjects. Heroes become models which can influence our behavior. They become standards which we can strive to emulate. A hero is an example. Heroes don't have to be alive, or your next door neighbor. They can come from paintings, books, from teachers, or from anywhere that you can discover them. As an example to help you with your classes, here are some heroes that have made a great impact on world art:

HEROES IN THE WORLD OF ART

Fernand Leger	French
Auguste Renoir	French
George Grosz	German
Claude Monet	French
Edgar Degas	French
Edward Hopper	American
Milton Avery	French
Henri Matisse	American
Pablo Picasso	Spanish
Albrecht Durer	German
Paul Cezanne	French
William Harnett	American
Winslow Homer	American
Andrew Wyeth	American
Kathe Kollwitz	German
Rembrandt	Dutch
da Vinci	Italian
Henry Moore	English
Tamayo	Mexican
Thomas Benton	American

The above lists of possible heroes may serve as inspiration to have your class discover who they are, when they lived, and what they created in art. The next step is to have the class build a list of their own heroes as they discover them through reading, looking at paintings, and discussing artists, art historians, and art critics. Heroes can be found (and used as models in any field or subject) in various places. Here are some other hero lists that your class might also be interested in building:

The Best Movies I have ever seen.
The Best Books I have ever read.
The Greatest Sports Figures I know about.
The Best Teachers I know.
Great Discoveries I have made that will help me in my art.
Great Museums and Galleries to visit.
Great Art Works that I remember seeing.

Hero lists can be built on practically anything, and for any reason. They will serve as models in helping children to grow in their artistic vision.

Professional Careers In Art: Tell Children Early, And Build It

It is never too early to discuss career possibilities with children. They often express their dreams, and what they want to be when they grow up. Classroom teachers could informally mention possibilities that exist in the wonderful field of art. Many children will have no other way to know what careers exist in art, except by what the classroom teacher reveals. In many of the art fields, as in any field, it's really the *interest* that counts, and not the greatest of talent. In other words, if a child has a great interest in some area of art, this type of personal momentum can carry far toward a future career if it is encouraged. Just look at the many possibilities:

Archeology:
Illustrator
Photographer
Historian

Architecture:
Designer
Draftsman
Architect

Art Director:
Advertising agency
Magazine agency
Newspaper

Art Teacher:
Public school
College
University
Art school
Private school

Craftsman:
Ceramicist
Leathersmith
Metalsmith
Wrought iron sculptor
Glassblower
Weaver
Jeweler

Designer:
Fashion
Advertising
Interior designer
Commercial: greeting cards, books, layouts
Medical illustration
Lettering
Photographer
Filmmaker
Industrial designer
Stage designer
Textile designer
Graphic designer
Art critic
Museum director

These are just a few of the countless opportunities which exist for young people today. Any public library will have further information on career opportunities. The nearest college or high school counseling office should have material available to assist in career planning. An interesting possibility would be to have the children write to artists in various fields, or to companies, and ask for information to be sent. Surprisingly, many corporations are pleased to be able to assist young people. They will often have printed material and photographs to send. Any grade level could do this, from first grade on up. Remember, it is the things that we learn as a child that carry through with us in life.

Teaching Aids

Selected examples of teaching aids for the teacher and student to use in developing aesthetic judgment and art heritage:

1. Art Education, Inc., Blauvelt, New York. An art appreciation Print Program consisting of sixty-four mounted and varnished prints, prepared by Oliver L. Riley and Eileen Lomasney.
2. Grolier Education Corp., New York. *The Book of Art*, ten volumes, a pictorial encyclopedia of painting, drawing, and sculpture.
3. American Book Company, 300 Pike St., Cincinnati, Ohio. "Teaching Through Art," a multi-purpose art print program designed by Robert J. Saunders for the elementary school. Series A, B, and C each contain twenty prints and a teacher's manual on how to extend the lesson.
4. Barton and Cotton, 2604 Sisson St., Baltimore, Md. "Guidelines for Learning through Art," a complete program in a comprehensive series for grades one through eight, edited by Clyde M. McGeary and William Dallam. Each set in the program contains ten six-by-nine inch student prints for the child's collection, lesson guidelines and procedures, information, bibliographies and correlative prints for comparing and contrasting the prints with other subjects and artists.
5. "Junior Museum," Educational Dimensions, Box 126, Stamford, Conn. 06904. This set of 6 sound filmstrips, approx. 10 minutes each with teacher's guide, covers painting, sculpture, ceramics, weaving, mosaics, and printmaking. They are designed as a comprehensive art appreciation program for elementary school. They give students an understanding of the basic principles of design and techniques that have been used by major and minor masters throughout the ages.

"King David With a Boy,"
Hans Memling
Courtesy: The Art Institute of Chicago

"The Artist's Son, Jean,"
Pierre Auguste Renoir
Courtesy: The Art Institute of Chicago

"On the Stage," Edgar Degas
Courtesy: The Art Institute of Chicago

6. "The Artist Looks at Life," Visual Publications, 716 Center Street, Lewiston, New York 14092, is a set of 7 filmstrips with handbooks that introduces the young art student to works of art by subject or theme as well as chronologically. The 7 themes selected in this set are: (1) landscapes and seascapes, (2) portraits, (3) music and dancing, (4) animals, (5) children, (6) food, drink, and flowers, (7) sports, games, and entertainments.
7. "Visual Sources for Learning," Sandak, Inc., 180 Harvard Avenue, Stamford, Conn. 06902, is a four-unit resource unit consisting of 28 filmstrips. Each filmstrip has a list of suggested points, art activities, related classroom activities, and book sources. The four units are (1) Man and Society: portraits, family, work we do, recreation and sport, performers—circus and theatre, masks and figurines, costume and fashion; (2) Forms from Nature: birds, flowers and foliage, landscapes, sun and sea, nightfall, weather; (3) Man-made World: the city, bridges, the machine, everyday forms and objects, words, numbers and letters, crafts in America, spaces and enclosures; (4) Visual Themes: lines and pathways, color and light, movement, shapes, structure, textures and patterns, still life and collage. This set is designed for use by the classroom teacher and is basically art appreciation and art history, but in addition has a lot of suggested art activities.
8. "Little Adventures in Art," Warren Schloat Productions, Inc., Prentice-Hall Media, Inc., 150 White Plains Rd., Tarrytown, New York 10591, contains 4 filmstrips and tape cassettes on animals in art from all around the world. Good to use to build understanding of importance of art in man's life and art appreciation, and good for art motivations involving three-dimensional materials.

Art and Arts Programs—3 Packages

1. "Meaning, Methods and Media," Guy Hubbard and Mary J. Rouse, Benefic Press, 10300 W. Roosevelt Rd., Westchester, Ill. 60153, is a set of six books for grades one through six. There is a teacher's edition and a student edition. They are designed as comprehensive art programs for each grade. They include perceptual training, learning the language of art, learning about artists, criticizing and judging art, learning to use art tools, and materials.
2. "The SWRL Elementary Art Program," 4665 Lampson Avenue, Los Alamitos, California 90720, is a complete package program for the classroom teacher to use from kindergarten through sixth grade. The SWRL Elementary Art Program provides materials and procedures for sequenced, systematic art instruction. It includes visual analysis area, production area, and critical analysis area, and is programmed to provide experiences for the child as artist, as art critic, and as art historian.
3. "The Aesthetic Education Program," developed by the Central Midwest Regional Educational Laboratory (CEMREL), and co-published by Viking Press and the Lincoln Center for the Performing Arts, are arts learning experiences for children in grades 1 through 6. The main objective of the program is to help children to use their senses meaningfully and joyfully. The program uses the arts, visual arts, language arts, music, dance, and theatre as resources for exploring these essential skills.

Summary

In summary the classroom teacher of art is responsible for projecting the *models* of *art critic* and *art historian* along with the artist model to children in the classroom.

Only about 10 percent of all students will continue to identify with the *artist model* in high school, and the other 90 percent will follow the *art critic* and *art historian models.* They will not necessarily take more art history or deal directly with aesthetic judgments in a classroom setting but will continue to function in this capacity most of their adult lives. This fact alone makes it vitally

"Corn Husking," oil on canvas, Winslow Homer

Courtesy: Oliver B. James Collection of American Art
Arizona State University, Tempe, Arizona

"Polka Dot Mushroom," pottery, Allan Widenhofer

Courtesy: American Art Heritage Fund
Arizona State University,
Tempe, Arizona

"Frogs Leaving from the L. A. Airport," David Gilhooly

Courtesy: The American Art Heritage Fund,
University Art Collections
Arizona State University,
Tempe, Arizona

"Fumador," Rufino Tamayo

Courtesy: Oliver B. James Collection of American Art
Arizona State University, Tempe, Arizona

"Osprey and the Otter and the Salmon," John James Audubon

Courtesy: Oliver B. James Collection of American Art
Arizona State University, Tempe, Arizona

"Italian Park," wash, Jean Honore Fragonard.
Courtesy: E. B. Crocker Art Gallery, Sacramento, California

"Meeting on the Bridge," wood block print, Utagawa Hiroshige.
Courtesy: E. B. Crocker Art Gallery, Sacramento, California

"St. Peter Liberated by the Angel," ink drawing, Rembrandt.
Courtesy: E. B. Crocker Art Gallery, Sacramento, California

Paintings help to provide insight into our own experiences and the experiences of others.

important for the elementary classroom teacher to emphasize the role of *art critic* and *art historian* as an important part of the elementary art program.

Learning to make aesthetic judgments based on critical evaluations of one's environment and one's own works will help children reflect on the value art has in their culture. This must be accomplished by active discussions in the classroom about art and through visits to places of art. Finally, consideration must be given to the cultural and artistic impact of the total environment on both child and adult.

Ways to Involvement

1. Plan a unit on study and appreciation of our art heritage. Use slides, reproduction or tear sheets from magazines about the art object or objects you plan to study. For specific helpful suggested approaches see the following:
    a. Clyde McGeary, *Actual Enrichment Program,* Barton-Cotton, Inc., 2604 Sisson St., Baltimore, Maryland 21211.
    b. Fred Gettings, *The Meaning and Wonder of Art,* New York: Golden Press, 1963.

References

[1]Eisner, Elliot W., *Educating Artistic Vision,* New York: The Macmillan Company, 1972, pp. 26-27.

[2]The National Art Education Association, *Art Educations Elementary,* Washington, D.C.: N.A.E.A., 1972, p. 34.

[3]Smith, Ralph A., "Aesthetic Experience: The Method of Aesthetic Education," *Studies in Art Education* 9, No. 3 (Spring 1968): 12-31.

[4]Feldman, Edmund, *Becoming Human Through Art: Aesthetic Experience in the School,* Englewood Cliffs, N.J.: Prentice-Hall, Inc., 1970, pp. 348-357.

[5]Gaitskell, Charles, and Hurwitz, Al, *Children and Their Art: Methods for the Elementary School,* second ed., New York: Harcourt, Brace & World, Inc., 1970, pp. 414-451.

[6]Smith, Bradely, *Mexico: A History of Art,* Garden City, New York: Doubleday and Company, Inc., 1968.

Additional References

Anderson, Donald M., *Elements of Design,* New York: Holt, Rinehart & Winston, Inc., 1961.

Baker, Samm, *Introduction to Art, A Guide to the Understanding and Enjoyment of Great Masterpieces,* New York: Harry N. Abrams, Inc., 221 pp.

Baldinger, Wallace S., *The Visual Arts,* rev. ed., New York: Holt, Rinehart & Winston, Inc., 1963.

Barr, Alfred, *What is Modern Painting?* New York Museum of Modern Art, 1956.

Berry, Ana M., *First Book of Paintings,* New York: Franklin Watts, Inc., 1960.

Borrison, Mary Jo, *Let's Go To An Art Museum,* New York: G. P. Putnam's Sons, 1960.

Brown, Margaret Wise, *The House of a Hundred Windows,* New York: Harper & Row, Publishers, 1945.

Cannaday, John, *Mainstreams of Modern Art,* New York: Holt, Rinehart & Winston, Inc., 1959.

Chase, Judith, *Afro-American Art and Crafts,* New York: Van Nostrand Reinhold Co., 1971.

Cheney, Sheldon, *The Story of Modern Art,* New York: The Viking Press, 1951.

Compton's Pictured Encyclopedia, Chicago: F. E. Compton and Co., 1963.

Conant, Howard and Arne Randall, *Art in Education,* Peoria, Ill.: Chas. A. Bennett Co., Inc., 1959.

de Barhegyi, Suzanne, *Museums,* New York: Holt, Rinehart & Winston, Inc., 1962.

Dover, Cedric *American Negro Art,* New York: New York Graphic Society, 1960.

Elsen, Albert E., *Purposes of Art,* New York: Holt, Rinehart & Winston, Inc., 1967, 455 pp.

Faulkner, R., E. Ziegfeld and G. Hill, *Art Today* 4th ed., New York: Holt, Rinehart & Winston, Inc., 1963.

Feldman, Edmund B., *Art as Image and Idea,* Englewood Cliffs, N. J.: Prentice-Hall, Inc., 1967, 512 pp.

Field Enterprises Educational Corp., *World Book Encyclopedia* vol. 14, Chicago: Merchandise Mart Plaza, 1963.

Fine, Elsa, H., *Afro-American Artists: A Search for Identity,* New York: Holt, Rinehart and Winston, Inc., 1973, 287 pp.

Fleming, William, *Arts and Ideas* rev. ed., New York: Holt, Rinehart & Winston, Inc., 1963.

Flexner, James T., *Pocket History of American Painting,* New York: Washington Square Press, Inc., 1962.

Gardner, Helen, *Art Through the Ages* 3rd ed., New York: Harcourt Brace & World, Inc., 1960.

"Closed Era"
by Jean Pratt
Woodblock Print

(Illustration for the Joseph Conrad novel, 'Youth")
Artist: Dewitt Jayne
Oil
Courtesy of the artist

"Transit"
by Walter Ball
Oil
Courtesy of the artist

The artist as interpreter uses art media in a manner which best expresses his ideas and experiences at any particular time.

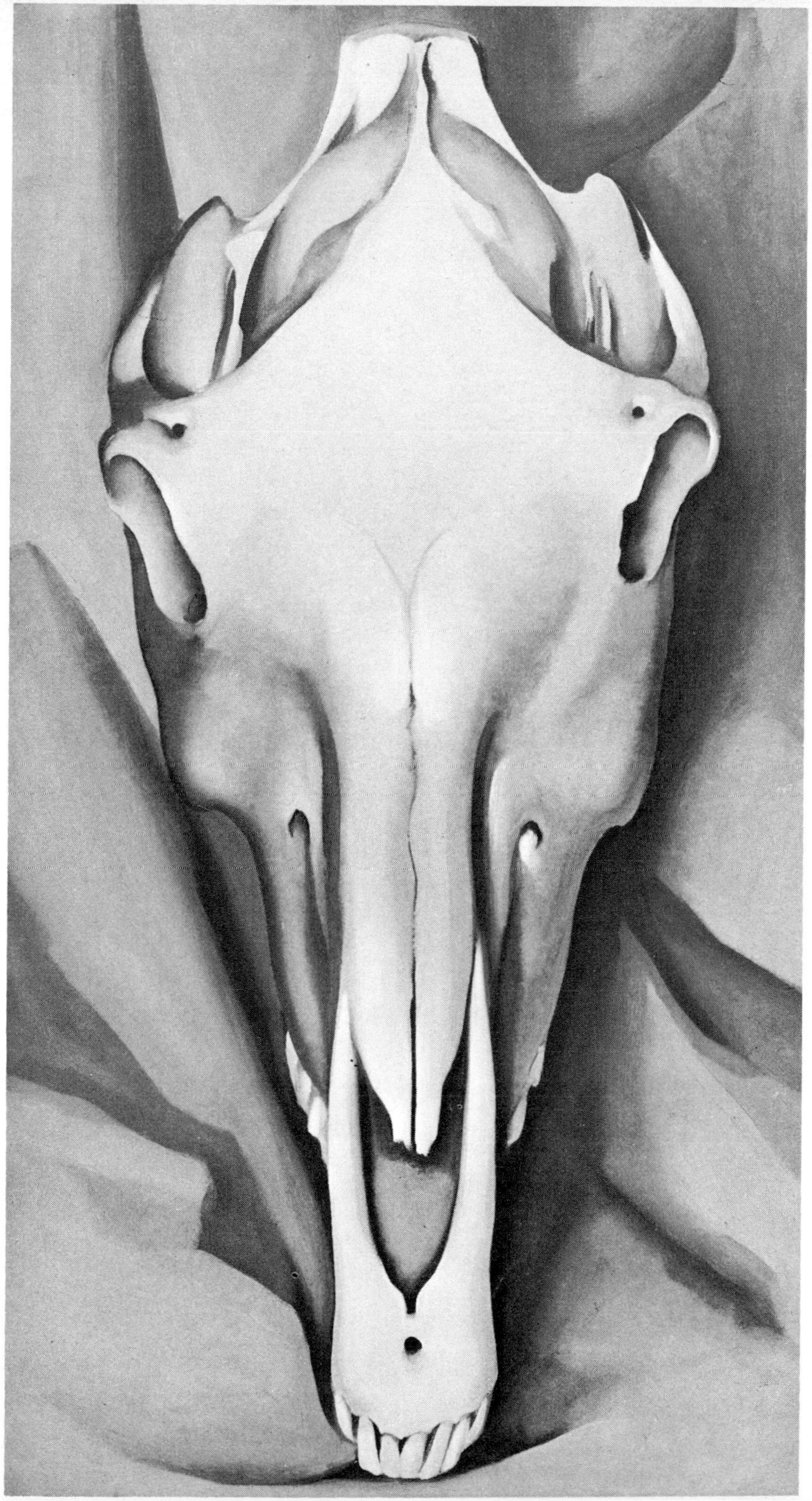

"Mrs. Stephen Peabody," oil on wood panel, Gilbert Stuart

Courtesy: Oliver B. James Collection of American Art
Arizona State University, Tempe, Arizona

"Horse's Skull on Blue," Georgia O'Keeffe

Courtesy: Oliver B. James Collection of American Art
Arizona State University, Tempe, Arizona

GETTINGS, FRED, *The Meaning and Wonder of Art,* New York: Golden Press, 1963, 91 pp.

GOMBRICH, ERNEST, *The Story of Art,* New York: Phaidon Publishing Co., 1954, 462 pp.

HUNT, C. and B. W. CARLSON, *Masks and Mask Makers,* New York: Abingdon Press, 1961.

HUNTER, SAM, *Modern French Painting* pap. New York: Dell Publishing Co., Inc.

JANSON, H. W., *History of Art for Young People,* New York: A Harry N. Abrams book for American Book Company, 1971, 412 pp.

JANSON, H. W. and D. J. JANSON, *The Story of Painting,* New York: Harry N. Abrams, Inc., 1952.

KNOBLER, NATHAN, *The Visual Dialogue,* New York: Holt, Rinehart & Winston, Inc., 1967, 342 pp.

LINDERMAN, EARL W., *Invitation to Vision,* Dubuque, Iowa: Wm. C. Brown Company Publishers, 1967.

———, "Let's Learn About Art," *Arts and Activities,* December, 1963.

———, "Appreciation Deserves An Early Start," *Arts and Activities,* October, 1962.

LINDERMAN, EARL W. and LINDERMAN, MARLENE M., *Crafts for the Classroom,* New York: Macmillan Co., 1977.

LOWRY, BATES, *The Visual Experience: An Introduction to Art,* Englewood Cliffs, N. J.: Prentice-Hall, Inc., 1967, 133 pp.

MACAGY, DOUGLAS and ELIZABETH, *Going for a Walk With a Line,* Garden City, N. Y.: Doubleday & Company, Inc., 1959.

MCCURDY, CHARLES, ed., *Modern Art: A Pictorial Anthology,* New York: The Macmillan Company, 1958.

MCDARRAH, FRED W., *The Artist's World,* New York: E. P. Dutton & Co., Inc., 1961.

MENDELOWITZ, DANIEL M., *A History of American Art,* New York: Holt, Rinehart & Winston, Inc., 1960, 622 pp.

MEYERS, BERNARD, *Understanding The Arts* rev. ed., New York: Holt, Rinehart & Winston, 1963.

MOORE, LAMONT, *First Book of Paintings,* New York: Franklin Watts, Inc., 1960.

MYERS, BERNARD S., *Art and Civilization,* New York: McGraw-Hill Book Company, 1967, 440 pp.

OCVIRK OTTO, ROBERT BONE, ROBERT STINSON and PHILIP WIGG, *Art Fundamentals,* Dubuque, Iowa: Wm. C. Brown Company Publishers, 1962.

O'NEILL, MARY, *Hailstones and Halibut Bones,* Garden City, N. Y.: Double-Day & Company, Inc., 1961.

OSMOND, EDWARD, *Houses,* London: B. T. Botsford, Ltd., 1956.

PASCHEL, HERBERT, *First Book of Color,* New York: Franklin Watts, Inc., 1959.

PLUMMER, GORDON S., *Children's Art Judgment: A Curriculum for Elementary Art Appreciation,* Dubuque, Iowa: Wm. C. Brown Company Publishers, 1974, 137 pp.

PORTER, JAMES, *Modern Negro Art,* London: Dryden Press, 1942, reprinted by Arno Press and *New York Times.*

SCHINNELLER, JAMES A., *Art: Search and Self-Discovery,* Scranton, Pa.: International Textbook Co., 1961, 322 pp.

SEIBERLING, FRANK, *Looking Into Art,* New York: Holt, Rinehart & Winston, Inc., 1959, 304 pp.

SEWALL, JOHN IVES, *A History of Western Art* rev. ed., New York: Holt, Rinehart & Winston, Inc., 1963.

SHAHN, BEN, *The Shape of Content,* Cambridge, Mass.: Harvard University Press, 1957, 131 pp.

SIMPSON, MARTHA, *Art Is For Everyone,* New York: McGraw-Hill Book Company, 1951.

SMITH, BRADLEY, *Mexico: A History of Art,* Garden City, New York: Doubleday and Company, Inc., 1968, 296 pp.

TAYLOR, JOSHUA C., *Learning To Look: A Handbook for the Visual Arts,* Chicago: University of Chicago Press, 1957.

VALE, EDMUND, *Cathedrals,* London: B. T. Botsford, Ltd., 1957.

———, *Churches,* London: B. T. Botsford, Ltd., 1954.

WECHSLER, HERMAN J., *The Pocket Book of Old Masters,* New York: Washington Square Press, Inc., 1961.

YOUNG, MARY, *Singing Windows,* New York: Abingdon Press, 1962.

Monographs and Papers

Planning Facilities for Art Instruction, National Art Education Association, 1962, 44 pp.

The Essentials of a Quality School Art Program, National Art Education Association, 1967.

Film References

Changing Art In A Changing World. A Paul Burnford Production in association with Jack Stoops, Ed. D., 21 min.

Figures, ACI FILMS, INC., 16 west 46th Street, New York 10036, 12 min.

Folk Art In Latin America. Bailey-Film Associates, 2211 Michigan Avenue, Santa Monica, Calif.

Reinhold Visuals
Portfolio 1. Line
Portfolio 2. Mass
Portfolio 3. Organization
Portfolio 4. Surface
Reinhold Book Corporation
430 Park Avenue, New York, 10022

Index